Working Blessedly Forever

VOLUME 1
The Shape of Marketplace Theology

"In this volume, R. Paul Stevens embarks on a journey to guide his readers to live a blessed life through working for the glory of God. The book integrates marketplace theology concepts with the author's personal stories and experiences, providing readers with provocative insights towards being blessed, blessing, and staying blessed in our daily work. We learn that we can experience spiritual growth and actively contemplate God's presence through our daily work."

—JEAN LEE, professor of theological studies,
China Graduate School of Theology

"In a world of anxiety, societal breakdown, global insecurities, and the all-pervasive threat of climate change, it is easy to become self-focused and defensive, even as Christians. But R. Paul Stevens's marketplace theology calls us into a very different way of thinking and being. Rather than only a Sunday faith, marketplace theology provides the vision of living the kingdom of God in the most basic of human activity—our daily work. What a vision! How incarnational! How practical! And so needed, today!"

—CHARLES RINGMA, professor emeritus of missions and evangelism,
Regent College

"R. Paul Stevens's approach is grounded in practical and life-giving interpretations of Scripture, avoiding fluff and generic recipes. He uses history and contextualization to synthesize the essence of the marketplace, making the theology both highly academic and intensely practical. The writing style is accessible to both academics and non-academics. The author does not seek to convince but rather enlightens readers with his insights. His approach is compelling, providing a rich and relevant understanding of work through a theological lens."

—WILLY KOTIUGA, chair of the Board of Regents,
Bakke Graduate University

"R. Paul Stevens is the most experienced teacher of the theology of work in our generation—and possibly in any generation. He is also the rare theological professor who has taught as many marketplace Christians as he has pastors and academics, maybe more. Here he distills a lifetime of experience, study, wisdom, and passion for anyone who wants to understand how the Bible applies to work."

—WILLIAM MESSENGER, executive editor, Theology of Work Project

"R. Paul Stevens had sensed 'something missing' in his experience of working, so he left his pastor-role for several years to become a day-laborer. No wonder his words on work are so authentic. Now, decades later, as he says, 'Marketplace theology takes time, indeed a lifetime.' Stevens has spent his own long lifetime exploring God's revelation about our daily work. Now, in this book, he has distilled for us the essential elements of his hard-won insights."

—LARRY PEABODY, author of *God Loves Your Work*

"Much of marketplace theology starts with the hands (right action) or the head (right orthodoxy) or the heart (right passion). Each is helpful but limited. R. Paul Stevens, in this beautiful book, *The Shape of Marketplace Theology*, calls us to see the interaction between these often-isolated views. With helpful and personal examples from his sixty years on this journey, Stevens brings these parts together in a wonderful way."

—AL ERISMAN, author of *The Accidental Executive*

"In *The Shape of Marketplace Theology*, R. Paul Stevens has once again showcased his erudite insights in the study of marketplace theology. Stevens provides a fresh integrated and effective framework to reflect on how faith can best be expressed in the marketplace in the broadest sense of its context, be it in the workplace, at a commercial hub, on a political area, or at home. Stevens is to be applauded for offering a fresh perspective and a unique addition to the discussion of marketplace theology."

—ENOCH WONG, director, Centre for Leadership Studies,
  Tyndale Seminary

"For many decades, R. Paul Stevens has called for liberating the laity not just in the church but for the work of God in the world. In this volume, he harvests a lifetime of teaching, practice, and friendships to give us a transformative vision and real-world practices for the 'marketplace' that can—and must—be lived if the gospel is to be made known in a time when the church has been dismissed by most of our culture."

—JONATHAN R. WILSON, senior consultant for theological integration,
  Canadian Baptist Ministries

Working Blessedly Forever

VOLUME 1

The Shape of Marketplace Theology

R. Paul Stevens

Foreword by Steven Garber

CASCADE Books • Eugene, Oregon

WORKING BLESSEDLY FOREVER, VOLUME 1
The Shape of Marketplace Theology

Copyright © 2024 R. Paul Stevens. All rights reserved. Except for brief quotations in critical publications or reviews, no part of this book may be reproduced in any manner without prior written permission from the publisher. Write: Permissions, Wipf and Stock Publishers, 199 W. 8th Ave., Suite 3, Eugene, OR 97401.

Cascade Books
An Imprint of Wipf and Stock Publishers
199 W. 8th Ave., Suite 3
Eugene, OR 97401

www.wipfandstock.com

PAPERBACK ISBN: 978-1-6667-5710-1
HARDCOVER ISBN: 978-1-6667-5711-8
EBOOK ISBN: 978-1-6667-5712-5

Cataloguing-in-Publication data:

Names: Stevens, R. Paul, author, 1937–. | Garber, Steven, foreword.

Title: Working blessedly forever, volume 1 : the shape of marketplace theology / R. Paul Stevens ; foreword by Steve Garber.

Description: Eugene, OR: Cascade Books, 2024. | Includes bibliographical references and index.

Identifiers: ISBN 978-1-6667-5710-1 (paperback). | ISBN 978-1-6667-5711-8 (hardcover). | ISBN 978-1-6667-5712-5 (ebook).

Subjects: LCSH: Work—Religious aspects—Christianity. | Theology. | Christian life.

Classification: BR118 S74 2024 (print). | BR118 (ebook).

References to the Bible unless otherwise noted are from The New International Version 2011. Used with permission.

To Gail
Beloved lifelong companion and spiritual friend

Contents

Foreword by Dr. Steven Garber | xi
Introduction: What Is So Good about Marketplace Theology? | xv

THE SCIENCE

1. Doing Marketplace Theology from Above | 3
2. Doing Marketplace Theology from Below | 17

THE MEANING OF WORK

3. Going to Work with the Professor | 35
4. Thinking and Praying about Work | 50
5. The Practice of Work—The Handiness of Theological Learning | 65

BLESSING THE WORKER

6. Working with the Trinity | 81
7. Growing Spiritually through Work | 94

BLESSING OTHERS

8. Blessing Your Neighbor | 111
9. Blessing the Workplace | 124

BLESSING GOD

10. Work and Worship | 141
11. The Beatific Vision and the Marketplace | 154

WORKING BLESSEDLY FOREVER

12. Contributing to a Down-to-Earth Heaven | 171

Epilogue: A Summary | 185

Contents

Bibliography | 195
Author Index | 203
Subject Index | 207
Scripture Index | 221

Foreword

Dr. Steven Garber

OVER THE SHOULDER, THROUGH *the heart*—an image, a reality, a deeply born pedagogical practice at the very heart of the truest teaching, the most profound learning.

And it is this that Paul Stevens offers us in his new book, *Working Blessedly Forever*, inviting us to come along with him, to see and hear what he has learned through the years of his faithful life, one marked by thousands upon thousands of friendships with students from all over the world—his own North America, of course, but all through Asia, into Latin America, across Africa and Europe, time and again opening himself to yet another person who longs to learn why and how "the other six days" matter to God.

Reading these pages, I am astounded, even as I know him well. A serious student for the years of his life—because a good teacher must be that—Stevens weaves together a centuries-long conversation, offering a wonderfully rich apprenticeship, an opportunity to learn something of what he has learned through years of patient, persistent study. Of course he begins with the biblical revelation, taking the text of Scripture with all the seriousness it deserves, attending to the very beginning of the story in Genesis, patiently listening to its history through the patriarchs, poets, and prophets, lingering as he must in the story of the incarnation, interpreted by the apostles, and then finally coming to the conclusion of the story in the Revelation to John, paying focused attention to the final words of the Word. Anyone with ears to hear will learn more than ever imagined as Stevens allows us to read along with him, the Story of stories shaping him, and us.

Drawing us into a conversation through the centuries, we read with wonder at Professor Stevens's knowledge of the most seasoned thinking about human life under the sun, and therefore about what work means to God and to the world. From Irenaeus to Augustine 1,500 years ago, to

Luther and the Puritans in the last 500 years, on into the great streams of the contemporary church—the Catholic, the Orthodox, the Protestant—we look over his shoulder, though his heart, as he weaves together a remarkable tapestry of the most time-tested wisdom on human labor which the church offers us. From this last century we are introduced to the Polish Catholic Stefan Wyszynski, the Russian Orthodox Alexander Schmemann, the British bishop of the Church of South India Lesslie Newbigin, and so many more too, *viz.* Ellen Charry, N.T. Wright, even on into Matthew Kaemingk and Cory Willson, all together a good course on the nature and meaning of vocation in God's world.

And then, because he must, Stevens surgically addresses the disposition to dualism written into the human heart that is the great plague on the church through history, "the great heresy" he calls it, insisting that we pay attention to the Bible in its more coherent and comprehensive reading of what worship and work mean for God and for us. With time-worn wisdom he presses in, showing us another way—something more seamless, of course, where the holiness of God is the foundational truth of the cosmos, and with it calling his people to be holy in every area of life, personal and public, at work and at play. Threaded through are chapters on the Trinitarian character of the universe, and its meaning for who we are and what we do as image-bearers of God; and then chapter by chapter we are drawn in more deeply to the biblical and theological rootedness of "working blessedly forever," coming to a very rich conclusion in a reexamination of the beatific vision, asking about its meaning for the marketplace, opening the eyes of our hearts to seeing more clearly what it means to be human, "fully alive" as Irenaeus taught us, our work holy as God is holy.

Page after page we are graced with his community through the centuries, but if there is one who stands out as Stevens' interlocutor it is his long friend, Robert Banks. The two together are the great fathers of all good thinking about work in the world, as teachers aptly named "professor of marketplace theology" (Stevens) and "professor of the laity" (Banks) respectively, through-a-glass-darkly efforts to honor the unique gifts of these good men, even great men. With his characteristic twinkle in his eye, twined together with his equally characteristic seriousness of heart, Stevens often writes about "my friend Robert Banks"—and if we are listening carefully to this conversation over time, we can hear the affection and respect of the one for the other. A Canadian and an Australian, separated by oceans, joined together by a commitment to the good work of work, this book is

Foreword

the fruit of a collegial and collaborative labor of love formed through years of life together.

What is plain is that both have wrestled with the Word and the world, at the same time, always willing to read one more book, to teach one more course, to take a walk with one more student, and yes, to write one more book, further up and further into their common calling, an unusual and wonderful calling to teach the church about the meaning of calling.

They have influenced generations, their gifts very good gifts to those who have entered into their questions, seeing ourselves implicated in and by them, our own vocations formed through them.

In a day long past when human communication came through letters in the mail, I opened one from Robert Banks, then-professor of the laity at Fuller Theological Seminary. He dreamed of a book about work in the world, inviting people from all over to contribute a chapter on the meaning of their own work—and so a farmer, an artist, a technologist, a businessman, a journalist, and more, including me, a teacher. We were to do theological reflection on our vocation, writing something for the wider world, offering a window into why we did our work and what it meant. I knew of him through his writing, which is why I responded with gladness, but not until several years later did I meet him, surprised to find an honestly humble man, more interested in me than he needed me to be interested in him, attentive to others around him with unusual grace.

Different men as they are, differently placed as they are, the very same could be said of Paul Stevens, who many years later has become my friend, which is one of the great gifts of my life. The author of many books, from *Liberating the Laity, The Other Six Days, Down-to-Earth Spirituality, Doing God's Business, Taking Your Soul to Work, Work Matters, The Kingdom of God in Working Clothes*, and more, he has labored lovingly to bring this good book into being. A man with a very deep heart, he thinks carefully and critically about life and the world—which is to say that he thinks Christianly—giving himself away in hope that "work matters" to God, and therefore to God's world.

If the language "as theologically mature as one is professionally competent" comes to us from his own Regent College colleague, James Houston—leaving the steeples and spires of Oxford, longing for another way to imagine the work of theology in service to the world—Paul Stevens embodies this uniquely, and I honor him here.

Foreword

A teacher's teacher, a professor's professor, a friend's friend, a neighbor's neighbor, he is known as a man of rare winsomeness, with an indefatigable strength for the things that matter most. Born of a vision for his own vocation that has been growing for the eighty-five years of his life, a calling worked out in careers of all kinds, from carpenter to pastor, from professor to author, with the saints through the centuries whom we trust with our souls, Stevens has become a wonderfully wise man whose counsel is sought by kindred spirits the world over. From Bratislava to Beijing, young and old alike, his students long to spend time learning *over his shoulder, through his heart*.

Always and everywhere, the truest teaching is that, the most profound learning is that.

Introduction

What Is So Good about Marketplace Theology?

> The best theology is compressed prayer.
> P.T. FORSYTH[1]

> I have come to believe that the true mystics of the quotidian [occurring every day] are not those who contemplate holiness in isolation, reaching godlike illumination in serene silence, but those who manage to find God in a life filled with noise, the demands of other people and relentless daily duties that can consume the self.
> KATHLEEN NORRIS[2]

FOR MANY PEOPLE, THEOLOGY is an off-putting word. But actually, as Linus van Pelt is reported to have said in *Peanuts*, there is nothing more comforting than good theology. And marketplace theology is no exception. This volume, the first of three, explores the *shape* of marketplace theology, its posture and methodology. A second volume concerns the *practice* of marketplace theology. And a third will cover the *spirituality* of marketplace theology. In the second and third volumes I am joined by a group of thoughtful practitioners.

It is very important to understand what I mean by using the word "marketplace." It is now more common to use "workplace" when speaking

---

1. Forsyth, *Soul of Prayer*, 44.
2. Norris, *Quotidian Mysteries*, 70.

Introduction

or writing about work in the public or private sphere. But I intend that these three volumes will encompass all the arenas where work is done: the home, the office, the factory, the medical clinic, the school, the government office, including work done in the church and other not-for-profit organizations. Work is simply the energy expended whether manual, mental, or both, whether or not it is remunerated. But I am deliberately using the word "marketplace" even though it tends to suggest business in particular. I do so because I wish to explore the context of work in which exchange takes place globally and cosmically including the principalities and powers that resist our work in this world. Of course, values and skills are exchanged in homes and charitable organizations. Knowledge and hopefully some wisdom is exchanged in educational contexts. And health is gained in doctors's offices and hospitals.

I am painfully aware of the fact that I have neglected in this volume to deal with matters such as economics, advertising, money, and profit.[3] In the next volume we will deal with the theology and practice of human enterprise, business being part of this but not all. And in the third volume we will deal with spiritual growth in the workplace and consider workplace disciplines for our journey inward, upward, downward, and outward. Many people, including some you will meet in volumes 2 and 3, have contributed to this book and I am grateful for their influence.[4] But in this volume we are merely exploring *the shape of marketplace theology*. To do this we must have a working definition.

For a simple definition we are taking a cue from the English Puritan William Perkins who in the sixteenth century defined theology simply and sublimely as "the science [it involves study and investigating] of living [not esoteric realities but life] blessedly [in the light of God's presence and purpose] forever [and not just for this life].[5] So understood, **marketplace theology is the science of working blessedly forever.** But what is the good

---

3. On the last—money—Clive Lim and I wrote the book *Money Matters: Faith, Life, and Wealth* (Eerdmans, 2021) and Economics and Advertising I suggest that entries in Banks and Stevens, *The Complete Book of Everyday Christianity* (InterVarsity Press, 1997), can be consulted.

4. I am especially grateful for the careful reading of this manuscript by Dr. Jonathan Wilson, Dr. Larry Peabody, Dr. Jean Lee, Dr. Willy Kotiuga, and especially my dear friend, Dr. Steve Garber, who wrote the foreword. They have contributed ably to this volume.

5. Perkins, *Golden Chain* (1592), 177.

Introduction

of marketplace theology? Why is there a blessing, as I affirm, in studying, practising, and doing marketplace theology?

The Goodness of Marketplace Theology

Marketplace theology is good because it helps us make sense of where we spend most of our waking hours. It is good because it draws us into the grand purpose that God has for everything. It is good because it could unleash a whole new missional energy for the world. Why is that? As people come into the lovely reality of the kingdom of God with Jesus as King, an alternative word for Messiah, they will flourish and want others to flourish. And flourishing is what God wants for the human race and for all of God's creation. So, I ask a question: What would be the most strategic thing we could do to reach the world with Jesus and his good news of the kingdom of God? Could it not be to touch the world where it aches and hopes, where people spend most of their time and life?

Marketplace theology is good for the body, soul, and mind. For believers this theology means integration, bringing work and faith together for the glory of God and the benefit of neighbors. Marketplace theology has benefit for spiritual formation, motivation for daily work, and ethical working. It is good because it tells us why we work, who we work for, how to work well, and what is the end or purpose of our work. Through it we get "the big view" of how our efforts to offer goods or services fits into the grand scheme of things. In short, we gain a worldview for work: truly a work-view. It is good because it explains why we feel such resistance and sweat in the workplace and how to grapple with it.

It is good because anyone can do it. Indeed, lots of people are doing it every day without knowing it. In the end, it is good because it links us with God who is a worker and came as a tradesperson in Jesus. But it is not just good in that God models good work. We can come to know the God who is a worker. That link can be in spiritual formation, in prayer, in joy, in play, and in the grace that God gives. Through it we gain a vision of God.

The Book in Brief

In this first volume I am gathering sixty years of working, praying, reflecting, teaching, and writing on the shape of marketplace theology. Along

Introduction

with my other books I am breaking some fresh ground in this volume.[6] But I would encourage the reader to consider reading my companion work on the marketplace entitled *The Kingdom of God in Working Clothes: The Marketplace and the Reign of God*. Besides elaborating on the primary theme of the Bible—the kingdom of God—and its relation to the marketplace, this book deals with marketplace ministry, mission, leadership, and, above all, the relation of the church to the marketplace.

In the present volume, following the modified version of William Perkins's definition, we will explore four dimensions of marketplace theology. First, we will ask what the investigation or the **science** of marketplace theology involves, certainly more than thought and theory. Marketplace theology which seeks to understand and practice the relationship of God with the marketplace must, in my view, take a cue from the Great Commandment (Mark 12:30–31) which involves loving God with head (thought), heart (soulful prayer), and hands (practice). In our approach to doing theology we will weave together insights from the global church on doing theology *from above*, starting with the revelation of God and God's purpose. But we also will do theology *from below*, starting with concrete life and work situations.

Second, we will explore the meaning of **working**, taking a comprehensive, biblical approach. We have defined work above as energy expended purposively whether manual, mental, or both, whether or not it is remunerated. Importantly we will discover the meaning of work. We will do this by taking a plunge in an Old Testament book, Ecclesiastes, and by exploring a theology of work with head and heart (thought and prayer) and hand. In this last emphasis I do some theological reflection on my own lifetime of work—surveying over sixty years of work.

Third, we will inquire how the worker, the neighbor, the workplace, and even God are normally **blessed** through human enterprise. In exploring "working blessedly" we will consider how the worker is blessed through working with the Trinity and how we grow spiritually through our work. We bless others through our work including the neighbor, the world, and the workplace. And we bless God through work as worship. And we come

---

6. See Stevens, *Other Six Days: Vocation, Work and Ministry in Biblical Perspective* (Eerdmans, 1999), published in the UK by Paternoster under the title: *The Abolition of the Laity; Doing God's Business: Meaning and Motivation for the Marketplace* (Eerdmans, 2006); (with Alvin Ung) *Taking Your Soul to Work* (Eerdmans, 2010); *Work Matters: Lessons from Scripture* (Eerdmans, 2012); *The Kingdom of God in Working Clothes: The Marketplace and the Reign of God* (Wipf & Stock, 2022).

Introduction

to know God at least partly in what has been called the beatific vision of God in the marketplace.

Finally, we open up the ultimate future of humankind and all creation. We will examine whether anything done in this life other than preaching and witnessing will last into the next, and whether we will work in the new heaven and new earth. This means **forever**.

In the **Epilogue** we attempt to summarize the entire book. Some might consider reading the Introduction and the Epilogue before reading everything in between.

What can you hope to gain by reading this volume? You will discover for yourself God's purpose in your work. You will see how work affects you as a worker, both in spiritual growth and, in the case of a toxic work environment, in demotivating you. You will pray more, both before and after work but even during it, as did Brother Lawrence, a monastery chef who said that "his greatest business did not divert him from God." You will relish the fact that God the worker still works, as does Jesus, and that he made you in his image as a worker. You will gain some ability to do theology from below, that is, starting with concrete human experience in the workplace and reflecting theologically on it, gaining God's perspective. You might even discover that God has called you right where you are. Here is someone who has been exposed to the content of the book.

> For a while now I had this huge inner conflict trying to decide what to do with my life. I was particularly torn between the desire to go into full-time ministry or working in my field of Engineering because I had an incorrect view of what full-time ministry is and a false hierarchy of occupation. I only saw my work as a way to produce income and make relationships with people. But I never took pride in what I did nor did I ever think that it was glorifying God. I now know that my calling is to be in the engineering field.

Who am I writing for? For the thoughtful person who is working in an office, home, medical clinic, or a craftsperson's studio. This book is for the person who wants to know why they work and for whom. And, of course, I am writing for the professional theologian and for pastors who wonder what they can do to inspire and equip people with their Monday to Saturday service in the world (Eph 4:11–12).[7] So read and enjoy. And may you

---

7. I well remember as a young student translating the Greek of Ephesians stumbling on chapter 4:11–12 where Paul says pastor-teachers are not to do the ministry alone but their ministry is to equip the saints (meaning the ordinary Christian) to do ministry and

Introduction

be edified as you work blessedly forever, whatever is your marketplace. For the marketplace is not merely where goods and services are exchanged but where values and ideas are given and received.

---

that ministry is primarily in the world, as mentioned in "filling the universe" with the glory of God. I have been trying to fulfill that verse throughout my life.

THE SCIENCE

1

Doing Marketplace Theology from Above

By living, even by dying and being damned, make someone a theologian, not by understanding, reading and speculating.

MARTIN LUTHER[1]

The spirit of persistence [in prayer] springs from an inward conviction that life is but one single way that leads to the kingdom of God.

MATTHEW THE POOR[2]

If you are a theologian you will pray truly.
And if you pray truly, you are a theologian.

EVAGRIUS PONTICUS (346–99 AD)[3]

MY INTEREST IN MARKETPLACE theology didn't start from "above," that is, from the perspective of God's revealed truth. In fact, it began quite early, without, of course, even having the language to call it "marketplace theology," and certainly decades before I became a professor of marketplace theology. As a young boy growing up in Toronto, Canada, son of a CEO of

---

1. Luther, *Luthers Werke*, 5.163.28–29; "Vivendo, immo moriendo et damnando fit theologus, non intelligendo, legendo aut speculando." Quoted in McGrath, *Luther's Theology of the Cross*, 210–11.

2. Matthew the Poor, *Orthodox Prayer Life*, 164.

3. Spidlik, *Spirituality of the Christian East*, 327.

a steel fabrication company producing steel strapping for shipping containers, I received a small weekly allowance with which I could go into a store and buy a vanilla ice cream cone for five cents.

I knew that I was exchanging money for something I wanted, a soul need or want, though not yet understanding that behind this simple transaction in a confectionary store lay a whole series of exchanges. A dairy farmer exchanged his milk for money for which he was able to buy feed for his animals and give his daughter a small allowance. That was just one of dozens of exchanges made before I got my ice cream cone in my hand. So it has always been.

There is an amazing list of exchanges internationally in the ancient world in the Lament over Tyre in Ezek 27, including the men of Rhodes who "traded with you, and many coastlands were your customers; they paid you with ivory tusks and ebony" (27:15). There is a mystery in the marketplace, as Jeff Van Duzer says in his masterful book, *Why Business Matters to God*. There is what he calls a common grace, involving a whole host of persons, including the farmer, the delivery person, the milk processor, the ice cream manufacturer, the company that makes the cone from wheat products, packagers, advertisers, and transporters, until it finally arrives at the confectioner on Yonge Street in Toronto. I have simply exchanged five cents (yes that is what it cost) for a treat.

But we are built for such exchanges. We are all individuals, unique. You have something I need, and I have something that you need, and we must exchange to survive and thrive. We live by giving and receiving.[4] We are all uniquely gifted and we are built for community. And we work communally. Marketplace theology explores the meaning, the God-given purpose, the spirituality, and the practice of that young boy buying his ice cream—and the work involved. Exchange is business. Years later I had the opportunity to see how exchange works in a village marketplace in East Africa.

For ten years my wife and I lived in a village of three hundred people in Kenya. Our little house was right next to a public marketplace. People would arrange their tomatoes on the ground in an attractive way, piling them up in pyramids, alongside others selling used clothing on temporary racks, and behind them a row of dukas, small shops, where you could buy milk, bread, Ono, and malaria drugs. Old people came to the marketplace daily to catch up on the news and to exchange values.

---

4. I owe this sentence to Dr. Jonathan Wilson who kindly reviewed this manuscript.

For be sure, values are exchanged in the marketplace even in the huge office towers where transactions of millions, even billions of dollars, take place daily, as well as the transactions over coffee breaks and water cooler stops. And the global marketplace means that before I have finished breakfast, I have literally eaten my way around the world. But also, before I have finished breakfast I have engaged in a serious problem, the haves and the have-nots of the world, the principalities and powers and the spirituality of the system by which I can enjoy my toasted crumpet, peanut butter, jam, and tea. And just where did that tea come from?

As with all good theology, marketplace theology helps us make sense of our lives in this world. But it does more. It enables us to practice our work righteously, in a way that is upbuilding to our near and far neighbors. Finally, it shows us that we *take our souls to work, so there is a spiritual theology of the marketplace*, as we encounter the principalities and powers in the marketplace, and the conflict of the flesh and the Spirit in ourselves and others while we work.[5] And we can meet God in the context of our work. So, in developing a marketplace theology that is fully biblical we are eschewing the modern fragmentation of theology into systematic theology, moral theology, historical theology, spiritual theology, and applied theology. We are attempting to integrate theology, as it was in the West in the Middle Ages, as *habitus*, a disposition to the soul, or as Ellen Charry so cogently shows, theology was meant to be *sapiential*, which means providing wisdom for life. In reading many of the ancient theologians she concluded that "taking the doctrines of the Christian faith seriously was assumed to change how we think and act—to remake us.... They were interested in forming us as excellent persons.... They understood human happiness to be tied to virtuous character, which in turn comes from knowing God."[6] But there is a problem with this.

---

5. We will explore later in the book the fact that when Paul uses the word "flesh" in most cases he is not referring to the actions of the human body but rather to the whole person turned in on oneself, sinful human nature, living as though Christ had not come, in contrast to the life in the Spirit. Misunderstanding "flesh" as referring to bodily activity easily contributes to a non-biblical dualism that life in the body is unholy whereas life in the Spirit is holy.

6. Charry, *By the Renewing*, vii. Charry read Paul, Matthew, Athanasius, Basil the Great, Augustine, Anselm, Aquinas, Julian of Norwich, and Calvin and concluded that "the divisions of the modern theological curriculum began making less and less sense to me. I could no longer distinguish between apologetics from catechesis, or spirituality from ethics, or pastoral theology. I no longer understood systematic or dogmatic theology apart from all of these. In the older texts, evangelism, catechesis, moral exhortation,

The Problem of Doing Theology Today

Charry, who teaches systematic and historical theology at Perkins School of Theology, put it this way:

> Sapiential truth is unintelligible to the modern secularized construal of truth. Modern epistemology [the study of the nature, origin, scope, and limits of knowledge] not only fragmented truth itself, privileging correct information over beauty and goodness, it relocated truth in facts and ideas. The search for truth in the modern scientific sense is a cognitive enterprise that seeks correct information useful to the improvement of human comfort and efficiency rather than an intellectual activity employed for spiritual growth. Knowing the truth no longer implied loving it, and being transformed by it, because the truth no longer brings the knower to God but to use information to subdue nature. Knowing became limited to being informed about things, not as these are things of God but as they stand (or totter) on their own feet. The classical notion that truth leads us to God simply ceased to be intelligible and came to be viewed with suspicion.[7]

This is the case in the West. In the East there are other challenges to developing a marketplace theology for Asia. My colleague Bruce Nie from Qingdao, China, has expressed it this way:

> In the East, Chinese culture represented by the Confucian tradition did not seek to understand the world from a metaphysical [more than physical] approach. Instead, it focused on seeking the

---

dogmatic exegesis, pastoral care and apologetics were all happening at the same time because the authors were speaking to a whole person" (viii). She suggests that the modern concept of truth and knowledge developed in the Western world in stages. "Locke separated faith from knowledge, denying the importance of trust as an element in truth. Hume insisted on the repeatability of events as a sign of their truth and disallowed inferential reasoning, tentativeness, and discerning judgment. Kant pointed out that the conditions for knowing lie within the mind itself and that human knowing cannot transcend the limits of time and space within which the mind operates" (10). Giving examples, Charry notes that "for Paul the cross and sealing of the Holy Spirit change a person's status before God, dignifying those who had been aliens or sinners. For Athanasius, the resurrection destroyed the fear of death, empowering people to take God, rather than reifications of human sin masquerading as pagan gods, as a model for human striving. For Augustine, knowing the triune God should promote human dignity and uplifted behavior based on the principle of the *imago Dei*" (18). She argues for the "virtue-shaping function of the divine pedagogy of theological treatises," calling these treatises "aretegenic," drawing on the ancient Greek word *arete* which usually means conducive to virtue (19).

7. Charry, *By the Renewing*, 236.

wisdom of life from a social and ethical perspective, emphasizing the connection among all things. The harmony among heaven, earth and human beings is the *telos* to pursue for all human cultivation. This Eastern wisdom is undoubtedly a great complement and balance to the epistemology of Western metaphysics and the epistemology of empirical analysis. However, in the Chinese culture represented by the Confucian tradition, the lack of the sense of transcendence and its total this-worldliness leave the society to fall into the swamp of static harmony which cannot generate the critical power of moral vision to facilitate the social transformation towards the ultimate goodness.[8]

But earlier in the Western world Martin Luther confessed that theology was wrung from life and was to be lived as expressed in his celebrated statement concerning the qualifications for a true theologian: "living, or rather dying and being damned make a theologian, not understanding, reading or speculating."[9] A little later, as noted in the introduction, the Puritan Williams Perkins, defined theology as the "science of living blessedly forever."[10] The late J. I. Packer, a person with profound Puritan inclinations, says that "theology is for achieving God's glory (honour and praise) and humankind's good (the godliness that is true humanness) *through every life-activity*."

If that does not put fire in our bones to be a theologian, I do not know what would! But let's work with Perkins's pithy modified definition. So, for those who say, "Everyone is talking about marketplace theology, but no one knows what it is," I offer an adaptation of Perkins's cryptic definition as follows: *Marketplace theology is the science of working blessedly forever*. Marketplace theology is a focused expression of biblical and contextual theology. But let me amplify this last comment both negatively and positively.

What Marketplace Theology Is NOT

Negatively, marketplace theology is *not a mere segmented sphere of application* in the so-called Applied Theology division of theology, an unfortunate result of the Enlightenment in Western theology that split wholistic

---

8. Email correspondence on June 1, 2021.

9. Luther, *Luthers Werke*, 5.163.28–29, quoted in McGrath, *Luther's Theology of the Cross*, 152.

10. Perkins, *Golden Chain* (1592), 177.

theology up into systematic theology, historical theology, moral theology, spiritual theology, and applied theology, the last being the "Cinderella of the seminary."

All theology is meant to be applied and in application there is further revelation. As such, marketplace theology requires the de-Westernization of theology. We observe that the "faith and work" movement has tended to become a "how-to" movement" exemplified by some forms of "Business as Mission." We wish to contribute our grasp of marketplace theology through the Institute for Marketplace Transformation (IMT) to the larger faith and work movement, to seminaries and to thoughtful practitioners.

Marketplace theology is *not a mere compensatory theology*, as has been the case with a theology of the laity,[11] compensating for the clerical and churchly paradigms of theology. As such, marketplace theology must include "street theology," that are down-to-earth and "bottom up" expressions of the meaning of our work so that street sweepers, blue-collar workers, and homemakers, as well as professionals, can be grasped and transformed by it. But *neither is marketplace theology genitive theology* with the emphasis on the word "of" (e.g., the systematic theology *of* the marketplace) as has been the case with the theology *of* the laity. So, what is it?

What Marketplace Theology Is

Positively, marketplace theology engages the whole of biblical theology in the understanding, practicing, and spirituality of work, the worker, and the workplace. Accordingly, marketplace theology engages the Triune God as the ultimate worker and humankind made in God's image as co-Creators or sub-Creators to work and worship in community. It includes understanding creation as made by God to be stewarded by humankind in both its material and immaterial existence including the principalities and powers that have become fallen, intransigent, and taken on a life of their own.

So, these powers affect work, workers, and workplace, forming an anti-kingdom. But central in the New Testament is the good news of the true kingdom of God. The kingdom is the integrating theme in the Bible and marketplace theology shows how we can participate in the partially come and "fully to come" kingdom of God through our work, thereby flourishing now and forever.

---

11. See Stevens, *Abolition of the Laity*, 6, reprinted in the USA as *The Other Six Days*.

Doing Marketplace Theology from Above

Jesus, the Son of God and the Son of Man, came to earth as a tradesperson. The divine missionary was a tentmaker—literally a homemaker in both senses of the word.[12] Having laid down his life for our redemption he now reigns through his resurrection and ascension as Son of Man at the right hand of God the Father anticipating the full coming of his kingdom in his second coming. Meanwhile the people of God are the sign, servant, and sacrament of the kingdom, especially through the church's scattered life. The church does this through witness, its whereabouts in the neighborhood and in the workplace through work.[13]

Marketplace mission originates in the Triune God who is Sender, Sent, and Sending itself,[14] as noted in the thirty-one occasions of sending within and by God in the Gospel of John. Through this divine incarnational sending (John 20:21) the Holy Spirit empowers believers to undertake the "work of the Lord," in both witness and work having been equipped with the fruit of the Spirit. The end of it all is the second coming of Jesus, the resurrection of the body, the judgment of all, the consummation of the kingdom, the new heaven and new earth, and the vital energetic rest of the people of God in a multicultural, multi-language community where some of the fruits of this life will be found and we will work unhindered by the curse. Such is the Grand Story of God and God's purpose and it is a great place to begin theological inquiry. But not the only place to begin.

The Integral (Wholistic) Shape of Marketplace Theology

Traditionally theological enterprise has started "from above" with God, God's Word, and God's purpose. It has been concerned with orthodoxy, which is right belief, though technically the word spells out "right worship." It has been, especially for the West, a largely rational enterprise. But we are expanding marketplace theology to combine heart and hands with head! This means that (*orthodoxy*—*ortho* for "right" or "true," and *doxy* for "glory"), needs to be joined to heart (*orthopathy*—meaning "right

---

12. As a carpenter Jesus designed and built homes; as a missionary he said, "My Father . . . will come to them and make our home with them" (John 14:23).

13. See chapter 13, "What about the Church," in Stevens, *Kingdom of God in Working Clothes*.

14. I note this parallelism with God as Lover, Beloved, and Love itself as proposed by Augustine and Moltmann.

passion"), and hand (*orthopraxy*—"right praxis" or "right action").[15] Orthodoxy (which actually means right worship, or right glory) is primarily conceived as a mental and rational exercise, a mind without a soul, in contrast to orthopathy.

While espousing *orthopathy*, marketplace theology awakens passion such as what moved the prophets who were gripped with the heart of God.[16] In the film adaptation of Chaim Potok's novel *The Chosen* a Hassidic rabbi cries out to God for his son. "I went away and cried to the Master of the Universe, 'What have you done to me? A mind like this I need for a son? A heart I need for a son, a soul I need for a son, compassion I want from my son, righteousness, mercy, strength to suffer and carry pain, that I want from my son, *not a mind without a soul!*'"[17] So marketplace theology recovers the Western medieval synthesis of theology as *habitus*, the disposition of the soul or heart, *the more than rationality* of theology, as represented by the Eastern church where a theologian is one who prays. But orthodoxy and orthopathy need action, or as Paul says in Gal 5, "The only thing that counts is faith *expressing itself* through love" (v. 6, emphasis mine).

So, through using the term *orthopraxy*, we are saying that marketplace theology is implicitly practical and must be embodied and done in conformity to the action of God. But marketplace theology is not just the *application* of the truth of orthodoxy and orthopathy. In actual service in the workplace, we discover truth about ourselves as workers, truth about our work, truth about our workplace, and truth about our God who is a worker. So, as a consequence of this discovery through practice, a marketplace theologian ideally needs to be working in the world and to reflect prayerfully and thoughtfully on that work, not merely to read and study in the academy.[18] In this way wholeness is recovered.

The following is admittedly an oversimplification but a suggestive one: In the Western Church a theologian is someone who mainly *thinks*. In the Eastern Church, the Orthodox Christian community, a theologian is someone who *prays and worships* in the mystery of God's ways.[19] And in the

---

15. See Stevens, "Living Theologically," 243–55.

16. The word "orthopathy" was coined by Richard Mouw and derives from the writings of the Jewish theologian, Abraham J. Heschel who said that the prophets embodied the divine passion. Heschel, "Anthropopathy," 48–58.

17. I owe this quotation to Dr. Steve Garber, senior fellow of the Institute for Marketplace Transformation, email November 18, 2022.

18. I do this in chapter 5 where I review and reflect on my lifetime of work.

19. Evagrius said, "If you are a theologian you will pray truly. And if you pray truly,

Doing Marketplace Theology from Above

Asian church a theologian is someone who *acts*.[20] Head, heart, and hands. But in much theological work these are largely kept separate. To the church fathers and mothers in the Middle Ages of the West, and earlier leaders in the East, nothing could be further from the truth than the rationalized, systematized theology that has emerged in the West.

So says Tomas Spidlik in *The Spirituality of the Christian East*: "spirituality is lived dogma."[21] *Christian theology, then, is the pondered, prayed, and practiced study of God, God's purpose, and God's presence. And marketplace theology is the pondered, prayed, and practiced study of God, God's purpose, God's calling, and God's presence in our work, the worker and the workplace.* So, marketplace theology should be wholistic, integral. Why? Matthew the Poor, an Egyptian monk, quoted above, said that "life is but one single way to the kingdom of God."[22]

The theological task has been short-circuited. We in the West have exported to the world the distortion of a bifurcated, compartmentalized theology. Many if not most Asian theologians teaching in seminaries have been theologically circumcised in the West. The result is this: we have theology divided into systematic theology, moral theology, spiritual theology, historical theology, and finally, to the Cinderella of the seminary, practical or applied theology. This last is usually where theologians place marketplace theology. Who, I ask, would want to be a professor of applied theology exclusively in that system? But, and I say this as an "applied theologian," I certainly would not want to be a professor of unapplied theology.[23] Why?

Christian theology based on the Bible is like love for God (Mark 12:30). It is wholistic, engaging head, heart, and hands. This same wholistic pattern

---

you are a theologian." Spidlik, *Spirituality of the Christian East*, 327. Spidlik notes that in the Christian East contemplation was crystalized in a definition based in a false etymology: *theoria* meant *theo oran*, to see God in everything (327).

20. I realize that this is a blanket statement and only offer it as a viewpoint. But in my experience when I lecture in Asia the usual critique, not from the formal theologians who have largely been educated in the West, but from working people, is that my presentation is not practical. Interestingly the Parable of the Ten Minas is a case in point. The Greek word used for "Put this money to work" (Luke 19:13), *pragmateusasthe*, is the origin of the English word "pragmatic." The Chinese language itself is pictoral and practical. And Confucian culture is a pragmatic attempt to order society in a harmonious way.

21. Spidlik, *Spirituality of the Christian East*, 37.

22. Matthew the Poor, *Orthodox Prayer Life*, 164.

23. I am happy to share that I have worked with systematic and biblical theologians who were truly applied theologians. But the system seems to keep these disciplines separated.

also exists in the kingdom of God, which means not just thriving spiritually or mentally but socially, emotionally, and vocationally (Luke 4:18–19; Isa 61:1–7). Usually, when we do theology today, we divide the human person up: first the brains, then the heart, and finally the hands. Why cannot we start, for example, with hands as a way "in" and proceed to the heart and head? This is really doing theology from below, the subject of the next chapter, and then proceeding to do theology from above. Or why not start with the heart, with prayer, and proceed to the head and hands? Or better still, why not comprehensively engage head, heart, and hands together? Spiritual theology, for example, is not an add-on to systematic theology but a dimension of the whole. And practical theology is not, as Chan suggests, "more broadly concerned with action in the world"[24] but part of the whole. But that, however, is not the only problem with the fragmentation of theology.

Earlier I quoted, as a basic definition of theology, the Puritan William Perkins.[25] In a similar way, the Puritan William Ames defined theology as "the doctrine of living unto God."[26] Marketplace theology is a part of living and working unto God. But it must be inclusive no matter where we start.

For example, Simon Chan suggests in his magnificent volume on *Spiritual Theology*, a book which incidentally reflects an Asian perspective, that spiritual theology starts with the mystery of the faith and "leaves the theological formulations to provide the backdrop."[27] Chan rightly goes on to state that "spiritual theology seeks to discover the transcendent within every sphere of life and every area of experience."[28] So, to summarize, Martin Luther once said, "True theology is practical . . . speculative theology belongs to the devil in hell."[29] But is there an integrating principle, an integral experience, and a wholistic practice in general theology and marketplace theology in particular?

---

24. Chan, *Spiritual Theology*, 19.

25. Perkins, *Golden Chain* (1592), 177.

26. Chan, *Spiritual Theology*, 16n6. Chan notes that this was the opening sentence of William Ames's highly influential work, *The Marrow of Sacred Divinity*, published in 1642 (p. 240).

27. Chan, *Christian Spirituality*, 19.

28. Chan, *Spiritual Theology*, 19.

29. Luther, *Luther's Works*, 54:22, quoted in Maddox, "Recovery of Theology," 654.

Doing Marketplace Theology from Above

The Integrating Theme for Marketplace Theology

The lack of an integrating theme is everywhere manifest. Thus, to take spiritual theology as an example, spiritual theology gets dissected into ascetic theology (from the Greek word *askesis*, "to train"—spiritual development or a kind of "practical soul work" through a systematic and disciplined method), and mystical theology (seeking union with God and engaging in the contemplation of the supernatural dimensions of life with God). Further delineations of spiritual theology include the charismatic approach (concerned with power encounters, with signs and wonders, what Jonathan Edwards calls the "surprising works of God"[30]) and the evangelical approach (arising from a conversionist approach to spiritual theology and focussing on the gospel understood as new birth and a way to heaven).[31]

That being said, I am grateful to Simon Chan for his emphasis on the *two basic components of Christian spiritual theology: the Spirit* (note: this is not referring to the human spirit but to the Holy Spirit) *and the Word of God*. And *we discover in the Word of God a single integrating principle for marketplace theology in the kingdom of God embodying head (orthodoxy), heart (orthopathy), and hand (orthopraxy).*[32]

As *orthodoxy* the kingdom is the truth about God's effective, transformative, and life-giving rule over creation and life, bringing human flourishing and the thriving of all creation under the beautiful rule of God. That includes our work in the world. The kingdom starts in Genesis with the enlistment of the first human beings to bring in the kingdom through *their* God-given rule and their attempts to "fill the earth" with the glory of God through their presence and work. They were to take the sanctuary—a place of beauty, safety, and prosperity—into the world. God says in effect, "Work with me and in harmony with my purposes in bringing in the kingdom, developing the potential of creation and bringing human flourishing everywhere." In calling humankind to "rule" (Gen 1:28) over everything except themselves, God made Adam and Eve and their descendants vice-regents over everything on earth.

---

30. Quoted in Chan, *Spiritual Theology*, 38.

31. Sadly, this is what many people think of as the Gospel of Jesus—a ticket to heaven, rather than the very gospel Jesus actually proclaimed—which is the good news of the kingdom of God, God's life-giving rule which has already begun, in the here and now, but also not yet and coming at the second coming of Jesus. See Stevens, *Kingdom of God in Working Clothes*.

32. See Stevens, *Kingdom of God in Working Clothes*.

Regents serve the monarch when the king or queen is out of the country or is too young to serve. Bruce Waltke in his grand *Old Testament Theology* expresses it this way: "Genesis 1 confers this authoritative status of God's image to all human beings, so that we are all kings, given the responsibility to rule as God's vice-regents and high priests on earth."[33] That is, the man and woman were to *bring in* God's kingdom, to exhibit his rule "with power to control and regulate it, to harness its clear potential, a tremendous concentration of power in the hands of puny man! What authority he thus possesses to regulate the course of nature, to be a bane or a blessing to the world!" says William Dumbrell, former Dean at Regent College.[34] Then comes Jesus.

Jesus saw the kingdom as the integrating principle of his entire ministry of teaching and doing good through life-giving signs of the kingdom having come. He announced in his home synagogue that the kingdom has come *in himself* (Luke 4:16–21; Isa 61:1–7). So, for good reason the early church fathers used the term *autobasileia* (the kingdom of God in his own person) when referring to Jesus. But there is more than orthodoxy in announcing the kingdom of God. There is heart and soul.

Orthopathy enlists our inner life, our prayers, and our passion for the kingdom and the King. For example, the kingdom is simultaneously here and now, and not-here and not-now but coming (in fullness). This is the mystery of the kingdom, and how hard it is to live with mystery! The kingdom will be consummated at the second coming of Jesus. Consequentially the last book of the New Testament provisions our imagination, prayers, and work with the hope that eventually "the kingdom of the world [will] become the kingdom of our Lord and his Messiah, and he will reign for ever and ever" (Rev 11:15). Indeed, Jesus says in the Gospel of John that we cannot even *see* the kingdom without being born again (3:3). We need our spiritual eyes to see the kingdom. But we cannot enter the kingdom without being born again (3:5). Jesus commenting on this in Luke 16 indicates that the kingdom is not for the mildly interested but the desperate, "Everyone is forcing their way into it" (v. 16). We need passion and prayer to see and to enter the kingdom of God especially through our work. In a similar way Paul tells the Colossian slaves, "Whatever you do, work at it *with all your heart*, as working for the Lord, not for human masters" (emphasis mine, Col 3:23). Head, heart, but also hands.

---

33. Waltke, *Old Testament Theology*, 218.
34. Dumbrell, "Creation, Covenant and Work," 17.

Orthopraxy. Knowing the kingdom in actual practice is expressed by Jesus in the parables of the kingdom but especially a parable given near the end of his earthly reign, the Parable of the Ten Minas in Luke 19. There he tells the story of a person who goes away to be made king (there are some allegorical dimensions to this parable) while he trusts his servants with a mina each (three months' wages). Significantly he says to them, "Put this money to work until I come back" (v. 13). The word in the Greek language used for this practical action is the basis of the English phrase, "Be pragmatic" (*pragmateusasthe*). The first servant was pragmatic and made ten times the amount. He was given ten cities to rule over. He was called to advance the kingdom of his master. How does he rule? Primarily through his work. But the last servant was not pragmatic and, even with what he thought he had, kept his one mina intact. It was taken away.

We do marketplace theology with head, heart, and hands. The shape of marketplace theology in orthodoxy, orthopathy, and orthopraxy. The integrating theme of marketplace theology is the kingdom of God. We must now consider four ways that we will integrate faith and work.

How Marketplace Theology Is to Be Done

We can conceive of this as a quadrant. In one segment we have the intellectual truth of the marketplace under the purpose of God, the theology of work commonly called theology. We could give this the title "meaning." (I am deliberately using four titles which start with "m" for easy memory.) But meaning comes not just from the mind, but the heart and the hand. This, however, is mainly a matter of orthodoxy. In a second quadrant we deal with "mysticism" or spirituality, the more than rational dimension of our engagement in the world, both in ourselves and in the workplace. In short, "soul" or orthopathy. In the third and fourth quadrants we deal with "mission" and "morality" (ethics) as we engage in God's mission practically in and through our work in the world, and in the moral complexity of whatever society in which we are working. This is orthopraxy.[35] But this cannot be done merely in the academy or in the library.

Consequentially, marketplace theology needs to be done from "top down" and "bottom up." "*Top down*" or "from above" means starting with the revelation of God and God's purpose in Scripture and the tradition of the church. But we will apply it in life. But "*bottom up*" or "from below"

35. I have adapted here the matrix first proposed by David Miller in *God at Work*.

means beginning with practice through using case studies, work experiences, and workplace situations as the starting point, not just the endpoint. "Bottom up" theology could partially be crafted through *narrative and story*, seeing the intersection of the divine story with our own stories. This is what is called theological reflection. But "from below" theology does in fact depend on "from above" which primarily through Scripture and biblical theology provides perspective, correction, and inspiration. All of this involves a global perspective as we have seen—West and East, North and South—enriching the whole. So, Paul says to the Ephesians that it is only "together with *all* the Lord's holy people" (Eph 3:18, emphasis mine) that we can know the fullness of Christ and the gospel of Christ as it relates to work, worker, and workplace—head, heart, and hand together. So where does this leave you the reader (and me the author)?

If you and I ponder about (head), pray about (heart), and practice (hands) our work, as a worker and about the workplace in the light of God's presence and purpose as revealed in Scripture, we are becoming marketplace theologians. Let's see how this works out in forthcoming chapters starting with doing theology from below.

2

Doing Marketplace Theology from Below

Only experience makes a theologian.

MARTIN LUTHER[1]

The crucified Christ is to be seen with the eyes of the heart.

ALISTER MCGRATH[2]

THE VISION WE HAVE for this volume on marketplace theology is this: every person in the marketplace could become a theologian of practice. But to accomplish this the marketplace theologian must be *in* the marketplace, and preferably actively so. It is not obvious that one cannot learn well the doctrine in the classroom and do it later. In contrast *the best education is education in service*. It is transformative, not preparatory. And behind this is an important principle of spirituality: the attempt to know God apart from the activities of life is unreal. So, we in the Institute of Marketplace Transformation are attempting to raise up a generation of marketplace practitioners that are theologically reflective. We desire that people in the workplace should understand the meaning of what they are doing, find God in their Monday to Friday engagement, and engage in God's mission in and through their daily work.

---

1. Luther, *Luthers Werke*, 1:16. "Sola autem experiential facit theologum." Quoted in McGrath, *Luther's Theology of the Cross*, 207.

2. McGrath, *Luther's Theology of the Cross*, 207.

Chapter 1 introduced a wholistic approach to marketplace theology. In it we affirmed that an integral Biblical marketplace theology involved thought (*theoria*), prayer (*ora*), and practice (*praxis*). It is hard to imagine how radical this view is because we have become acculturated to an applied theology as a discipline taught in seminaries to prepare people for their clerical duties in the church: apologetics, preaching, pastoral care, equipping, counseling, and evangelism. But, as we have already seen, if people ponder (think), pray, and act reflectively on their life in the marketplace, not just in a linear way, but in a spiral of learning and growth (acting and reflecting, reflecting and acting, praying and acting, acting and praying), they are beginning marketplace theologians—perhaps without knowing it!

Chapter 1 included my adaptation of William Perkins's definition: "Marketplace theology is the science of working blessedly forever." In this chapter we are continuing to explore that second phrase in our definition, the *science*, the investigation of marketplace theology, especially as it involves doing theology from below (starting from concrete human experiences in the workplace) as well as from above (starting with the revelation of God in Scripture). There are strong biblical and educational reasons for this synergistic approach to the relationship of thought, prayer, and action.

Practice, Pondering, and Prayer in that Order

Many of the commands of Jesus link revelation with obedience and practice: "If you keep my commands, you will remain in my love" (John 15:10); "If you hold to my teaching, you are really my disciples" (8:31); "Whoever obeys my word will never see death" (8:51). Sometimes, Jesus invited people to "believe this"; more often Jesus said "do this and you will live" (Luke 10:28; see also Matt 19:21; John 7:17). Jesus issued a call to the early disciples, and to all disciples today, to follow him (Luke 5:11, 27; 9:1–2, 59). Following Jesus was and is a total life apprenticeship to and communion with the Lord.

Especially in the Gospel of Luke, Jesus teaches that obedient action is the organ of further revelation. "If they do not listen to Moses and the Prophets," he said, "they will not be convinced even if someone rises from the dead" (Luke 16:31). Jesus puts these words on the lips of Abraham in the parable of the Rich Man and Lazarus and proclaims that even his own resurrection will have little evidential value if they are not acting on what they presently know. Many of the disciples were not able to verbalize their faith in Jesus as Messiah and Son of God when they started to follow him (Matt 16:13–20). For them belonging preceded believing; following led to knowing; acting led to revelation.

So, knowing is wholistic. It is active. Consequently, Francis of Assisi once said, "Humankind has as much knowledge as it has executed." That means that what you really know—in the fully biblical and Hebraic sense of intercourse—is how you live and work. For example, James Houston, founding principal of Regent College, said at a pastors' conference—shockingly—that the curriculum vitae of a pastor is written on the face of his wife. But Francis and Houston are not the only theologians of practice.

Christian philosopher from Denmark, Søren Kierkegaard, affirmed that we learn by doing. "The law for the communication of ability is: begin by doing it. The student says: 'I cannot'. Then the teacher answers: 'Now, now, do it as well as you can'. Thereby the instruction begins. Its end is to be able."[3] Kierkegaard freely attributes this idea to his mentor Socrates who argued that virtue cannot be taught, but must take the form of a "being-able, an exercising, an existing, an existential transformation," says a student of Kierkegaard, Christian Breuninger.[4] For Kierkegaard, "Christianity is not doctrine, it is an existence, an existing. Christianity is not the doctrine about denying yourself . . . Christianity is to deny oneself."[5] According to Kierkegaard, "the best school for learning Christianity is in the world . . . In other words, Kierkegaard is groping for a way to mobilize Christianity out of the Church and into the world: 'from a Christian point of view, to confess Christ is to do it in the situation Christianity assigns: the actual world.'"[6] In truth we are facing the same kind of corruption of Christianity Kierkegaard faced. Another voice in asserting the need to learn, believe, and grow by doing is Dietrich Bonhoeffer, theologian and Second World War martyr.

Bonhoeffer remembers a conversation he had with a French Christian in which that person said he wanted to become a saint. Bonhoeffer admits that he was impressed, and thinks he, the French Christian, may have well done that. But Bonhoeffer responded that he wanted to learn to have faith, not realizing at the moment what a contrast that was.

3. Kierkegaard, *Journals and Papers*, 1:#656.

4. Kierkegaard, *Journals and Papers*, 1:#1060, quoted in Breuninger, "Usefulness of Soren Kierkegaard's Strategy," 39.

5. Kierkegaard, *Journals and Papers*, 1:#1061, quoted in Breuninger, "Usefulness of Soren Kierkegaard's Strategy," 40.

6. Kierkegaard, *Journals and Papers*, 4:#4056, quoted in Breuninger, "Usefulness of Soren Kierkegaard's Strategy," 40.

> I discovered later, and I'm still discovering right up to this moment, that it is only by living completely in this world that one learns to have faith . . . By this-worldliness I mean living unreservedly in life's duties, successes, and failures, experiences, and perplexities. In doing so we throw ourselves completely into the arms of God.[7]

So too, I am arguing that the marketplace is an arena for growth in faith, growth in the knowledge of God and God's purpose in and through work. We have lost doctrine as a way of life. How could we have missed this fundamental truth, especially in the Western world?

The Decline and Fall of Applied Theology

Initially practical or applied theology in the West was not a separate discipline but a way of speaking of theology itself. Theology was considered a *practical* science as early as Duns Scotus. "Widespread from the Middle Ages through the seventeenth century is the view that 'theology' names a *habitus* or a disposition of the soul . . . of a practical not just a theoretical kind. Theology is, accordingly, a practical knowledge having the character of wisdom since its object is God and the things of God grasped in the situation of faith and salvation."[8] So says Edward Farley in reviewing the history and promise of applied theology. But in the seventeenth century in the West something happened.

Moral theology in general expanded to include ministry activities. An isolated instance was seventeenth-century Reformed theologian of Holland Gisbertus Voetius. He proposed broadening practical theology to include both moral theology and the activities of ministry. In the eighteenth century the clericalization of applied theology was furthered. Applied theology became pastoral theology which emerged as separate from moral theology—concerned with *poimenics* (the activities of the minister). The isolated instances of this in the seventeenth century became more widespread in the eighteenth century. N. H. Gundling (1753) claimed that practical theology included pastoral, casuistic, and homiletical subjects.[9] In the nineteenth-century, practical theology became fully clericalized, a fourth theological discipline, but not including ethics. Applied theology then had five

---

7. Dietrich Bonhoeffer in a letter from Tegel prison, 1944, quoted in Melanie Morrison, "As One Stands Convicted," 15.

8. Farley, "Interpreting Situations," 18.

9. Farley, "Interpreting Situations," 19.

subdivisions: homiletics, catechetics, liturgics, church jurisprudence, and pastoral care.[10] It was limited to a science in the university/seminary setting, and further narrowed from a church-clergy science to a solely clergy science. A stunning example of this is the lovely work, Richard Baxter's *The Reformed Pastor*. Then comes the Enlightenment, that European intellectual movement of the late seventeenth and eighteenth centuries that emphasized reason and individualism rather than tradition. It was heavily influenced by seventeenth-century philosophers such as Descartes, Locke, and Newton, and its prominent exponents included Kant, Goethe, Voltaire, Rousseau, and Adam Smith.

Enlightenment definitions of theology reduced theology to the God-talk of Job's miserable comforters: rational, objective, and abstracted. Following Enlightenment assumptions, theological colleges separated the "academic" (rational) subjects—biblical studies, history, systematic theology, philosophy, and ethics—from the practical subjects. The result of this was that the "academic" subjects themselves became fragmented and distorted, conformed to university disciplines (as though practice had no intrinsic place in these disciplines), and the practical theology field was reduced largely to how-to techniques.[11] The "nineteenth-century consensus," however, was critiqued by Roman Catholics—who wanted applied theology returned to the church. Then came the twentieth century.

With the twentieth century, the ascendency of technique brought further specialization in the fields of applied theology: counseling, leadership, equipping, discipline, church growth, urban mission, and evangelism. At the same time both Catholics, especially following Vatican II, and Protestants called for a comprehensive discipline of praxis in the world, an applied theology of the whole people of God, not only in the life of the church but in the world. We are now being challenged by postmodernism to be more wholistic[12] though we should not abandon reason in the process! In the twenty-first century, with the decline of Christianity in the West, and the emerging of Christianity in some of the majority world, seminaries are slowly beginning to offer courses for non-clergy people of God, not only to serve better in the church, but for their service in the world. And in North America, institutes, including the Institute for Marketplace Transformation, are multiplying like the proverbial mustard seed and attempting to do

---

10. Farley, "Interpreting Situations," 3–4.
11. Dykstra, "Reconceiving Practice," 55.
12. See Grenz, "Star Trek and the Next Generation."

what the seminaries and churches would not do. But why did it happen in the first place?

If all the disciplines of the theological academia were consistently taught as the Bible proposes—"faith expressing itself through love" (Gal 5:6)—would there be any need for a separate discipline of applied theology? In this context Craig Dykstra does a fine piece of analysis on right practice.[13] He wonders whether the teaching of other disciplines in a wholistic way—taking praxis into consideration—would eliminate the need to teach applied theology at all! Dykstra thinks this is too idealistic a dream. But I would personally welcome the demise of applied theology as a separate discipline. And this chapter takes the view that marketplace theology must be wholistic involving thought, prayer, and practice. So, we are asking, what does it mean to have a theology of doing and especially doing in the marketplace (the third dimension in our theological triad of pondering, prayer, and practice)?

Towards a Theology of Good Works: Orthopraxy[14]

We are in desperate need today of a theology of good works, especially among evangelicals. We are saved by grace through faith and not by works; that is part of the gospel. But faith without works is dead and that is an implication of the gospel too. So, the Roman Catholic mentor of the late Pope John Paul II, Cardinal Stefan Wyszynski, uses the term "salvation" for what Protestants might prefer to use the term "sanctification." Wyszynski says,

> Work by its difficulty, redeems, liberates, ennobles, and sanctifies.... The sweat of a man's toil-stained face marks a suffering that purifies not so much the body as the soul. In this suffering is the whole Calvary of man who dies every day on the cross of his life to destroy death by this slow-death agony, and so attain the glory of resurrection.[15]

Is this what Luther meant when he said that there is a cross to be taken up in the marketplace? And is this not what Paul was referring to when he

---

13. Dykstra, "Reconceiving Practice."

14. Some of the following is abstracted from "Living Theologically."

15. Wyszynski, *All You Who Labor*, 98. Wyszynski continues to write, "Work becomes an instrument, one of the means of salvation" (p. 99). This is to be distinguished from the kind of works righteousness about which Luther reacted in a time when he viewed the monastery as a kind of salvation machine.

wrote in Phil 2:12–13: "Continue to work out your salvation with fear and trembling, for it is God who works in you to will and to act in order to fulfill his good purpose." So, faith engages the whole person in thought, prayer, and action. What, however, is right practice? When is a deed, or work itself, "Christian?" I propose as an answer the following: What makes an activity Christian is not the husk but the heart. It is faith, hope, and love.

Martin Luther deals with this brilliantly in his "Treatise on Good Works." In that treatise, Luther describes the works of a husband who is confident of his wife's love, and even a little thing or a small gift to her will please her since it arises from this confidence. He compares this to a husband who is in a state of doubt and worries whether even a big gift or a great action can win his wife's favor. Luther then compares this to our relationship with God. The person who has gospel confidence can sweep the floor or give a cup of coffee gladly and generously knowing as David says in Ps 41:11, "I know that you [the Lord] are pleased with me." The second person, he says, is "in a state of doubt, worries and starts looking for ways and means to do enough to influence God by his many good works."[16]

The unselfconsciousness of such faith-action is a matter raised by the disturbing parable of the Sheep and Goats (Matt 25:31–46) where both the righteous and the unrighteous are *surprised* that what they did or did not do to "the least of these my brothers and sisters" was *done or not done to Jesus himself*. We onlookers are caught up in the parable and are surprised by the implication that loving and compassionate actions (surely intrinsically Christian practices) are Christian precisely because they did not have a spiritual reward in view!

They are Christian, Luther would say, because they arise from gospel confidence, from the generosity of a heart set free by acceptance with Christ. It is this element of surprise for which we are least prepared when we ponder the parable. Perhaps one of the purposes of theological education is to set us up to be the righteous ones surprised on the day of judgment when we discover we acted in love when we shared a cup of coffee with a neighbor, visited someone in prison, shared a meal with someone, built a home for someone, or repaired a broken gear for a printing company, without knowing it was directly for and to Jesus. Received by Jesus. So, it is not the religious character of our actions—the Bible open, the name of

---

16. Luther, "Treatise on Good Works," 27.

Christ proclaimed—that makes our actions Christian, but faith, hope, and love.17 But there is more.

On a most basic level *orthopraxy*—right action—is about practices that are in harmony with God's *kingdom* in the church and world, that bring value and good into the world. Good work does that. Good work, theologian Karl Barth notes, improves, and embellishes human existence, does not use human beings as tools, provides time and space for reflection, and is limited by Sabbath.18 But there is much more to *orthopraxis* than the *application* of rational and mental truth. There is revelation and illumination—knowing through doing. We should speak of this as a spiral of learning—theory, prayer, and practice—as we keep re-entering each phase at a deeper level.

The *orthodoxy-orthopraxy* tension in the West reflects the intrinsic dualism of Western Christianity, and the lingering effects of the Enlightenment. In contrast, the Bible invites us to wholistic living that embraces truth, as truth learned through faithful pondering, praying, and practice, all in a seamless robe. The late Ray S. Anderson notes, "Paul's theology and mission were directed more by the Pentecost event which unleashed the Spirit of Christ through apostolic witness rather than through apostolic office. This praxis of Pentecost became for Paul the 'school' for theological reflection."19 The gospels and the Acts point to the same unity of knowledge.

Every action has implicit theory just as every theory has implicit action. So theological reflection in a societal occupation (or church ministry for that matter) is essential for living theologically. But in these matters, we are not trying to squeeze blood from a rock. Daily life is bursting with theological meaning. What a strange marriage psychology that would require one to love fully and then only to kiss, rather than to kiss in order to love! What a strange perversion of the Christian life that would forbid one to act until one knows fully, and to forbid someone to act in order to know! So we are left with the basic question: How can we do theological reflection on our actual practice?

---

17. I wrestle with working in faith, hope, and love in chapters 1–3 of Stevens, *Seven Days of Faith*.

18. Preece, *Changing Work Values*, 178–79.

19. Anderson, *Praxis of Pentecost*, 163.

Inside Christian Practice

Can we do theological reflection by introspection, plumbing the depths of our own soul for clues as to whether we are acting in faith, hope, and love? Or is it a mostly unconscious thing that we are acting, like Luther's gospel-confident person, out of true acceptance with God? Can we do theological reflection through prayer? Or pondering (thinking)? As we have already seen, theological reflection is done both from above and below and involves all three of head, heart, and hands. Let me offer some ways of doing it.

A case study is a great way to do theology "from below." In a case, a person tells or writes the story of a concrete dilemma, but the case turns out to be universally significant—the more personal the more universal. In a case study we are starting not with the revealed truth of God's Word but with a life or work situation.[20] We deal with the case by beginning to identify the central issues in the case. Then we ask whether there are verses of Scripture, taken in context, that apply directly to this situation, addressing the core issues. Sometimes there will be a biblical story that illuminates the situation described in the case, for example, the story of Joseph, Daniel, or Esther. We then consider biblical theology—creation, fall, redemption, and consummation—asking whether these great biblical themes give insight into the situation. And finally, we explore options for action and then we act. The aim in doing case studies is that people will be formed, as Jonathan Wilson proposes, so that they just do it well without reflecting and deciding as great athletes do all the right things to score a goal, or people show mercy as a matter of course.[21] But there are other ways of doing theology from below.

We can listen to the questions people are asking and reflect on them. Or we can identify what is happening in the world and reflect on it. We can explore felt needs such as work-life balance, shame, time, significance, security, and vocational transition. We can do theology from below by hearing the stories of people and discerning the meaning of their work, as well as how they are doing the work of God. In my experience it takes a full hour (minimum) to hear a person's story. Examining and reflecting on evocative dimensions in so-called secular culture is another way of doing this.

---

20. For a good example of a case study and the development of it see the opening paragraphs of Stevens, *Other Six Days*, ch. 5, and the notes at the end of the chapter.
21. Email correspondence on November 15, 2022.

Interviewing ordinary people in the workplace either privately or possibly in the church service can be a great way of doing theology from below. Questions to ask are: What do you do for a living? What are the issues you face in your daily work? How does your faith impact and make a difference to how you deal with those issues? And finally, how can we pray for you for your ministry in the workplace? Do that with ordinary church members once each week for fifty-two weeks and you will have turned the church inside out, and in the process "ordained" fifty-two people for their full-time ministry in the workplace. So, there is a theology of application or, as it is sometimes called, theological reflection on life. For further reading I am providing a bibliography on this subject which is found in the footnote.[22]

I especially encourage you to note the book edited by Irene Alexander and Charles Ringma on *Pub Theology: Where Potato Wedges and a Beer are a Eucharistic Experience*. In it they tell the story of how they arranged with a pub in Brisbane, Australia, that one Friday night each month the pub would be available for theological presentations, really as life story, by someone they knew, especially not inviting professional top-down theologians. These stories are wrung out of personal experience, the good and the bad of it: loss, anger, loneliness, unemployment, divorce, immigration, marginalization, laughter, provision, mission, and neighboring, just to mention a few. In the introduction Alexander and Ringma explain what they were doing:

> First of all, theology in the pub is a "lay" theology. In other words, it is grassroots and bottom up. . . . This theology has ordinary persons of faith talking about what sense they have made about important decisions of life in the light of their religious values.
>
> Secondly, theology in the pub is free-flowing theology. . . . Pub theology is not an exercise in apologetics. Rather, this theology is more one of testimony.

---

22. A bibliography for doing theology from below would include Alexander and Ringma, *Pub Theology*; Stone and Duke, *How to Think Theologically*; Volf and Bass, *Practicing Theology*. The closing chapter by Volf on "Theology for a Way of Life" is especially worth reading (pp. 245–63); Graham et al., *Theological Reflection*. In this book the introduction (pp. 1–21) is especially worth reading. In the context of outlining various ways of doing theological reflection, this book also contains fascinating examples of how theological reflection has been done by believers throughout Christian history; O'Connell Killen and de Beer, *Art of Theological Reflection*. This text has a number of helpful perspectives but is light on biblical authority; Chan, *Grassroots Asian Theology*. "Grassroots theology . . . reflects the lived theology of Christians in their ecclesial experiences. It is not bound by elitist sociopolitical or individual experiences, but is 'essentially an ecclesial endeavor requiring cooperation between the people of God and the theologian.'"

Thirdly, pub theology is more dialectical. The speakers do not present some tidy theological system. Instead, they are wrestling with issues and as they deal with ambiguity. Theirs is a theology "on the road," rather than a theology of destination.[23]

But, lest I be misunderstood I must clarify something.

As described in the previous chapter we must do theology not only "from below" but also "from above." Theology from above starts with divine revelation in Scripture and insists that it not be mere information about God and God's purpose but enacted revelation, fleshed out in the nitty-gritty of everyday life, including the workplace.

So, for example, as we open the Bible we discover God as a worker who still works, as Jesus said in John 5:17: "My Father is always at his work to this very day, and I too am working." But Gen 1:27 says that God made humankind in his own image, which must include the work that we share with God as co-Creators or, as some prefer, sub-Creators, but not on the same scale. And God does work we cannot do. So, all our work in the marketplace, provided it is good work, enters into God's ongoing work of creation, sustaining, redemption, and consummation. We will take this up more fully in another chapter.

Biblical Examples of Doing Theology from Below

Doing theology "from above" is normal in theological thinking. But I am proposing a shift from the "applied theology" mentality—which largely has been hijacked to the service of practical strategies for churchmanship as part of the clerical captivity of the church—to the "theology of application." Why? Because Scripture models doing theology from below. For example, there are at least three books in the Old Testament and part of the New Testament that in my view start with life and ask questions about our experience of life and work in the presence of God. The first is Ecclesiastes.

Ecclesiastes and Thinking about Life

There are at least two views of this professor's dark reflections on life "under the sun," the code word in the book for *not* referring to a transcendent and personal God—in short, two-dimensional life.[24] One view is that he

---

23. Alexander and Ringma, *Pub Theology*, 2.
24. For an excellent and recent scholarly work on Ecclesiastes I recommend Charles,

knows the answer but is confronted by a thoughtful secularist and takes this inquirer's questions to their logical conclusion, namely that life without God is meaningless. It is, *hebel*, "a puff of smoke." But the other view is the one I take, namely that the professor is asking *his own questions* about the meaning of money, work, pleasures, religion, and success without God and with God. In so doing he concludes where Proverbs begins with the affirmation that life is meaningful if we "fear God" (Eccl 12:13), which surely means intimate, affectionate respect, and reverence of God—in short, a three-dimensional life. In my view this professor has discovered meaning through *examining his experience of life* both "under-the-sun" and "under-heaven." We will explore this further in chapter 3. But there is a second Old Testament book that starts with life from a different angle—Job.

Job and Praying about Life

Unlike the Professor in Ecclesiastes who, as a thinker, asks, as I have proposed, his own questions in the presence of God, Job addresses God directly with the terrible experiences he is having in life. In this case, theology is wrung out of experience, not simply applied to his experience. His traditional theological "friends," if we dare call them this, were orthodox and "top down" theologians and their speeches could have been published in a fine Christian journal. But they were damned.

As George MacDonald, an influence on C. S. Lewis, suggests, "There is nothing so deadening to the divine as a habitual dealing with the outsides of holy things."[25] Indeed when God finally speaks to Job's "friend" Eliphaz, God says "I am angry with you and your two friends, because you have not spoken well of me, *as my servant Job has*" (42:7, emphasis mine). To speak well of God is to be a theologian. But Job, who is a good theologian by God's standards, though a dismal failure before his friends, attacked and pestered God, like the widow before the unjust judge in Jesus's parable (Luke 18:1–8). Job lamented about his situation directly to God and, surprisingly, is affirmed in the end by God. And blessed by God.

In passing we should note that Job in his blustering attacks on God stumbled on the gospel in three remarkable ways. First, he became

---

Wisdom and Work. Charles masterfully develops the main thrust of Ecclesiastes, namely that "nothing in life has meaning apart from a theistic outlook" ("Wisdom Literature," 40). By a theistic outlook Charles is referring to the fear of YHWH.

25. MacDonald, *Curate's Awakening*, 176.

convinced that if God could become human they would settle this issue once and for all—"He is not a mere mortal like me that I might answer him" (Job 9:32). Second, he believes he has an advocate in heaven, a lawyer who will plead his case—"my witness is in heaven; my advocate is on high" (16:19). Third, Job affirms that he has a *goel*, a family kinsman with the power to redeem him, but this *goel*, this redeemer-relative, is in heaven and that "in the end he will stand on earth. And after my skin has been destroyed, yet in my flesh I will see God" (19:25–26).

Job discovers the gospel through his agony. And then, but only then, Job has a revelation of God (38–41). The issue for Job is whether he has gratuitous faith, that is, faith that is not dependent on the benefits of believing. So, Satan says to God in the opening dialogue, "Does Job fear God for nothing?" (1:9). But Job proves he is a true believer, that he has gratuitous faith, when he cries out, "Though he slay me, yet will I hope in him" (13:15). Why the difference in the Lord's evaluation between the friends, whom I am calling orthodox (Western) theologians, and Job?

It is simply this: while the friends of Job talked *about* God to Job, Job talked *to* God about his life situation. The friends were top-down theologians, thinking and talking; Job prayed. I have in my Bible all the verses underlined where Job prayed to God. It is his most common theological strategy. For the friends there are no prayers, only the constant handling of the outside of holy things. Remarkably, the liberation theologian Gustavo Gutiérrez says that Job shows us that it is more important to contemplate God than to understand (intellectually) God's justice.

> The truth that [Job] has grasped and that has lifted him to the level of contemplation is that justice alone does not have the final say about how we are to speak of God. Only when we have come to realize that God's love is freely bestowed do we enter fully and definitively into the presence of the God of faith . . . God's love, like all true love, operates in the world not of cause and effect but of freedom and gratuitousness.[26]

Job was doing theology from below. But there is a third book in the Bible that demonstrates doing theology from below—the Psalms.

---

26. Gutiérrez, *On Job*, 87.

The Psalms and Praying Emotionally

In the Psalms the whole range of human experience is brought before God in prayer. John Calvin said of the Psalms that they are "an anatomy of all the parts of the soul."

> There is not an emotion of which any one can be conscious that is not here represented as in a mirror. Or rather, the Holy Spirit has here drawn . . . all the griefs, sorrows, fears, doubts, hopes, cares, perplexities, in short, all the distracting emotions with which the minds of men are wont to be agitated.[27]

The word of God in the Psalms is this: you can bring your entire experience to God. You can tell the whole truth about yourself to God, expressing your emotions without reserve. There is no situation you can be in which you cannot take it to God. And in the process, you will be able to worship God even though God's ways are largely inscrutable. It is this metamessage of the Psalter that is, in my view, as important as the message of the individual Psalms. So, the Psalter shows us how to find meaning in life through *existential experience and prayer*. But what about the New Testament?

Starting with Life Experiences in the New Testament

Paul became a Christian and saw Jesus as the Son of Man partly through his intense opposition to the Christian sect, so much so that he dragged men and women who followed Jesus out of their homes and into jail. Paul was there when they stoned Stephen, holding the coats of those who stoned this first missionary to death. He heard Stephen announce as he died that he could see Jesus standing at the right hand of God as the Son of Man, that enigmatic figure found in the book of Daniel, chapter 7. In that Old Testament book the Son of Man was a boundary breaker. He brought the non-Jewish world to God and introduced the kingdom of God to the entire human race (Dan 7:13–14). Not surprisingly, the Son of Man was the favorite self-designation of Jesus.[28]

This encounter with Stephen prepared Saul for his encounter with the risen Christ on the Damascus road. Following Saul/Paul's being apprehended by Christ it seems that Paul hammered out the doctrine of justification

---

27. Calvin, *Commentary on the Psalms*, Part 1, 1:xxxvii.
28. Marshall, "Son of Man," 776.

by faith through grace in the context of the gentile mission, doing theology from below as well as above. His encounters in the gentile world, his disputing with the Judaizers who wanted gentile believers to come to Jesus through the law and circumcision, was revelatory for Paul and led him to interpret Scripture differently from his peers.

And not only Saul/Paul but a second apostle, Peter, discovered through a dream and a Spirit-led encounter with the gentile Cornelius that God does not play favorites, that God includes the outsider in his kingdom (Acts 10). This experience of revelation through action accords with the theological template for exploring practical experience known as the Methodist quadrilateral. According to this template, four things must be considered to gain truth—Scripture, reason, tradition, and experience.[29]

So, having typified the three ways of doing theology as Eastern—through prayer (Psalms, Job), Western—through thought and reason (Ecclesiastes), and Asian—through practice (Paul and Peter), this last way—through practice—has merit as it is especially illuminated for us in the Asian context which is culturally grounded in Confucianism.[30] Taken together, head, heart, and hand, it seems that truly it is only *together with all the saints* that we can grasp the depth of the good news of the kingdom of God and the King (Eph 3:18).

Why do theology from below? We do it to make sense of life experiences. We do it to gain wisdom in perplexing life situations. We do it to seek God's guidance and direction when there is no clear biblical direction. We do it, as Job did, to find meaning in our lives in the light of God's story. A truly biblical theology of the marketplace must include head, heart, and hand—exactly what a kingdom theology of the marketplace provides.[31]

We turn now to a central dimension of marketplace theology, the theology of work. We do so remembering William Perkins's (modified) definition of marketplace theology: "Marketplace theology is the science of *working* blessedly forever."

---

29. Stone and Duke, *How to Think Theologically*, 46–56.

30. Undoubtedly Confucian thought continues to provide a profound influence on Asian theology. Confucius outlined the seven steps to gaining peace in the earthly kingdom—a very practical goal: 1. the investigation of things; 2. the completion of knowledge; 3. the sincerity of the thoughts; 4. the rectifying of the heart; 5. the cultivation of the person; 6. the regulation of the family; 7. the government of the state.

31. Please see my book, *Kingdom of God in Working Clothes*.

THE MEANING
OF WORK

3

Going to Work with the Professor

Only when a person has become so unhappy or has penetrated the wretchedness of his existence so deeply that he must truly say: for me life has no value—only then can he make a bid for Christianity.

SØREN KIERKEGAARD[1]

In spite of God's respect and love for man, in spite of God's extreme humility in entering into man's projects, in the long run one cannot but be seized by a profound sense of the inutility and vanity of human action.

JACQUES ELLUL[2]

I AM A PROFESSOR but not like the one who forms the title of the Old Testament book of Ecclesiastes, a person who had enormous influence and a harem! I have been married to one wonderful woman for sixty years. I am calling the author of Ecclesiastes "The Professor" because the Hebrew form, Qoheleth, of the Greek title, Ecclesiastes, is based on the Hebrew word *qahal* which suggests that he is someone who gathers or convenes an assembly. He self-designates as a "Teacher, son of David, king in Jerusalem" (1:1), not quite calling himself Solomon after whom he styles himself. Other terms have been used to describe him: Preacher, Philosopher, Spokesperson, or President. This person I am calling the Professor is researching life. He is

---

1. Kierkegaard, *Journals and Papers*, 2:#1152.
2. Ellul, "Meditation on Inutility," 190.

starting with concrete experiences in everyday life and trying to find the meaning of it. Rather than doing theology from above, which starts with revelation and proceeds to application, the Professor is doing theology from below starting with life and proceeding to revelation. We have been considering work through thought (the head), through prayer (the heart), and now through doing it (the hand).

Doing Theology from Below

So, to elaborate the conclusions of his research the Professor uses a word that appears over and again in the book: *hebel*, which is usually translated "meaningless," in which he concludes, "Everything is meaningless" (1:2). The word suggests a puff of smoke, a vapor, futility, or meaninglessness. And meaning is what keeps us alive, keeps us working, keeps us contributing to the common good, keeps us enjoying our work, as Victor Frankl discovered in the concentration camp during World War II. The Professor, whether in his own journey or as an apologist, is starting where the people are, with the futility of life, with the world, or with pure unadulterated secularism. And he does this through using a code word in the book that occurs some thirty times: "under the sun."[3]

It is a way of saying, "here is what life is like when viewed and experienced without any reference to a transcendent God." In this context the Professor asks repeated rhetorical questions about life "under the sun." "What do I gain for all my hard work?" (1:3). "Who knows what is good?" (6:12). "Who can tell what will happen . . . after they are gone?" (6:12). And he asks these questions about pleasure, wisdom (meaning the wisdom of the world), religion, money, and critically as a major theme in the book, about work, which is our subject.

The Professor also uses the phrase "under heaven" (2:3) and in so doing refers to "God," meaning to say "here is what I have found life is like when viewed and experienced when a person has the fear of God." But he throws his research data both "under the sun" and "under heaven" together in a mixture of seeming inconsistencies. Jacques Ellul, the French theologian, says of Ecclesiastes, "Few books contradict themselves as much as this one, and I believe one of its main meanings resides precisely in these inconsistencies. They guide us to a point where we must recognize the true

---

3. Eccl 1:3, 9, 14; 2:11, 17, 18, 22; 3:16; 4:3, 7, 15; 5:18; 6:1, 12; 8:9, 15, 17; 9:3, 6, 9, 11, 13; 10:5.

character of human existence, and not just its reality: human existence is essentially self-contradictory."[4] Why, I ask, would he write this way? Why not sort out the inconsistencies and present a clear statement about the theology of work?

The Professor is a master of indirect communication for, as Ellul points out, we are faced here with "veiled truth."[5] In a footnote Ellul notes that "since truth remains immutable, transcendent, and absolute, we can reach it only through the most easily misconstrued, unstable, and fluid medium: the word."[6] He quotes Kierkegaard who thought that indirect communication was Jesus's primary suffering, "since he could not communicate directly to people that he was the Christ, the Son of God, God himself. (This explains why he never applies these titles to himself, using instead 'son of man'). Because of his indirect communication, this man who is God represents *both* the possibility of faith *and* the possibility of scandal."[7]

Kierkegaard himself in his *Journals and Papers* notes that "illusions are rarely destroyed directly."[8] In other words, "a direct attack elicits a defensiveness within one's listener which, in turn, fortifies their illusion."[9] Thus, not only when communicating about himself did Jesus use indirect communication but when he taught about the kingdom of God through parables he was casting down images through which the person hungry for God and his kingdom[10] might grasp the central message while others would listen but not hear. They won't get it. So, Robert Farrar Capon says,

> In resorting so often to parables, [Jesus's] main point was that any understanding of the kingdom his hearers could come up with would be a misunderstanding. Mention "messiah" to them, and they would picture a king on horseback, not a carpenter on a cross; mention "forgiveness" and they would start setting up rules about when it ran out. From Jesus' point of view, the sooner their

---

4. Ellul, *Reason for Being*, 39.
5. Ellul, *Reason for Being*, 119.
6. Ellul, *Reason for Being*, 118.
7. Ellul, *Reason for Being*, 119.
8. Kierkegaard, *Point of View*, 24–25, quoted in Breuninger, "Usefulness of Soren Kierkegaard's Strategy," 41.
9. Breuninger, "Usefulness of Soren Kierkegaard's Strategy," 41.
10. See J. Daryl Charles for evidence of the essentially negative approach to the book in his chapter, "Interpretive Strategy in Ecclesiastes."

misguided minds had the props knocked from under them, the better.[11]

The Professor does not use parables to communicate indirectly but he does use contradiction, and effectively so. What is the illusion that the Professor seeks to destroy? Is it the meaninglessness of work in the world? Or is it the illusion that if faith is embraced, work will automatically be successful, satisfying, and joyful?

The book of Ecclesiastes is sadly misunderstood, as evidenced by my Old Testament professor in theological school, several decades ago, who said that the person who wrote this book needed counselling! J. Daryl Charles suggests that it is possible that the writer is reflecting personally on his own experience—the view I personally take—though he prefers to see the writer contrasting two competing metaphysical outlooks as an apologist.[12] Essentially this book belongs to the genre of wisdom literature, which includes Job, Proverbs, Ecclesiastes, and some Psalms.[13] Unlike prophetic literature the message is not a cannon ball of inspiration, a blast from the other side. In this book wisdom comes to us with the force of a hint—a hint that God is present, whether bidden or not. It is a whispered suggestion that God does provide meaning in life. And so, the book is included in the canon, the books of the Bible that will not "defile the hands," just as much as Romans, Isaiah, or Zechariah.

This Professor is inviting us to do a thought experiment of what life is like without God and with God, for that is one of the characteristics of wisdom literature.[14] One characteristic of wisdom literature that is salutary is noted by Charles. "Wisdom knows no vocational dichotomy, no 'sacred-versus-secular' or tiering of classes."[15] So while we focus on the work passages in Ecclesiastes with its two views—the secular view "under the sun" and the sacred view "under heaven"—there is no dichotomy between so-called "sacred work," such as the work of a pastor, and so-called "secular work," such

---

11. Capon, *Parables of the Kingdom*, 8.
12. Charles, "Wisdom Literature," 59. Charles outlines the nature of wisdom literature in his chapter, "Wisdom Literature and the Wisdom Perspective."
13. Namely Pss 1, 37, 49, 73, 78, 91, 126.
14. Charles notes for us the characteristics of wisdom literature in the Bible: Its focus on how to live; its accent on actions, human labor, and economics; its pedagogical use of nature through analogy to reflect lessons for human nature; its implicit theology; its accent on experience and observation. Charles, "Wisdom Literature," 23–24.
15. Charles, "Wisdom Literature," 39.

as a merchant shipping grain across the Mediterranean. In fact, he says that the work of a pastor or a person seeking God through religious activity is, like other work, meaningless "under the sun." They are making a "sacrifice of fools."[16]

The interpretative key to the whole life and thought experiment of the Professor is found in verse 11 of chapter 3: "He [God] has made everything beautiful in its time. He has set eternity in the human heart; yet no one can fathom what God has done from the beginning to end" (3:11). So, what I now wish to do is to separate the "under the sun" statements—which the Professor has interspersed with the "under heaven" statements about work—something which the Professor has left strangely and intentionally connected.

Work "Under the Sun"

"What do people gain from all their labors at which they toil under the sun?" (1:3).

"I undertook great projects . . . houses, parks . . . a harem . . . My heart took delight in all my labor, and this was the reward for all my toil. Yet when I surveyed all that my hands had done and what I had toiled to achieve, everything was meaningless, a chasing after the wind; nothing was gained under the sun" (2:4–11).

"So I hated life, because the work that is done under the sun was grievous to me. All of it is meaningless, a chasing after the wind. I hated all the things I had toiled for under the sun, because I must leave them to the one who comes after me . . . What do people get for all the toil and anxious striving with which they labor under the sun?" (2:17–23).

"And I saw that all toil and all achievement spring from one person's envy of another. This too is meaningless, a chasing after the wind" (4:4).

"There was a man all alone . . . 'For whom am I toiling?' he asked . . . This too is meaningless—a miserable business" (4:8).

"Whoever loves wealth is never satisfied with their income" (5:10).

"The sleep of a laborer is sweet, whether they eat little or much, but as for the rich, their abundance permits them no sleep" (5:12).

"No one can comprehend what goes on under the sun. Despite all their efforts to search it out, no one can discover its meaning" (8:17).

---

16. Eccl 5:1–7; 7:16–18

"Enjoy life with your wife . . . all your meaningless days. For this is your lot in life and in your toilsome labor under the sun. Whatever your hand finds to do, do it with all your might . . . for in the realm of the dead, where you are going, there is neither working, nor planning nor knowledge nor wisdom" (9:9–10).

But meaninglessness is not the whole truth. Interspersed with these dreary and soul-deadening thoughts there are hints of another way. In his literary-rhetorical strategy[17] the Professor provides an alternative way of finding life's meaning—a theistic one.

Work "Under Heaven"

"A person can do nothing better than to eat and drink and find satisfaction in their own toil. This, too, I see is from the hand of God, for without him, who can eat or find enjoyment? To the person who pleases him, God gives wisdom, knowledge, and happiness, but to the sinner he gives the task of gathering and storing up wealth to hand it over to the one who pleases God. This too is meaningless, a chasing after the wind" (2:24–26).

"I know that there is nothing better for people than to be happy and to do good while they live. That each of them may eat and drink, and find satisfaction in all their toil—this is the gift of God. I know that everything God does will endure forever . . . God does it so that people will fear him" (3:12–14).

"So I saw that there is nothing better for a person than to enjoy their work, because that is their lot" (3:22).

"God is in heaven and you are on earth" (5:2).

"Much dreaming and many words are meaningless. Therefore fear God" (5:7).

"This is what I have observed to be good; that it is appropriate for a person to eat, to drink and to find satisfaction in their toilsome labor under the sun during the few days of life God has given them—for this is their lot. Moreover, when God gives someone wealth and possessions, and the ability to enjoy them, to accept their lot and be happy in their toil—this is a gift of God. They seldom reflect on the days of their life, because God keeps them occupied with gladness of heart" (5:18–20).

---

17. Charles, "Wisdom Literature," 56.

"I know that it will go better with those who fear God, who are reverent before him. Yet because the wicked do not fear God, it will not go well with them, and their days will not lengthen like a shadow" (8:12–13).

"So I commend the enjoyment of life, because there is nothing better for a person under the sun than to eat and drink and be glad. Then joy will accompany them in their toil all the days of the life God has given them under the sun" (8:15).

"When I applied my mind to know wisdom and to observe the labor that is done on earth—people getting no sleep day or night—then I saw all that God had done. No one can comprehend what goes on under the sun" (8:16–17).

"As you do not know the path of the wind, or how the body is formed in a mother's womb, so you cannot understand the work of God, the Maker of all things" (11:5).

"Sow your seed in the morning, and at evening let your hands not be idle, for you do not know which will succeed, whether this or that, or whether both will do equally well" (11:6).

"You who are young, be happy while you are young, and let your heart give you joy in the days of your youth . . . but know that for all these things God will bring you into judgment" (11:9).

"Now all has been heard: here is the conclusion of the matter: Fear God and keep his commandments, for this is the duty of mankind. For God will bring every deed into judgment" (12:13–14).

Derek Kidner in his concise and pithy commentary on Ecclesiastes notes that the

> compulsive worker of chapter two, over-loading his days with toil and his nights with worry, has missed the simple joys that God was holding out to him. The real issue for this worker is not between work and rest but between meaninglessness and meaningful activity. As verse 24 points out, the very toil that tyrannized him was potentially a joyful gift of God (and joy itself is another, in verse 25), if only he had the grace to take it as such.[18]

So I must ask out of this survey a question. What are we to make of this contrast, of this futility in everyday work and, at the same time, the hint of God's presence, his inscrutable presence in the affairs of the world and the details of our work life? What does the theistic view of work, work seen from and experienced under God, actually mean?

---

18. Kidner, *Time to Mourn*, 35.

Work Is a Gift

Charles does a study of the keywords in the book. *Hebel* (meaninglessness) appears thirty-eight times, the noun and verb forms of *simha* (enjoyment, pleasure, contentment) and *samah* (to enjoy, to be content) together appear seventeen times. And *tob* (good) appears fifty-two times.[19] Dorothy Sayers has it right. Work was meant to be a way of life, a source of delight, a way in which human beings can find fulfilment and a means of glorifying God. Work should be undertaken for the love of the work itself.[20] In the Genesis narrative, especially chapter 3, it is not work that is cursed but the ground that is cursed. Thorns and thistles will impede the work of Adam and Eve but it is the workplace that bears the worst effects of the fall. What does it mean to say "work is a gift" east of Eden? It means we are given this opportunity for self-expression and neighbor love. We are given the joy and satisfaction that comes with work in the presence of God. It means we are given a calling to work—it is vocational not merely aspirational.[21] It means we are created with the capacity to be like God in that we work.

But what if work is not satisfying? What if, as the joyless worker in chapter 2 discovered, it is just plain hard. What if we will be followed by a fool? What if we must leave all we have worked for to someone else? What if we find ourselves so occupied with the sweat of work, whether mental or physical, that we cannot sleep at night? The inspired author, I assume, is genuinely searching for an answer. This question plumbs the depths of our experience of work. It is a question asked not only by people at the end of a long hard day at the office or home, or by workaholic professionals who have discovered that their exciting careers are mere vanity and emptiness. Perhaps we can understand this kind of questioning.

But it is sometimes also secretly asked by people in Christian service careers who wonder if their preaching, counseling, and leadership is, in the end, useless and to no avail. Yet, taking account of the book of Ecclesiastes as a whole, it is crucial to observe that the Professor is not "down on life" as a matter of principle. On the contrary, he affirms that "A person can do nothing better than to eat and drink and find satisfaction in their own toil."

---

19. Charles, *Wisdom and Work*, 154n.

20. Sayers, "Why Work?," 89.

21. See Charles on the influence of Martin Luther on the Protestant doctrine of vocation in his reading of Ecclesiastes, *Wisdom and Work*, 141–47.

In fact, he says that this positive disposition to work is "from the hand of God" (2:24). So, the Professor is in a bind and, as a consequence, so are we.

Work as an Evangelist

This question about the uselessness of work probes our souls deeply. If work, even volunteer work in Christian service, proves to be meaningless, then perhaps we are being invited to conclude that we were not made for work in the first place, but rather made for God. The frustration, futility, resultlessness, and meaninglessness of much of our work life drives us to seek God, who has set eternity in our hearts, that God-shaped vacuum in our souls. This is the "heavy burden God has laid on mankind!" (1:13), namely finding meaning, true fulfilment, and happiness in life.[22] If the Professor is right, then we will not find satisfaction in our work even with the help of our faith, but rather find our satisfaction primarily in God in the experience of our work. It is a subtle but telling distinction.[23] And when we come to the Lord and take a theistic approach to life we find work is not utterly meaningless but rather satisfying and a gift of God.[24] It is true that God's ways are past our finding out, but God is providentially involved in our lives. Let me illustrate.

A young woman I taught in Africa graduated with a certificate but was assigned to a job that was much less than she dreamed of, and this work was a burden laid on her (3:10). I asked her a simple question, a silly, stupid, Western question: "Do you like your new job?" But she answered from the perspective of "under heaven." "I like it *in Jesus*," she replied—a sublimely simple shift from intrinsic to extrinsic meaning, though the extrinsic then becomes intrinsic to the work itself. That is to say, the shift is from the meaningfulness of the work itself, taken at face value, like extracting oil from the ground, to the extrinsic meaning that is experienced in the context of our work. God brings to us the meaning of our work. In God we bring meaning to our work.

Thus, work becomes an evangelist to take us to Christ. And the gospel we hear from Jesus is not that if we accept him we will be insanely happy and successful in our jobs, but that we will find our work to be satisfying "in

---

22. Charles, *Wisdom and Work*, 7.

23. This section on "Work as an Evangelist" was first published in Stevens, "Uselessness of Work."

24. Charles, *Wisdom and Work*, 12.

Jesus." He alone can fill the God-shaped vacuum in our souls. So, it is not just the Old Testament Professor but Jesus who asks the probing question we have been pondering. With absolute courtesy Jesus comes to us in the workplace not to tell us what to do with our lives but to ask what meaning we are discovering in our work. And then, with infinite grace, he offers himself.[25] But that is not all we learn about work from the Professor.

Work Is God's Work

All of the above comes to us with the force of a hint, a suggestion, because the ways of God are past our finding out. Kidner says, "the fascination of the book throughout its length arises largely from such collisions between obstinate facts of observation and equally obstinate intuitions."[26] There is providence involved, and this means that we are called vocationally to the work we do. Our lives are not a bundle of accidents, but God is engaged with us in a hidden way, bidden or not bidden. This means there is mystery in God. If God could be fitted into our puny brains he would be too small a God to worship. As Job said, "These are but the outer fringe of his works; how faint the whisper we hear of him!" (Job 26:14), or as the Professor put it, "As you do not know the path of the wind, or how the body is formed in a mother's womb, so you cannot understand the work of God" (Eccl 11:5). "Ecclesiastes constitutes a necessary reminder that God cannot be calculated, manipulated, localized, or humanly understood," so says Charles.[27] But what a pregnant hint! The thought goes deeper in chapter 11.

If God makes everything, if God is the "maker of all things" (11:5), then why work? But, says the Professor in effect, if you do not work you will not know that God is working! So Ellul reflects on this amazing truth:

> If you do nothing, if you fail to sow, if you keep staring at the clouds, you will not know the work of God who does everything. These words astonish: God does everything, yet I must do something! God will cause one thing or the other to succeed, or both things. But you and I must do them! . . . If you do nothing, you will be unable to perceive the work of God, because there may be no

---

25. Some of the above two paragraphs have been abstracted from Stevens, *Work Matters*, 21–24.
26. Kidner, *Time to Mourn*, 82.
27. Charles, *Wisdom and Work*, 83.

work of his to observe! . . . Let God do his work through you (but his action is through you, so your action is necessary!).[28]

Kidner expresses it this way: "Even as procreators we do no more than activate the mysterious process in which God brings into being a new life."[29] Here is a further indication of indirect communication. We are placed in a contradiction. "Everything lacks consistency. [Yet] God makes everything," Ellul points out.[30] And the Professor is not a skeptic. He believes that God has made everything beautiful in its time. But that too is a word that applies to work. As Ellul says, "the time when a thing is beautiful is God's time. In our action we must try to discover how to accomplish, in our time, the work God wants beautiful in his time. This amounts to discerning God's time." Ellul continues, "We need to learn how to work at just the moment God makes it beautiful, when he will take it up and take it over."[31] So we need to discern when to invest, when to create, or in the Professor's words, when is the best time to ship grain across the Mediterranean, because of the risk involved in work.

Work Involves Risk

In *Against the Gods: The Remarkable Story of Risk*, Peter Bernstein observes that "the word 'risk' derives from the early Italian *risicare*, which means 'to dare.'"[32] Thus Bernstein opens up a fascinating commentary on the role of risk. "In a sense," he continues, "risk is a choice rather than a fate. The actions we dare to take, which depends on how free we are to make choices, are what the story of risk is all about. And that story helps define what it means to be a human being."[33] But far older than this modern assessment of risk is the Professor's admonition to "Cast your bread on the waters," which in the NIV is interpreted as "Ship your grain across the sea" (11:1). If you see a cloud the size of a man's hand on the horizon and fear a storm, through which your investment may be lost, you will never take the risk. In

---

28. Ellul, *Reason for Being*, 226.
29. Kidner, *Time to Mourn*, 15.
30. Ellul, *Reason for Being*, 227.
31. Ellul, *Reason for Being*, 237.
32. Bernstein, *Against the Gods*, 8.
33. Bernstein, *Against the Gods*, 8.

the same way, "Whoever watches the wind will not plant; whoever looks at the clouds will not reap" (11:4).

So, the Professor wisely counsels investment in more than one venture, indeed seven or eight (11:2), as you do not know which will be fruitful, this or the other. The Greek dramas show human beings as helpless before the impersonal fates.[34] In some societies, luck determines the outcome. So, in his history of risk and risk management Bernstein reflects on the impressive achievement of the Arabs in inventing the mathematical symbols we universally use today. He notes how Christianity spread across the Western world and how "the will of a single God emerged as the orienting guide to the future, replacing the miscellany of deities people had worshipped since the beginning of time. This brought a major shift in perception."[35]

Bernstein asks, "Why, given their advanced mathematical ideas, did the Arabs not proceed with probability theory and risk management?" "The answer," he ventures, "has to do with their view of life. Who determines the future: the fates, the gods, or ourselves? The idea of risk management emerges only when people believe they are to some degree free agents."[36] Bernstein continues to assert that the Renaissance and the Protestant Reformation "would set the stage for the mastery of risk."[37] "Trade," he asserts, "is . . . a risky business. As the growth of trade transformed the principles of gambling into the creation of wealth, the inevitable result was capitalism, the epitome of risk-taking."[38]

Of course, the Professor writing in the third century BC was not advancing sophisticated, mathematically based risk management. But in the context of a personal God who is sovereign rather than impersonal fate, whimsical gods, or luck, he is assuring the merchant in Alexandra that it is not gambling to ship his grain to Rome, or to sow seed in the ground even though there are clouds on the horizon. Providence, which in Ecclesiastes is rightly deemed as inscrutable, means that God is ceaselessly operative in human affairs "even when this working is unseen and indescribable."[39] But there is more to our experience of work than this.

---

34. Bernstein, *Against the Gods*, 17.
35. Bernstein, *Against the Gods*, 19.
36. Bernstein, *Against the Gods*, 35.
37. Bernstein, *Against the Gods*, 20.
38. Bernstein, *Against the Gods*, 21.
39. Charles, *Wisdom and Work*, 16.

Work Is Joyful in God

Joy is the hallmark of the Christian person. It is a dominating theme in Ecclesiastes. We are to be inundated with joy—"God keeps them occupied with gladness of heart" (5:19). This is a remarkable reflection on our calling and is an amazing gift of God. Charles says that "joy [is] depicted in the *carpe diem* [enjoy the moment] refrains from 2:24–26 through 11:7–12:1. This joy mirrors the inbreaking of 'eternity' (3:11), as it were. Joy is intrinsic to the life of faith, not merely an antiseptic, or palliative from the pain of normal living. Rather, joy is "internal, constitutive, and grounding in their character."[40]

When we accept the presence of God we do not become suddenly and insanely happy with our work life. But we have joy, the mark of God's presence. The joy we experience is not just intrinsic to the work itself, like a treasure buried in the soil waiting to be found. The joy is in God. But we experience the joy of God in the context of our work, our marriages, and in everyday life. Derek Kidner opines on chapter 5:18–20, "we catch a glimpse of the man for whom life passes swiftly, not because it is short and meaningless but because, by the grace of God, he finds it utterly absorbing."[41] All of the above—the gift, the evangelistic role of work, the sense that we are working with God and doing God's work, the risk implicit in much work, and the joy of working—are viewed "under heaven" or in the "fear of God," to which subject we must finally turn.

Work Is Meaningful When We Fear God

In this book God is Creator, Sovereign, and Unsearchable Wisdom. This last descriptor drives us to admit that God is hidden and "reduces our most brilliant thoughts to little more than guesses," as Kidner says.[42] But God is also described in Ecclesiastes as a Judge who "will bring every deed into judgment, including every hidden thing, whether it is good or evil" (12:14). The professor is bringing us to the point where, when we say that nothing matters "under the sun," that all of life is meaningless, it is only so that we can hear "as the good news that it is" that "everything matters."[43]

---

40. Charles, *Wisdom and Work*, 125.
41. Kidner, *Time to Mourn*, 58–59.
42. Kidner, *Time to Mourn*, 16.
43. Kidner, *Time to Mourn*, 20.

And when we come to Jesus, in the fear of God, as the professor encourages us as his stated conclusion in 12:13—"Fear God and keep his commandments"—in reverent, awesome affection for God, we find meaning in work as well as meaning in life. The fear of God is not sheer fright of God, though some philosophers, especially Rudolf Otto, has proposed that we experience a *mysterium tremendum* and "numinous dread" in the presence of God. But we experience this mystery, this awesome One beyond ourselves, in the context of a relationship of grace from God and affection towards God, who is not a mere It, in the sense of raw impersonal power. As Martin Buber once said in his famous book, *I and Thou*, God is to be experienced as a Thou, not an It. My Thou. Personal.

The fear of the Lord in the Old Testament, says Old Testament scholar Bruce Waltke, "involves both the non-rational and the rational: the former, fear, love, and trust; the latter, ethics, justice, and uprightness."[44] Waltke continues to expound on the non-rational: "The heart that both fears and loves God at one and the same time is not divided but unified in a single religious response to God . . . both emotions are rooted in trust: faith in his threats, causing one to fear, and faith in his promises, causing one to love."[45] So he concludes that "without the felt awareness of God's holiness humans would not throw themselves through the veil of God's wrath against sin upon his merciful heart. As Newton taught us to sing, 'Twas grace that taught my heart to fear, and grace my fears relieved.'"[46] "Such fear," Dr. James Houston says, "brings blessing in every sphere of life."[47]

Blessings, not *hebel* (meaninglessness), is what we can experience in the workplace. So concludes Charles,

> Humans are created with a sense of the transcendent—the eternal (*'olam*)—in their hearts (3:11) . . . In its implications the statement is utterly profound, suggesting that human person's deepest longings cannot be filled by that which is temporal. It suggests that in the experience of true joy, something of the transcendent—something of the eternal—manifests itself. It is the antidote to the *hebel* of life "under the sun."[48]

---

44. Waltke, "Fear of the Lord," 21.
45. Waltke, "Fear of the Lord," 25.
46. Waltke, "Fear of the Lord," 24.
47. Houston, *I Believe in the Creator*, 189, quoted in Waltke, "Fear of the Lord," 31.
48. Charles, *Wisdom and Work*, 108–9.

Thus the Professor's ruminations can be considered eloquent, though down-to-earth, research (as theology done "from below"), anticipating the statement of the apostle Paul in Rom 8. "For the creation waits in eager expectation for the children of God to be revealed. For the creation was subjected to frustration [*hebel*], not by its own choice, but by the will of the one who subjected it, in hope that the creation itself will be liberated from its bondage to decay and brought into the freedom and glory of the children of God" (Rom 8:19–21).[49] Jacques Ellul concludes his meditation on Ecclesiastes with these probing words: "Qoheleth knows wisdom can follow only one first step: relationship with God . . . everything begins with this fear of God . . . God has led us by the hand to this last door, which is the first door to life."[50]

Now let us consider a theology of work based on the head (orthodoxy), and the heart (prayer and orthopathy), and, in chapter 5, the hand (orthopraxy).

---

49. See Charles for other NT confirmations, Acts 14:15; Rom 1:21; 1 Cor 3:20; 1 Cor 15:17; Eph 4:17; Titus 3:9; Charles, *Wisdom and Work*, 65.

50. Ellul, *Reason for Being*, 303.

4

Thinking and Praying about Work

> Meaning is the new money.
> DANIEL PINK[1]

> Every [believer] in his occupation or handicraft ought to be useful to his fellows, and serve them in such a way that the various trades are all directed to the best advantage of the community, and promote the well-being of body and soul, just as the organs of the body serve each other.
> MARTIN LUTHER[2]

> There is no work better than another to please God; to pour water, to wash dishes, to be a souter [cobbler], or an apostle, all are one, as touching the deed, to please God.
> WILLIAM TYNDALE[3]

OVER THE YEARS MY own work has included making steel rivets by hand (it was boring), preaching (complex feelings of awe and inadequacy), filing (restful work), committee work (I like committee meetings!), listening (not especially good at it), building houses (terrific, you can see what you have done), teaching (love it), writing (a total surprise), grading papers

---

1. Pink, *Whole New Mind*, 61.
2. Cited by Cyril Eastwood in *Priesthood of All Believers*, 12.
3. Summarized from Tyndale, *Parable of the Wicked Mammon*, 98, 104.

(instructive), and doing some domestic work (it is good). Will some of this work last into eternity and other work just be fluff? What is good work? What is the point of this work? Who benefits? Does work have both intrinsic and extrinsic value? What does work mean? Whose work matters to God? These are some of the questions that must be answered by a theology of work. I am defining work as any *purposeful* expenditure of energy, whether manual, mental, or both, whether remunerated or not. Work is counterpoised with leisure, rest, and Sabbath, though the line between them cannot always be drawn exactly. This is especially true with children for whom work is play and play is work.[4]

In the last chapter, "Going to Work with the Professor," we explored a theology of work by researching a life experience of a professor and reflecting theologically on it. But here we do it by thinking and praying, head and heart. But the head has been uppermost in almost all theologies of work, especially as we review the history of work.

A Brief History of Work

Over the last two centuries work has become a job. Australian ethicist Gordon Preece outlines the seismic shift that the job has caused in our understanding of ourselves, our world, and even our God.[5] Whereas earlier generations did not usually "go to work" or "have a job" their work was mostly related to their household economy, whether as farmers, homemakers, or tradespeople. Even the apostle Paul, a tentmaking pastor-apostle, did not have a job. He was a self-employed tradesman who did not report to anyone. Indeed, in rural East Africa I have seen a ninety-year-old grandmother carrying a few stalks of corn from the field to assist in the domestic (household) economy. She was still working. She has not retired from a job she never had.

Today it is different. The vast majority of people work for someone else, and their work takes them away from home. And when they retire, they no longer work (or think they do not work when they are usually still working). In the modern and post-modern world, the hardest hit by the job-concept of work are the overworked, the unemployed, housewives, the forcibly retired, and "the attention-deprived children."[6] Until the job came

---

4. Diddams, "Good Work, Done Well," L4 (pp. 423–33).
5. Preece, "Work," 1124.
6. Preece, "Work," 1124.

along work was simply part of life, which it is, and which is why we have selected "work" as a part of Perkins's definition of "theology as the science of living blessedly forever." So, it is not surprising that the concept of a theology of work is a fairly recent development, coming into the Western world after the Second World War largely as a result of Roman Catholic theologians.[7] But, having attempted a definition of work, are there others?

John Stott's definition of work is as follows: work is "the expenditure of energy (manual, mental, or both) in the service of others, which brings fulfilment to the worker, benefit to the community and glory to God."[8] In my view this is a definition of *good* work, *kingdom* work, *holy* work. But, by this definition, people working in a cigarette factory or making a product that is harmful to people or to the environment might not be working at all. They are, I propose, doing *bad* work or simply engaging in a destructive activity, whereas a recycling dumpster dipper, a street cleaner, a volunteer helper in school are actually doing good work. But there is a further problem with work today, especially in the Western world: the disintegration of faith and work.

The sources for this disintegration are manifold. One source is the Greek cultural world that was like a totally enveloping fog to the early Christians. In the Greek world, work was called "unleisure" and reserved mostly for slaves.[9] The Greek city of Thebes apparently issued a decree that its citizens were forbidden to work. Who kept the city running? Slaves did the work and made the city thrive. Freed persons gave themselves to politics and friendship. So, the apocryphal wisdom of Ecclesiasticus, influenced by Greek thinking, exalted the scribe over the tradesperson, the contemplative over the person engaging in material action. The merchant or business person, "can hardly remain without fault" (26:29) for "between buying and selling sin is wedged" (27:2).

Sadly, this view is cherished by many Christians who exalt the pastor or missionary at the top of the holiness hierarchy, to be followed by people in the helping professions, with business people, and politicians near the bottom. The very bottom is reserved for unacceptable occupations such as currency traders and prostitutes. It is thought that if people are really serious about following Jesus they should quit their job, go to seminary, and become a pastor. In the Middle Ages in the Western world Mary, the

---

7. Cosden, *Theology of Work*, 4–5.
8. Stott, *Issues Facing Christians Today*, 162.
9. See Barkman, "Dualism and Work; Wong, "Intrinsic Value of Work."

contemplative, was exalted over Martha, the active person. But there was a temporary recovery of the dignity of ordinary work in the Protestant Reformation.

It is well known that Martin Luther was reacting to the medieval monastery as a salvation machine. In contrast Luther exalted the God-given dignity of ordinary work. What you do in your work in your own house, he would say, is just as if you did it to the Lord God in heaven. Whereas medieval Europe viewed only the priest, nun, and monk as having a vocation, a calling from God, Luther insisted that everyone is called to their station in life. "Therefore," said Luther,

> I advise no one to enter any religious order or the priesthood, indeed, I advise everyone against it—unless he is forearmed with this knowledge and understands that the works of monks and priests, however holy and arduous they may be, do not differ one wit in the sight of God from the works of the rustic laborer in the field or the woman going about.[10]

Imagine putting that quotation over the entrance to a Christian theological seminary today! Unfortunately, by the time of the later English Puritans, work became largely secularized as typified by the deist Benjamin Franklin with his famous lines, "Early to bed, early to rise makes a man healthy, wealthy and wise" and "time is money." The Industrial Revolution put the finishing touches on the separation of faith and work with the reduction of work to a job. In spite of the economic gains of the Revolution, it took people away from the home, mainly the men, and today it is both men and women who are taken away from children and from each other. Now we live mostly in a culture, at least in the developed world, characterized by information and creativity. And the old hierarchy of occupations has been adjusted but still remains.

The following is really an executive brief on a *thoughtful* theology of work with the emphasis on the head.

Toward a Thoughtful Theology of Work

Darrell Cosden describes this new post-Second World War discipline as "a theological exploration of work itself by exploring work with reference to a number of doctrines within a systematic theology."[11] Most attempts

---

10. Luther, *Luther's Works* (American Edition), 36:78.
11. Cosden, *Theology of Work*, 5.

at elaborating a theology of work concentrate on *one* of those doctrines, doctrines such as the Trinity, creation, image of God, the curse, new creation, the kingdom of God, vocation, the Spirit, and the New Heaven and New Earth. I list these theological themes in *Work Matters: Lessons from Scripture* with a partial list of representative authors taking each viewpoint in the footnotes.[12]

A better way, I propose, is to approach it through biblical theology. *Work Matters* is an approach to a comprehensive *biblical* theology of work. It constitutes a *theology* of work because it explains what work *means*— what is its origin, effect, and endurance. It is *biblical* because it draws on the entire revelation from Genesis to Revelation by telling the stories of people, people like Adam and Eve, Joseph, Ruth, David, Daniel, Esther, Nehemiah, Jesus, Paul, Priscilla and Aquila, Lydia, and John, all of whom worked serving God and others in the marketplace. In the process we see how contextualization has actually been done within biblical history in a diversity of contexts. At the same time, we uphold the fundamental unity of Scripture. It is certainly a "head" approach to the theology of work. In this context we need to explore the extrinsic and intrinsic meaning of work for, as Daniel Pink above says, speaking for a portion of people in the West and in other parts of the developed world, meaning is the new money. But is the value of work intrinsic to work or is it only extrinsic?

The Extrinsic and Intrinsic Value of Work

First, we start with the *extrinsic* value, what work means in its effect. We gain this from observation and Scripture. From *observation* we observe that work is good for the worker, good for the neighbor, good for the world, and good for God. Let me take each of those in turn. Good for the worker is evident, as Dietrich Bonhoeffer says in his delightful classic *Life Together*, because it takes a person out of themselves; it gives a person dignity; it involves him or her in the world outside of his own internal world. The English writer, Dorothy Sayers, says that "the characteristic common to God and man is apparently that: the desire and the ability to make things."[13]

Further, drawing on *Scripture*, work enables a person to sustain themselves so they will not be a burden on others, as Paul so passionately persuaded people to work. Indeed Paul worked so that the gospel would not

---

12. I have quoted this list from Stevens, *Work Matters*, 2–4.
13. Sayers, *Mind of the Maker*, 17.

be "hindered" (1 Cor 9:12; 1 Thess 2:9; 2 Thess 3:6–10). But it is also good for the neighbor, providing the possibility not only of goods and services for our neighbor, whether that neighbor is seen or unseen, but even, when there is a surplus, enabling a person to help others directly (Eph 4:28). It is good for the world, as the creation narrative says, that "there was no one to work the ground" (Gen 2:5), for which reason, in part, God created the man and the woman to "work the earth and take care of it" (2:15). This surely includes developing the potential of creation by harvesting some of the earth's crust in minerals and stone to humanize planet earth. And it is good for God, a subject we will return to, though for now we can say that God is pleased that his intent in creating humankind is largely being fulfilled. So, after making everything, including the man and woman, God says "It was very good" (1:31). Paul says that even the slaves can "glorify God" through their work (Col 3:22–24). But what about the intrinsic, the internal and hidden, value and dignity of work?

Second, the *intrinsic* value of work is beautifully expressed by my student and former teaching assistant, Siew Li Wong from Malaysia, who wrote her Regent MA thesis on this subject, nicely condensed into an article published on the Institute for Marketplace Transformation website.[14] Biblical theology in contrast to systematic theology is grounded solely in Scripture. It takes the main themes of the Bible from Genesis to Revelation and sees it as a grand story about the coming of the kingdom of God. This kingdom is partially brought to earth through the founding of the people under the old covenant, but the kingdom comes substantially with Jesus whom early church fathers described as the kingdom of God in his own person. Finally, the kingdom comes fully in Christ's second coming. Thence the major themes around the coming of the kingdom of God are (1) creation and the creation of God-imaging creatures to bring in the kingdom; (2) the fall into sin of both people and the invisible powers, short-circuiting God's intention; (3) redemption in Christ who embodied the kingdom and conferred a kingdom on his followers; and finally, (4) the consummation of the kingdom with the second coming of Jesus involving the renewal of earth and heaven. Let us look at some of these themes.

The Creation of Everything. The Bible opens with God working. "In the beginning God created the heavens and the earth" (Gen 1:1). God is not sitting in heaven drinking ambrosia as do some of the mythical gods of ancient literature. But God not only worked in creating everything but is

---

14. Wong, "Intrinsic Value of Work."

still working, or so Jesus says (John 5:17; Rev 21:5). Throughout the Bible, we see different images of God as a worker namely: shepherd (Ps 23), potter (Jer 18:6), physician (Matt 8:16), teacher (Ps 143:10), vineyard dresser (Isa 5:1–7), and so on.[15] God is as active and creative today—creating, sustaining, redeeming, and consummating—as God was when this 93 billion light year universe was begun.

Human beings are "like" God and made "in the image of God" in at least two ways: first, in being relational like the Father, Son, and Spirit ("male and female he made them in his image") thereby becoming *human beings*, and, second, by working (Gen 1:26–8). Human beings are also *human doings*, workers by God's design. So, we are commanded to work (1:28). The Bible makes it clear that we are vice-regents over creation and therefore are commanded to act as stewards of God's created world. As workers, human beings and doings are called to extend the sanctuary (the garden) into the world, to "fill" it not only by populating the earth, but to fill it with the glory of God by humanizing the earth. As God delighted in his creation (1:31), humans too find fulfilment when they do good work. Hence, we acknowledge that our enjoyment of work is also a gift from God (Eccl 3:13; 5:18).

The two words used by God in his command to Adam and Eve to work are *abad* (work) and *shamar* (take care; Gen 2:15); interestingly, these words are also used to mean "service to God" and "keeping of his commandments" respectively. This implies that no distinction between sacred and secular work is to be made. Likewise, the Greek word *diakonia* is used both for the ministry of the word and service at tables in Acts 6:2, 4. It is important to note that the command to work was given *before* the fall and hence work is meant to be a blessing and not a curse. So intrinsically work is a good thing, a God thing, a holy thing. It is not a diversion from the righteous life of Adam and Eve but part and parcel of their dedication to God and God's purposes. And what makes a person holy is his or her dedication to God. But then something happened.

The fall of humankind into sin and the revolt of the powers into autonomy. Genesis 3 tells the story succinctly of this literal event but told in a figurative way. The innocent couple are told they have limits to their lives. They could eat of any tree in the garden except one, the tree of the experiential knowledge of good and evil, sometimes called the autonomy tree. This tree was to be a test of their obedience and their God-centredness.

---

15. See Banks, *God the Worker*.

Testings are good for us, but they can become temptations.[16] The serpent was wily and approaching them with an appeal to their pride turned their being tested by God into a temptation by which they would fall flat on their faces. Note the parallelism of the three testings of Adam and Eve in Gen 3, the testings of Jesus in the wilderness at the commencement of his public ministry in Matt 4:1–10, and the testing of every disciple of Jesus in 1 John 2:16 in the following triad of testings in *provision*: "good for food," "turn these stones into bread," "the lust of the flesh;" in *pleasure*: "a delight to the eyes," "throw yourself down [and be miraculously rescued]," "the lust of the eyes;" in *power*: "desirable for gaining wisdom," "all this [worldly power] I will give you," Satan said, "the pride of life" [or boasting of what one has and does].

These three testing are roughly parallel to the three most pressings tests we all face: provision or money, pleasure especially sex, and power. Well, you know what happened with the Adam and Eve test, and what followed. Instead of communion with God in their work caring for and beautifying the sanctuary garden, they hid from God. Instead of intimacy in their marriage they now knew they were naked and grabbed some fig leaves to cover their genitals. Instead of enjoying a side-by-side relationship, the woman will be ruled by her husband, but she will try to overmaster him.[17] Instead of work being a gift it becomes "painful toil" and the workplace, the "thorns and thistles," dog the worker's steps. Is this what God wants? No, it is what humans have brought about by their sin.

Toil and frustrating work, and conversely, the idolatry of work as in workaholism, are the *result* of the fall. The suspicion with which many Christians regard vocations in the marketplace may arise because they think such work is driven by selfish ambition for wealth and power as was the case with the Tower of Babel (Gen 11).

What is not clear in Scripture is whether those invisible forces and personages, called "powers," that provided an ordered environment in time and space for the first humans, became corrupted because of human sin or whether they acted on their own rebellion. But one thing is certain, even

---

16. The Greek word for "test" *peirazein* is the same word as "temptation." So, every test can technically become a temptation. See the three testings of Jesus in the wilderness in Stevens, *Seven Days of Faith*, chs. 16–18.

17. The Hebrew word for "desire" as in "your desire will be for your husband" (Gen 3:16) is the same word as is used in 4:7 where God says to Cain before he murders his brother Abel, "sin . . . desires to have you, but you must rule over it." Rule and revolt are the result of sin, not the design of God for the male-female relationship.

the "principalities and powers," originally created good and for our benefit by the Son of God and for Christ (Col 1:16) have become fallen, taken on a life of their own, and become enemies of the King and the kingdom of God, as well as dogging the steps of all working creatures on the planet. But that is not the end of the story.

Work and workplace have been substantially redeemed. Despite the pervasive effects of sin, God in Christ has redeemed the entire created order (note the repeated use of the words "all things" in Col 1:15–20 in regard to both creation and redemption). Apart from humans, creation also waits for the day when it will be set free from bondage (Rom 8:19–23). The cosmic scope of God's redemption means that everything affected by sin and the curse can be redeemed including human work. The scope of redemption is the same as the scope of creation. God redeems work now through his church when, by the power of the Holy Spirit, his people bring God's presence (Matt 5:16–17) and godly values (Prov 16:11; Matt 5:13–17; Prov 20:10; Amos 5:10–12) into the workplace. Even the powers have been "disarmed," "made a public spectacle," as Christ "triumphed over them by the cross" (Col 2:15). Mammon, idolatrous images, traditions, institutions, the demonic, and death itself have been substantially conquered. It is like D-Day during the Second World War when the beaches of France were invaded. People said the war was won that day. But peace was not attained until V-E Day almost two years later. Christ's death, resurrection, his ascension, and his pouring out the Holy Spirit were like D-Day, but the day of final victory will come at the end of history when Christ comes again.[18]

Meanwhile, we live in the "messy middle" time in the "now" and "not yet" of the kingdom. Jesus came as King, did kingdom work, and invites us to do kingdom work. We can also derive an idea of the holistic nature of God's mission from Jesus's ministry on earth. He not only met people's spiritual needs but also ministered to their emotional, psychological, and physical needs: he worked at his carpentry (Mark 6:3), fed the 5,000 (Matt 14:15–21), healed the sick and cast out demons (Matt 8:16), raised Lazarus from the dead (John 11:43–44), and washed his disciples' feet (13:4–5).

The kingdom of God is not just spiritual: it is personal, social, political, economic, and cosmic. Most good work in this world extends the kingdom of God and brings *shalom* and human flourishing.[19] The distinc-

---

18. I owe this analogy to Oscar Cullmann, Swiss theologian.

19. See ch. 5, "How the Kingdom Comes—Humankind's Initiative," in Stevens, *Kingdom of God in Working Clothes.*

tion often made between spiritual work (expressed as kingdom work) and so-called "secular" work is both unbiblical and harmful. Gospel work and societal work are interdependent and together they are ways of praying and acting "thy kingdom come." This would imply that all human work that embodies kingdom values and serves kingdom goals can be regarded as kingdom work. But what about the End in biblical theology and how does that contribute to the theology of work?

Our work will judged in the end according to its alignment with the purpose of God. At the culmination of God's purposes when Jesus comes again, Christians will be judged not only for their work that is directly related to evangelism and the church but also for their faithfulness as stewards of the resources and responsibilities that God has given them (Matt 25:31–36). The judgment criteria, when put into the perspective of God's expectations, thus validates our present human work in various capacities. The eschatological (end times) vision in the Old Testament is that of a humanity at work (Amos 9:13; Mic 4:3–5; Isa 11:1–9; Hos 2:18–23). We are devoting a full chapter to this prospect at the end of this book.

This picture is completed for us in the New Testament. Our work will last, and we will work in the new heaven and new earth. Our final destination as children of God is a glorified material destination described as a new heaven and a new earth (Rev 21–22; Isa 65). We will not be "saved souls" in "heaven" but fully resurrected persons in the new heaven and new earth. The redeemed community will inhabit this new creation in their glorified bodies (1 Cor 15; Phil 3:21). They will bring their cultures (Rev 21:24, 26) and their ethnic and linguistic diversities (Rev 5:9).

All this strongly suggests that there will be some continuity with our present existence which will undergo a dramatic, transformative, and cathartic renewal, alongside substantial discontinuity. In some ways which we do not fully understand, some of our human work and labour will surely find a way into the new creation (Rev 14:13). It is not just our spiritual work that will endure and matters to God, but all work and life undertaken with faith, hope, and love (1 Cor 13:13; 1 Thess 1:2–3). The kings of the earth bring their glories into the holy city (Rev 21:24) and that transfigured creation will be embellished by the deeds of Christians, deeds that "follow them" (Rev 14:13). So, our labour in the lord is "not in vain" (1 Cor 15:58).

That, ever so briefly, is theology of work in the head; now for a heart theology of work. And what exactly do we gain by praying about and through our work, and the work of others?

Heart—Toward a Prayerful Theology of Work

A spiritual friend of mine, my former next-door neighbor, now passed away, was a French tax lawyer. Among our many conversations he said, "I have never consulted God about a problem in my work without his substantially helping me to solve it." So, one thing that prayer teaches us about work is not only that God wants us to pray to him about our work, but through this we may gain answers to our questions, or at least perspective. But primarily through prayer we gain God. Often when we do not get an answer, we find that, along with the psalmist, we have a listening ear in God. There is no situation we face in the workplace that we cannot bring to God and pour out our hearts.

But further, we gain perspective on our work, but not to endorse the idolatry of work as in workaholism. And we discover that, as the Professor revealed in the last chapter, work is a gift. We will find that our work is a form of worship and glorifies God. We change as workers in how we respond to interruptions, to pressures, and to irritable workmates. We can celebrate and worship God when we have made important discoveries, when we finish a good job, and when we find love in our heart for a difficult-to-work-with person in our company. And we can go to God in prayer as Brother Lawrence did when we make a mistake and say, with him, "I will always do this unless you mend what is amiss in my life." And, at the end of the day we can ask for forgiveness when we have sinned in our work, or when we did bad work, which, most likely we have. In the next chapter I will review my six decades of work prayerfully. Praying *about* our work is difficult but praying *while* we work is even more difficult. Why? To answer we must explore the contours of prayer and work, work and prayer.

Prayer inhibiting work. While it is not common, there are people, not just monks and nuns, who are so occupied with prayer that they do not attend to the work they need to do to survive. A minister once asked an Indian Christian mystic Sadhu Sundar Singh, "Do we need to pray more, or work more, or to divide our time in doing both?" Singh replied: "Both are equally necessary. Prayer without work is as bad as work without prayer. As a clucking hen to satisfy its instinct continues to sit in some dark corner even after its eggs have been removed, so the life of those who remove themselves from the busy life in the world and spend their time wholly in prayer is as fruitless as is the hen's."[20]

---

20. Singh, *With and Without Christ*, 74.

Prayer versus work. This most common practice keeps Mary and Martha separated, with Mary the listener to Jesus and Martha the busy sister preparing a meal for Jesus and his friends (Luke 10:38–42). Work occupies most of our day. Prayer, in this view, is what we can do in discretionary time either before or after the workday is complete. Cardinal Wyszynski in his volume *All You Who Labor* comments on this tendency, "Conscientiousness in work and the turning of our attention to God are at odds. When we are fully absorbed in our work, we forget about everything, about the external world, and all the more about prayer."[21]

Prayer enabling work. This is prayer before you start to work, either at the beginning of the day or when we commence a new task. We seek God's energy and wisdom for the work. It also can be, as it was for Brother Lawrence, a cry for help in the middle of work: "Lord, I cannot do this unless you enable me," he would say to God. For Brother Lawrence, the monastic chef working in the clatter of pots and pans in the kitchen, his "greatest business did not divert him from God."[22]

Prayer inspiring work. Paul commented in Col 1:29 that he is working to present each person mature in Christ "with all the energy which Christ so powerfully works within me." Many new projects have been conceived in prayer. The Institute for Marketplace Transformation, for which I now mainly work, is such an entrepreneurial initiative formed as a result of prayer.

Prayer through work. Work reveals the worker. Wyszynski says that the "sweat of our brows lays bare the image of our soul and unveils its real expression." Without active work, this onetime mentor of the late Pope John Paul II, says, "it is usually hard to know yourself, for there is a lot of hidden evil in us, covered over with apparent calm."[23] When I worked in carpentry my business partner used to say to me, "I have never met anyone who can work in the mess that you work in." This comment made me ask about myself, what is it, Lord, that makes me this way and what can be done about it?

Prayer as work. Prayer can be a form of energy expended purposively as we have defined work. But in this case the work is not manual or mental but the work of the whole person, body, soul, and mind. The soul is not a

---

21. Wyszynski, *All You Who Labor*, 69.
22. Lawrence, *Practice of the Presence of God*, 22.
23. Wyszynski, *All You Who Labor*, 113.

spiritual organ inserted in an evil body. Rather, the soul is the longingness of the whole person, especially longing for God and life.

I remember one incident in my early work days as a pastor when, in talking with a young French pastor who, like me had not prepared his sermon for Sunday (it was Friday). We discussed our situation and he said to me, "You are fairly good in preaching but not so good in praying. I am good in praying but not so good in preaching. Why not I go downstairs and pray and you stay upstairs and write the sermon." It was a ridiculous proposal. But, after praying, we eventually agreed that we would preach the same sermon. Two hours later, after I received an incredible inspiration in writing the sermon, he knocked at the door of my study. His tie was untied and his hair all askew. He looked exhausted. He had been working at praying. "Are you done?" he asked. "Not quite," I said, "go down for a few more minutes and we will be done!" Which we were. Prayer as work. But let us reverse the order and consider how work and prayer interface.

Work inhibiting prayer. Some work is so demanding in what is sometimes called "extreme work" through which one's attention is so engaged that one cannot think of their need for God. Karl Barth once defined good work as work that does allow us to reflect on the meaning of the work. Bad work does not do this. And there is a lot of bad work out there. Some jobs are so demanding, so idolatrous, that they cannot be sustained for more than a few years. When the Three Mile Island nuclear reactor melted down at 4:00 a.m., March 28, 1979, in Pennsylvania, the workers, who used to go into the reactor and work for forty hours a week could go in for only forty minutes. Then their Geiger counters told them they had all the radioactivity they could take for the week. I see this as a metaphor of extreme work today. Some executives say things like, "I don't have time to think or pray." Some work inhibits prayer.

Work and prayer. The Benedictines live in a rhythm of eight hours of sleep, eight hours of work and eight hours of prayer. The prayer time includes the liturgy, "the work of the people" literally, but it also includes reading the Bible spiritually, *lectio divina*, and time for private and personal meditation. The manual and mental work period of their life together does not exclude prayer but to the extent that it is manual work, not requiring the full attention of the mind—the kind they prefer—they can pray. Even mental work can be reflective and contemplative. But the work needs to be done and it too is a discipline. Indeed, their motto is *ora et labora*, or "prayer and work."

Thinking and Praying about Work

Work inciting prayer. The exigencies of work, fellow workers, and the toxicity of the workplace, the pressures and the problems, the resistance we face from the world, the flesh, and the devil all get wrapped up in the apostle Paul's phrase "principalities and powers." These powers, which range from structures to invisible spiritual beings that are opposed to the kingdom of God, dog our steps, and require spiritual warfare, the primarily vehicle for which is prayer (Eph 6:12). But not just the negativity experienced in work but also the positive experiences, as we will see in chapter seven brings spiritual growth and blessing from God.

Work as prayer. Earlier I mentioned how prayer can be work. But now we are considering how work can be prayer. In his biography, Eugene Peterson tells how as a teenage boy he had a question about prayer and asked his mother, a Pentecostal preacher, what to do. She directed him to talk to John Wright Follette, a Pentecostal teacher visiting with the Petersons. Eugene tramped off to ask this esteemed person, "Dr. Follette, how do you pray?" He replied, "I haven't prayed in forty years!" Initially this shocked Eugene. But he came to realize that he was really saying he did not have a "prayer life," as something separate and holy. Rather he lived "a life of prayer."[24] Here is a pregnant suggestion: that even our work can be a prayer. How can this be?

First, when we do good work, we are actually doing God's work, entering into God's ongoing work. After all, Jesus said, "My Father is always at his work to this very day, and I too am working" (John 5:17). Second, we are actually working in the presence of God and prayer is attending to God, being present to the one who is always present, "bidden or not bidden," as the plaque in Carl Jung's study said. Surely this is part of the meaning of praying without ceasing or "continually" (1 Thess 5:17), a matter we will take up later. Third, in work we are acting as priests of creation, bringing God and God's purpose into this world and the people of the world. But priesthood is a two-way bridge between God and humankind. So, we also are presenting our work to God and the people around us, as a thank offering, as well as interceding for the world situation and the people with whom we work.

So, as Cardinal Wyszynski notes, "the prime virtue gained through our daily work is patience—a necessary virtue (Heb 10:6; Rom 5:3–5). Here is a ladder, as it were, by which we go ever higher in all our ordinary, daily

---

24. Collier, *Burning in My Bones*, 38–39.

work. The oppressive nature of our work, when understood correctly, gives rise to patience, and with patience goes extraordinary wisdom."[25]

But having considered the theology of work from the perspective of thought (head) and prayer (heart) we must now turn, once again, to the practice (hands) of work and its meaning. To do this I must tell you about my own work story.

---

25. Wyszynski, *All You Who Labor*, 123.

5

The Practice of Work—The Handiness of Theological Learning

WHY DO I TELL you my own work story? Because I have learned much about work through it, much about myself, and much about God's purpose in our work. So, it is theology gained through practice. This is a sample of theological reflection "from below" on the practice of work—the hands. And I encourage you to do the same. So here goes.

I have had many jobs in my eighty-five years and each one has taught me something.

Pastor—Assignment #1

My wife Gail and I started our marriage in 1961 in the inner city of Montreal, Quebec, Canada, where we pastored a dying English-speaking church. Its building was located in the midst of a racially mixed and needy community with seventeen ethnic groups of people. I learned that pastoral work is hard, very hard, and that one does not see rapid fruit from it. A pastor sets out to build a people, empowering people to use their gifts. The pastor wants to create a community that prizes people and serves the community outside the building. In the process I learned about myself as a worker that I love to be liked and that I do not like criticism. A pastor gets lots of the latter. I remember telling my spiritual friend, Bill, over a Montreal smoked meat sandwich in Lester's Deli, that I was quitting. When he asked why, I explained that I was spending most of my time putting out fires in the congregation (who is leaving? Who is disgruntled?). Bill asked me what kind of church I wanted to belong to.

I said, "No one would want it."

He said, "I might. Tell me about it."

So, we scribbled on serviettes in Lester's Deli the shape of the church for which God had given me vision. Then I tried it out on the board. We had a complex board structure and thirteen standing committees which were set in concrete when the church was a large suburban church. It was now a flea-bitten inner city church composed mainly of people commuting from the suburbs. These people gave me a year of their membership before they would join a suburban church.

But the board bought it. Then came a year of communicating, through sermons, letters, and intensive visiting of the members. All of which amended the vision but kept the substantial center. And years later it was substantially realized, including replacing the cumbersome church organization with a simple group ministry of which I was a member. I learned that without a vision the people perish, and so does the pastor. I learned that I needed to sound my own voice as a leader and not merely keep the ecclesiastical wheels turning. I also learned that if you change the culture quickly the culture will change you by giving you an exit visa! We spent years reinforcing the good things in the culture and ignoring most of the negative features. But the church did change and we reached out to the neighborhood. Why? The church was desperate.

When I was being interviewed to become their pastor the people said, "If you do not come, we will close the doors." There are three situations when a church or an organization is likely to accept fairly radical change. Number one is desperation. Number two is in a new church plant, a new business startup, or a new organization. Number three is a revival, a fresh infusion of the Holy Spirit. But, I have found since, the Holy Spirit seems limited in bringing renewal to a church or a business where the people are self-satisfied.

Where was God in that process? Where wasn't he? God gave the vision for the work. God gave me a mentor who encouraged me. God was in the process of sharing the vision with the people. God was in the meeting in which major changes were made. God was in the mission outreach that we did. But supremely God was in a person who emerged as the pastor to replace me.

Joseph Hovsepian was a young Greek-speaking Armenian who came to faith in the church. Little did I know that God was preparing him through the care and discipling which I and others did, to assume the role of pastor when I left. And he is there to this day, some forty years in all.

Baptist "Area Minister"—Assignment #2

After six years of pastoring, I was asked to become an area minister overseeing nineteen churches in the province of Quebec. I was too young for the job, twenty-nine to be exact. There are many positive things I experienced during that year, including a downtown Bible study on Wednesdays, but one in particular led me to resign within a year. As an area minister I needed to go to Toronto to meet with other staff monthly. The first item on the agenda was "Will we lick stamps or rent a postage meter?" We debated this for hours and came up with a compromise; for one month we would rent a postage meter and try it out. Next month when I walked through the mail room I discovered two boxes, one for metered mail and the other for stamped mail. You can guess what the first item on the agenda was!

I was, I thought, a misfit in an administrative job. I wanted to create something, not lubricate the machinery. I have since learned that I missed a golden opportunity to be mentored in the ministry of administration. I was actually gifted in administration but I did not see administration, running things, organizing, as a ministry. Once again, I was learning about myself and learning, at the same time, about the purpose of God in our work.

Martin Luther said one's daily work is the situation in which the Christian's sinful self must be put to death within and by the demands of daily life in vocation. "It is the place," Luther argued, "in which the person of faith chooses sides in the ongoing combat between God and Satan. The 'old self' must bear vocation's cross as long as life on earth continues and the battle against the devil continues."[1] So the pressures of the marketplace have a purifying result, even if we may shrink from saying, as does Cardinal Wyszynski, that the toil of work is salvic, and a remedy for original sin. Wyszynski says, "Christ wants us to take the whole burden of work on His cross, to become co-sufferers with him. The hardship of work is our daily cross."[2] Shocked at this when I first read it, I now wonder whether this really differs from Paul's exhortation to work out the salvation that God has

---

1. This quotation is from an article by Kolden, "Luther on Vocation," in which Kolden draws on the masterful work of Gustaf Wingren, *Luther on Vocation*, 250–51.
2. Wyszynski, *All You Who Labor*, 94.

worked into us, with fear and trembling (Phil 2:12). I was not ready for that fear and trembling. What followed was an abrupt change.

What was my theological reflection on this second job? Precisely I was running away from the gift that God had given me, that of being an effective administrator, truly a gift of the Spirit of God (Rom 12:8; 1 Cor 12:28). Political service, leadership, and management are all ways to serve God and others by providing an infrastructure whereby people and communities can flourish. But the year as a religious bureaucrat included a part-time involvement with the student Christian group at McGill University. And I thought I had found my home.

Coaching and Counseling: InterVarsity Staff Worker— Assignment #3

"Will you go anywhere in the world?" I was asked in the interview. Move to Halifax on the East Coast and cover the five Atlantic provinces, came the assignment. Which we did and loved living there, loved the students in the five universities I was responsible for, loved the creative opportunity to take students on canoe trips in the summer, and loved to counsel one on one with them. I loved teaching the Bible which I did weekly in a friend's house with students coming and going. There was, however, one major snag. I was travelling on the road 50 percent of the time, and that with a young family that needed their father to be present.

So, when InterVarsity asked me to move to the west coast, to Vancouver, and become divisional director for the province we felt this was the hand of God—less traveling but more administration. In reading what I am writing I realize that I must seem to be a person trying to find his vocation. And indeed, that is the truth. As Karl Barth once said we find our calling by experimentation, by trying out various service roles and contexts.

What was my theological reflection on the work of being a student mentor and a behind-the-scenes leader in InterVarsity Christian Fellowship? I was an equipper and that, whether in business or the church, is a very important, perhaps the most important, thing leaders are to do (Eph 4:11–12)—empowering others for their service in the church and/or the world. As a behind-the-scenes leader and with deep "needs" for approval I was not completely satisfied. There is a dark side to every gift, including the gift of leadership. Meanwhile the church of which we were members had hundreds of students. The leaders and the congregation invited me to pastor them. My wife and I prayed about this and felt that it was right.

Pastor—Assignment #4

The next four years were terrific, engaging, fun, and also trying. Pastoral work is a meat-grinder as one tries to reconcile the needs and desires of so many diversely inclined people. This time I was mainly using my communication gifts, speaking morning and evening to hundreds of students and families. It was a dream, but not a dream without a problem. So, when I resigned after only four years the people wondered what hit them. And when they realized that I was going to support my family through carpentry they thought I had "left the ministry." In fact, as I told my friends, "I have never left the full-time ministry. There is no part-time option available for followers of Jesus." But there were longings to be fulfilled, and one sturdy and persistent longing was to work in the world.

I had gone from university to seminary to first church and while some pastors work too hard, I felt there was something missing in my experience of work. I am also a mission-hearted person who wanted to engage with the marginalized and the outsider. I taught and worked with the congregation to substantiate that their dispersed life in the workplace was holy and pleasing to God, and a major mission field for the twentieth and twenty-first century; I needed to model this. Pastoral service has a unique hazard, and I soon began to realize that I was praying more as a carpenter than I had as a pastor. In George MacDonald's novel *The Curate's Awakening*, there is a fascinating interchange about church work.

> The great evil in the church has always been the presence in it of persons unsuited for the work required of them there. One very simple sifting rule would be, that no one should be admitted to the clergy who had not first proved himself capable of making a better living in some other calling . . . I would have no one ordained till after forty, by which time he would know whether he had any real call or only a temptation to the church from the hope of an easy living.[3]

I was thirty-seven not forty!

---

3. MacDonald, *Curate's Awakening*, 189–90.

What was my theological reflection on this work that I had done? First, I took an exit visa too quickly when the going went roughly. I tried to gather up the mission vision which I sensed for the people and presented it to the Board. Being less than a mature leader I failed to realize that it was too much too soon. My team person with whom I worked daily once said, "You are so far ahead of the people that they think you are the enemy." I have pondered that remark for years. I also pondered the fact that leadership is situational. And I wondered whether there is a place for an entrepreneur in the leadership of a church that is going very well. But I was a leader and reflected on what made me this way.[4]

Leaders can be born that way. Such people are usually gifted with charisma. Other people just want to be with these charismatic leaders and follow them. But charisma without character is dangerous—which is why the New Testament names character as the number one requirement for church leadership. But there are other ways one becomes a leader. The Spirit of God can come on a person and make them a leader through Spirit gifts of exhortation, healing, teaching, giving, or administration. Sometimes cultural circumstances draw out a person's leadership. Take, for example, Mohandas Gandhi in South Africa and later in colonial India, or Adolf Hitler in post-World War I Germany. Leaders can be made as the result of followers being made into leaders by the leader. This is what Jesus did with Peter when he said to him, "feed my sheep" (John 21:17). But there is another way that leadership is created that is part of my story.

Dietrich Bonhoeffer said that the "group is the womb of the leader."[5] So a group draws out leadership from some person in that group.[6] On reflection this happened to me when I was sixteen. I had been baptized that year and thought I was now a Christian (I was not). Church was boring so I sat at the back and made drawings of various carpentry projects I was doing. But my eye caught the newsletter of the church where I read that young people would meet at 7:00 p.m. Sunday. I was a Sunday School dropout at eleven years of age. But I thought I would try it. So, I went to

---

4. Some of this was published on the IMT website under the title "On Being a Biblical Servant Leader."

5. Bonheoffer, *No Rusty Swords*, 186–200.

6. It is fascinating to note that while most of the evangelical church has followed John Calvin in that the pastor has a call directly from God and of which the church is not witness, Martin Luther said that the call to church leadership comes not directly from God (with the exception of the apostles) but comes from the church, requesting that a person leads and ministers in place of and on behalf of others. See Stevens, *Other Six Days*, 152–59.

the room where the young people were supposed to meet. There were ten of them sitting in a circle with long sad faces. I said, "Hi, I'm Paul Stevens. I am here to join your group." They said, "That's too bad." I said, "Why is it too bad?" They replied, "It is our last meeting." I inquired why. "We can't find anyone to be president." Then they looked at me. Then they said "If you are willing to be president we will keep meeting." I said, "It's a deal." And it was. I organized Bible studies and prayer meetings in which I indeed became a Christian. In fact, I woke up one morning at a prayer retreat I had organized and told the group, their president had got saved last night! That group was the womb of my leadership.

Now as a more mature (in years) but still immature leader I for one whole year did not lead in the church. I simply maintained the status quo. But I prayed and sought God's will with a small group of people. We eventually conceived of a multiple house church that would be thoroughly missional, especially for the marginalized and the needy in the city. There were at that time literally thousands of young adults living on the beaches and the streets of Vancouver.

Did I make a mistake in leaving this thriving cause prematurely? Yes and no! Søren Kierkegaard once said that "life is lived forward but understood backwards." One thing I know and understand. God does not have a wonderful plan for my life, or anyone else's for that matter. He has something far better than a plan which, if not followed in detail, we will be doing God's second best. That better thing God has for us is wonderful *purpose*. And that purpose is to grow into Christlikeness and become mature. My next assignment took me even deeper into the discovering of what it means to do "the Lord's work" and to work "the Lord's way."

Carpentry and Business—Assignment #5

After a year of prayer and with the support of a small group I apprenticed as a carpenter and, at the same time, worked as a tent-making pastor of a church plant among street people in Vancouver, BC. I have written elsewhere about my experience in housebuilding and home renovation in Vancouver.[7] Suffice it to say that it was hard to start at thirty-seven in a very physical calling. Wheeling drain rocks with a wheelbarrow and dumping them into an excavation in a winter rain just above freezing was not easy. But, as my mentor and business partner kept reminding me, "the sleep of

---

7. Stevens, *Kingdom of God in Working Clothes*.

the labourer is sweet" (Eccl 5:12). It seemed to me that other carpenters were dancing on the thin-edged top of 2 x 10 floor joists and walking swiftly on top of 2 x 4 walls carrying one end of huge roof trusses without thinking about the risk (I did think of the risk but I did the job anyway).

One thing I discovered was the tremendous satisfaction of seeing a result from one's daily work. As I threw my nail belt into the trunk of my Chevy Nova I could look back and see that we had framed an entire floor of a house that day. And the business-end of the enterprise was also a learning experience. Further, I was learning that the average person spends a load of time as well as their primary energy at work. I also learned that manual work requires brains and not just brawn.

The ancient philosopher Anaxagoras as wrote, "It is by having hands that man is the most intelligent of animals." For the early Heidegger, "handiness" is the mode in which things in the world show up for us most originally: "the nearest kind of association is not mere perceptual cognition, but, rather, a handling, using, and taking care of things which has its own kind of 'knowledge.'"[8] Something is being lost in this information and creativity society. "What is new," continues Matthew Crawford, "is the wedding of futurism to what might be called 'virtualism': a vision of the future in which we somehow take leave of material reality and glide about in a pure information economy."[9] In the Bible, the first artisan is God—the worker, who makes things with imagination, creativity, and with his hands, things with both form and function.

My theological reflection on my "business years" was rich. I discovered that God gives us joy in work, that God wants us to see the results of our work. Did not God look over everything he had made and say, "It is very good" (Gen 1:31). I discovered that carpentry work, along with administration, is a real service to God and to our neighbor. In short, it was a ministry. I discovered that the balance of manual work and ministry work, technically called "tent-making," like the vocation of Aquila and Priscilla, and even the apostle Paul for much of his life, was lifegiving. How glad I was to get up early in the morning and meet with some men over Bible study and prayer, but then to go to work as they did, and, in the evening after supper to be engaged weekly with a house church meeting in our home. I have met lots of pastors who have burnt out. I have yet to see a tentmaker burn out. But once more I went to the church but this time with feeling.

---

8. Quoted in Crawford, *Shop Class as Soulcraft*, 68–69.
9. Crawford, *Shop Class as Soulcraft*, 3.

The Practice of Work—The Handiness of Theological Learning

Pastor—Assignment #6

Mark Twain, quoting someone else, said it well. "'Blessed is the man who has found his work'? Whoever it was he had the right idea in his mind. Mark you, he says *his* work—not somebody else's work. The work that is really man's own work is play and not work at all."[10] I was seeking my work but not sure I had found it. I returned to a dynamic though small church ministering to students and families near the university. It was a thriving cause, standing room only (in a small building) three times on Sunday. I was working in a plural eldership with mature people each of whom could have led their own church. But it was obvious that we needed to plant a new church, and church plant we did.

One Friday afternoon I received a phone call from the clerk of a church even nearer to the campus. "Mr. Stevens, you have a space problem." "Yes, we have," I answered. She continued, "We have the reverse one. We have a 700-seat church with only 40 people meeting in it. Would you like to rent our facility?" I immediately said, "Yes." So, the church was planted. And I remained in it for ten years but not as staff.

It was here that an elder said to me, "Paul, I don't know why you are such a driven person. But I think it would be a good thing if you found out why." I confess, I felt unneeded in the new church as all the staff and leaders came from the mother church to start a new one. The result of this was that the "mother church" nearly died in childbirth! But God was still leading me, recovering a sense of vocation, and sticking with me. He does not give guidance. He is a Guide. Especially in the next step.

Professor—Assignment #7

I was going into Carey Theological College on business and the President said, "I want you to apply for an open faculty position." I said, "You don't want me, I'm too controversial." He said, "That's why we want you. You are a maverick, and we need a maverick here." After two years at Carey, I moved to Regent College with whom Carey was, at the time, in partnership. And after two more years I became the academic dean in a strange way.

The selection committee chose me as the inside candidate, but they had an outside candidate who was better qualified. At the interview I realized that what the faculty wanted was a senior academic who would read

---

10. Twain, "Humorist's Confession," quoted in Witherington, *Work*, 14, emphasis mine.

and critique their academic articles. I was not a senior academic. So, I withdrew. But when they went to the outside candidate he withdrew as his marriage was dissolving. So, they came to me and asked me to do it for a year's interim. I said, "No. I am not an interim. I will tinker with it. Four years or nothing!" They came back and offered two years. I said, "Four years or nothing." They scrimmaged again and offered me three years. This time, my wife and I prayed furiously and agreed to do it for three years.

When I became the academic dean of Regent College, the president, my boss, Dr. Walter Wright, served me by saying four things when he hired me. First, "I guarantee your success. If you fail it is because I failed as your supervisor." How empowering that was! Second, "On your annual review there will be nothing negative. I will stay up the night before and write a long letter of affirmation and give it to you." (I remember reading these letters and thinking, Is that really me?) But third, "We will have breakfast each Thursday morning and will talk about everything. When things are not going right, we will deal with them then, not in the annual review. No surprises. And no secrets."

But the fourth thing he said was what marked him as a servant of the Lord watching over my soul. "In this job you will have to deal with yourself. You love to teach because you get strokes from your students. It feeds something in you. But you will get no affirmation in this job except from me. You will be criticized. And you will have to deal with yourself." Then he said something beautiful. "And I will help you." And he did.[11] Servant leadership at its best.

Something happened in me. *I realized what I had been fleeing all these years was a critically important ministry*, and that I was gifted in administration. Management is a practical way to love. It provides the infrastructure whereby people can thrive. I realized as an administrator I could define reality, prize giftedness, empower people, and say thanks to everyone in the organization.

What was my theological reflection on my academic dean years? I finally accepted the gift that God had given me. Finally, I was content where I was (Phil 4:11), and practising the "secret of contentment." Paul confessed in that chapter: "in every situation, *by prayer and petition, with thanksgiving*, present your requests to God" (4:6, emphasis mine).

---

11. I dedicated my book *Doing God's Business* to him as the most influential leader in my life.

Meanwhile, I was teaching full time, as well as writing a book annually. At the end of three years, I said to my wonderful assistant, "I am going back to faculty." She said, "You cannot." "Why not?" Then she looked at me and said, "I refuse to train another dean!" So, I did another three years, six in a block, and another year in an emergency. But they were the most spiritually formative years in all my work life because my president mentored me. I served at Regent from 1986 to 2005, nineteen years in a formal post followed by many years informally teaching and mentoring students.

Chairman, The Institute for Marketplace Transformation—Assignment #8

At sixty-eight I retired from the faculty of Regent College but kept teaching and writing. I had become the professor of marketplace theology and was traveling globally, teaching and encouraging my students who had returned to their home countries. Then at seventy-seven years of age one of my former students sent me an email. Dr. Dae Kyung Lee, an oral surgeon in Seoul and a Regent grad, wrote me that he was praying about a vision: an Institute (or school) for Christian Life, a Bible and Marketplace Institute for integrating faith and work "with you as President. I am wondering if you are able to be part of the plan. Possible location is Jeju Island, South Korea, and the main language would be English, with consideration of Chinese and Korean translation."

I was instantly interested. I had retired from Regent, but I had fifty years of teaching, publishing, modeling, and advocating for the marketplace under my belt and in my heart. But I was seventy-seven years of age. "Am I crazy to be starting something at this age?" I asked my physician and my accountability group. "Keep engaged," they both said. And now the IMT movement has become global with regional centers in Hong Kong, South-East Asia, China and Taiwan, South Korea, and North America. Why decentralized? Because a theology of work must be contextualized to the culture.

What is my theological reflection on being Chairman of the Institute of Marketplace Transformation? This has proven to be the best assignment in my life, gathering up the gifts God gave me, the experiences I have had, the extensive travel I have done cross-culturally, the passion that God has given me, and the people skills I have developed and were given by God. I have waited for more than half a lifetime for this thing. This near perfect fit.

Earlier I mentioned that the theology of work must be contextualized. So must leadership.

Here I am not speaking about the internal culture of the church or organization, a subject we will take up in a later chapter, but rather the external surrounding culture, be it Asian, Indigenous, African, Western, or Latino. It is the water we swim in. And it is precisely here that this second volume of *Working Blessedly Forever* on *The Practice of Marketplace Theology* with its international group of authors offers a unique help on the vexed and wonderful question of how the leader is to function. Every culture has its unique expectations of leadership and service which may or may not permit the servant leader to function. These expectations are innate, hidden, invisible to the naked eye—except in certain public ceremonies—but profoundly influential.

As you will see later, in Asia, Confucian culture assumes a hierarchy in the organization. This means that the pastor is the top of the church pyramid, just under the Lord himself. Whereas, in North America the pastor's authority is largely swallowed up in democratic expectations as well as anti-establishment postmodernity. In Africa it is who you know that makes you a leader, what tribe you belong to, what your position is in that tribe, and what it takes culturally to be a "big man" or (less likely) "a big woman." We have two great needs as followers and as persons who want to flourish: *the need to be we and the need to be me.*[12] In the West the need to be me is uppermost, because of the rampant individualism implicit in the culture. In Asia and in Africa, in contrast, the need to be we is uppermost. So, in Africa no one ever calls me "Paul." I am always called by my family name, "Stevens." I have a corporate identity. But in Canada most people call me "Paul" because I am an individual. Yes, they call me Paul even though I am eighty-five and many decades older than my students. But, and I cannot stress this too much, as servant leaders and servant followers we have both needs, the need to be me and we!

Remember that just as the internal culture of the organization "speaks," informs who is important and what is important based on values and implicit beliefs, so too the surrounding outside culture speaks more loudly than the president of a country! Can servant leadership thrive in your culture? Are there points of contact with the culture that we can build on, that will reinforce servant leadership? Are there innate resistances in

---

12. I learned this from Edwin Friedman, a Jewish rabbi and psychotherapist when he was lecturing in Vancouver sometime in the 1970s.

the surrounding culture that mean that servant leadership will be countercultural, subversive, and possibly even deemed to be heretical? But one thing for sure is this.

The ultimate servant leader is Jesus, whom author after author in servant leadership books expound like facets of a jewel. As a leader Jesus was *life on life*; he lived with his followers and shared his life with them. He was an *empowering leader*, giving away everything he knew and owned so they could become effective leaders. Jesus concentrated on the three, the twelve, and the seventy in order to serve the crowd, and ultimately the world: *concentration with a view to expansion*. His leadership was *situational*, not standardized. He led differently when faced with the opposition of the Pharisees than when he faced with a crowd of seekers, and, different again with potential followers. Jesus *attended to his own needs* dismissing the crowds (Matt 14:23) in order to be alone with the Father and sleeping in the boat between assignments. But here is the ultimate action of this servant leader: he *laid down his life for his followers*.[13] Can we do this as servant leaders? I confess I am still learning to do this.

But there was one more work assignment in my life.

Homemaking—Assignment #9

During the past four years, as my wife has become more frail and handicapped, I took on a new role alongside my part-time commitment to IMT. I have become a full-time homemaker, making meals, keeping the house, and making the house a home, which is why some people call homemaking "hearth-keeping."

Now along with IMT I am taking care of my wife, Gail, and managing the household (she has, since writing this, passed into her next assignment in the new heaven and new earth). I have a helper to do the laundry and house cleaning one day each week, but I do the cooking, entertaining, and people-work around the home, work which my wife has done for fifty-five of our sixty years of our marriage. It is just like any other work, sometimes hard but good, appreciated sometimes, and largely taken for granted, but is as pleasing to God as speaking the gospel to a vast audience. Perhaps more so, because you are pouring your life into a few people whom you know

---

13. In my opinion, the best book on Jesus as servant leader is Bruce, *Training of the Twelve*.

and love, including our three children, eight grandchildren, and three great-grandsons.

Whew! I have not even mentioned my other vocational pursuits that include photography, publishing photographic books, and building a cabin in the Gulf Islands off the coast of Vancouver Island. But each of these assignments has been revelatory, not just of who I am but what it means for me to be a worker under God.

My Learnings

So, what have I learned about a theology of work from the practice of my own work life? First, I learned that the theology of work is good for the body and the soul, it puts stamina in your energies, it reveals why work is hard but good, and it teases us with the thought that some of what we have done in this life "for the Lord" with faith, hope, and love will last and find its place in the New Heaven and New Earth. But what have I learned about being a worker?

Second, I learned that finding one's calling to the workplace is a lifetime process rather than a one-time word from God (except of course the word to love God and to love our neighbor).

Third, I learned that it is important not to leave work prematurely, as I have done more than once. The ancient desert fathers and mothers had a saying: "Stick to your cell, it will teach you everything." In other words, you can only learn about yourself, and God's purpose for your work, by an extensive commitment to a particular work. I believe in my Regent assignment and now with the IMT work I have discovered that.

Fourth, I learned that God gives approval and delights in your work that is well done because it is done for him even when people do not acknowledge that you are doing the work of the Lord. We are working for an audience of one. I have learned to be less dependent on positive feedback for my work.

Fifth, any work, and not especially religious or church work, is an arena for spiritual growth.

Yes, head, heart, and hands—all engaged in doing marketplace theology well. But now we must consider how God blesses the worker *internally*, in terms of working with the Triune God, and how we can grow spiritually through our work. What indeed makes work a **blessing to the worker**?

BLESSING THE WORKER

6

Working with the Trinity

Among world religions, the Trinity is unique to Christianity . . . The relevance of the Trinity is to emphasize both the individual and the state, as well as a large variety of mediating institutions.

BRIAN GRIFFITHS[1]

IN THE LAST THREE chapters we explored the wholistic triad of head, heart, and hands as it relates to work. But here we want to apply it to the worker herself. We will consider how the worker is inspired by, and participates in, the ongoing work of the triune God, Father, Son, and Holy Spirit. And in the process the worker is blessed by God.

The Blessing of Doing the Lord's Work

So often I hear people saying they are leaving secular work and "going into the Lord's work," meaning into pastoral or missionary service. I always ask, "What were you doing before? It was not secular work but sacramental work! God's grace is coming into the world through your work. You were doing the work of the Lord. But, of course, if God leads you to move from one kind of Lord's work to another kind of Lord's work that is fine. But don't say you are leaving secular work to do the Lord's work!" How could I dare to say this?

---

1. Griffiths, *Creation of Wealth*, 55.

Frequently Scripture says that we are "coworkers in God's service" (1 Cor 3:9). We are doing God's work with God, or rather God is doing his work through us. God is a Creator and he invites humankind to enter his ongoing work of creativity. So, people doing informational technology, entrepreneurship, art, music, carpentry, and engineering are entering into God's work. A friend who did his PhD in computer science said that he went into the field because he knew his work would be as close as possible to what God does when he created out of nothing!

God the Sustainer keeps the world running. Read Job 39–41 where God takes Job on an African safari or a tour of the far north and asks, in effect, you try running the world better than me! God shows Job his wild work. But God's ordinary work is done through human beings. We are his hands and feet to "keep stable the fabric of the world," as the book of Ecclesiasticus says. So, homemakers, people in politics, systems engineers, police persons, and garbage collectors are entering God's sustaining work. A city can manage for awhile without a mayor but not without garbage collectors.

God is also a Redeemer. People in transformative, fixing, and repairing work are also doing the Lord's work. Of course, none of us can redeem the world as Jesus did when he went to the cross for us all. But technicians, repair persons, house cleaners, street sweepers, snowplow operators, mechanics, IT repair persons, counselors, doctors, nurses, and lawyers are doing the Lord's work. Do they do it perfectly? No. Because in this life all good work is mixed with bad. But, essentially, they are doing God's work for God.

And, finally, God is a Consummator, bringing the whole human story to a wonderful conclusion in the new heaven and new earth, in the wedding supper of the Lamb, that grand rendezvous at the end of history. Parents raising children towards maturity, teachers pointing people to truth, pastors, media people, and reporters explaining where things are going, and spiritual directors are all doing sacramental work: the work of the Lord. All these people are fulfilling God's mandate in Genesis when he enlisted people to rule, to fill, to work, and to take care of the world—as God does. So work is a blessing to the worker to participate in God's ongoing work. It links her with God; it gets a person "out of themselves," as Dietrich Bonhoeffer said. But what do we mean by the word "blessing"?

I have on my bedroom dresser a birthday card sent by my daughter and son-in-law that pictures a moose sloshing and padding through a shallow lake in the morning, a sight I sometimes see on my canoe trips in Northern Canada. Underneath the photograph is a quotation from Henry

David Thoreau, "An early morning walk is a blessing for the whole day." In common speech, even among those with no connection with the Christian way, people speak about blessing when they say things like "Bless me," or "What a blessing!"

In our largely secularized world the word has gone out of favor being largely replaced by "luck." Robert Banks in his article in *The Complete Book of Everyday Christianity* says, "Blessings include such things as the gift and enhancement of life, fertility and other forms of tangible reward, the experience of salvation through Christ and the deepening growth of the believing community."[2] But we rarely associate what the word actually communicates—peace, well-being, wholeness, human flourishing—with our work, especially work in the marketplace. But that is what we are doing here. We are insisting, in this chapter, that our work is a means through which God blesses us, and in the next how God blesses others through our work. Here we explore how the triune God blesses us workers.

The Blessing of the Trinity

Father, Son, and Spirit exist in a reciprocal unit, each person enwrapping the others, each living in the others and for the others, so deep and so united that they are one God. Thomas Torrance expresses the importance of this truth in the following way:

> The doctrine of the Holy Trinity [is] . . . the fundamental grammar of our knowledge of God. Why is that? Because the doctrine of the Trinity gives expression to the fact that through his self-revelation in the incarnation God has opened himself to us in such a way that we may know him in the inner relations of his divine Being and have communion with him in his divine life as Father, Son and Holy Spirit.[3]

This means that we have access, albeit limited, to the inner life of Father, Son, and Spirit in their relationship, including their love and work *together*. And if human work is meant to reflect and participate in the character of God's work as Father, Son, and Spirit, what does this mean? It means that human work like God's work is not only redemptive and curative but creative and unitive, not only in saving souls and fixing/mending relationships

---

2. Banks, "Blessing," 72.
3. Torrance, *Trinitarian Perspectives*, 1.

but designing and building, as well as creating community. If God's work is unitive and creative as well as curative and redemptive, then what does doing "the work of the Lord" entail? But there is more.

Human work, like God's, is meant to be relational. God is a being in communion. Humankind is made in God's image as a being in communion, even in the workplace. Saint Augustine, followed by Jürgen Moltmann, said that God is a lover, a beloved, and love itself. This is marvelously explained by the Gospel-writer John and in the letter of John.[4] The world was created through the love of God. All human beings are born in the love of God. They are "love babies," no matter what the circumstances of their conception. And the world essentially runs on love. So, the worker in the kingdom of God does not yield to worker isolation but gladly works together, rather than doing solo work, in small groups or project teams.[5] The "body" metaphor used by Paul for the interdependence of members in the church is suitable for the workplace and work groups as well, with interdependent gifts, skills, and personalities.

Systems thinking is essential to understand how groups, families, churches, and corporations function and can be nurtured toward health.[6] In fact we love our neighbor through our work whether we see that neighbor or not, providing goods and services. So, we are mandated to build a relational work culture. Even the etymology of the word "company," made up of two Latin phrases—*cum* (together) and *pane* (bread), suggests a shared life and livelihood. And God meets us in our relationship with our coworkers, so invested is God in our relational life as God is, in fact, love itself. But there is more!

The great themes of God's work as revealed in Scripture include creating, sustaining creation and human life, redeeming, transforming, and consummating. These themes of divine work are apparent from Col 1:15–20 where Christ, the Son of God, is named in the following way:

> The Son is the image of the invisible God, the first born over all creation. For in him all things were created: things in heaven and on earth, visible and invisible, whether thrones or powers or rulers or authorities; all things have been created through him and for him. [creation] He is before all things, and in him all things

---

4. John 3:16; 13:34; 17:23; 1 John 4:7–12.

5. This team pattern can exist even on in virtual companies as shown by Elliott et al., *How the Future Works*.

6. See Collins and Stevens, *Equipping Pastor*.

hold together. [sustaining] . . . he is the beginning and the first born among the dead [consummation] . . . and through him to reconcile to himself all things, whether things on earth or things in heaven, by making peace through his blood, shed on the cross [redemption].

But while the Son implemented the Father's work, the same could be said of the Spirit who implements the Father's work but in a specific way. Each person brings a distinctive character to their work, and humankind, made in God's image to be "co-workers in God's service" (1 Cor 3:9), will find their own work expresses mainly one of the ways God is God, possibly all three.[7] Let's start with God the Father.

The Blessing of Working with the Father

Christian Schumacher in his book *God in Work* says the following about Father work:

> A person cannot reflect the Father in work unless he [or she] participates in the actual act of envisioning the object he wishes to make. That is to say, the creative idea must emanate from the worker—the intuitive act of the imagination which precedes the fashioning of the actual material.[8]

As workers, human beings are called to extend the sanctuary (the garden) into the world, to "fill" the earth not only by populating the earth, and so humanizing the earth, but filling it with the glory of God. How do we do this? Through our daily work, our presence, and our witness. The Bible makes it clear that we are vice-regents over creation and therefore are commanded to act as stewards of God's created world. Indeed, as Bruce Waltke has shown in his *Old Testament Theology*, previously mentioned, "Genesis 1 confers this authoritative status of God's image to all human beings."[9] So Father work is creative, stewardly, and providential.

So, when we are stewards of matter, creation, history, human talents, and giftedness in a company, a church, or an organization, we are doing Father work. When we are doing protective work, like the police, the military,

---

7. Dr. Jonathan Wilson compares the Father to the architect, the Son to the contractor, and the Spirit to custodian, but admits that these analogies are inadequate. Email correspondence on November 15, 2022.

8. Schumacher, *God in Work*, 75.

9. Waltke, *Old Testament Theology*, 218.

and security officers do, we are doing Father work. A specific dimension of this protective work will be the engagement and grappling with the principalities and powers, those largely invisible realities that, while originally created by Christ and good (Col 1:16), have fallen and become part of the anti-kingdom, resisting the rule of God in creation and in the community of people.[10]

Famously Ps 46 is frequently misquoted out of context. It begins with "God is our refuge and strength." But when the psalmist Korah later says, "Be still and know that I am God" (v. 10), he is not saying that if we can be quiet and shut out the world, we can know that God is God. This is actually true, but it is not what the psalmist is saying here.[11] Who is speaking here in verse 10? Not the psalmist but God! To whom is God speaking? Not to us, but to the powers. God is speaking to the tumult, to the controversy, to the opposition and resistance we feel. These powers are cosmic, "the earth gives way" (v. 2), "the waters roar" (v. 3), and "the mountains quake" (v. 3). The powers are "nations [that are] in uproar, kingdoms fall" (v. 6). Some of these devastations are caused by wars. And he "makes wars cease" (v. 9). And God speaking to the principalities and powers says, "Be still." "Desist." "Quit being so troublesome."

God is our refuge when we are attacked by images, institutions turned in on themselves, traditions that bind people to the tried and true but resist change, Mammon, the invisible powers of Satan and his demonic allies, and even death itself which holds people in lifelong bondage. These powers are called by various names in Scripture: the basic elements of the universe, thrones, powers, principalities, the demons, and death. And God says to them all, "Be still." The Father *protects*.[12]

But God the Father also *provides*. "There is a river whose streams make glad the city of God" (v. 4). God provides rain and sunshine, nurture and care for his world and for all creatures, human and otherwise. When we are doing steward work, protective work, and provision work we are working with the Father, doing Father work. But what about doing Son work?

---

10. See Stevens, "Anti-Kingdom in the Marketplace," 139–51.

11. David does say this in Ps 37:7, "Be still before the Lord and wait patiently for him."

12. See the extensive treatment of the powers in Scripture in Stevens, "Resistance: Grappling with the Powers."

The Blessing of Working with the Son of God

Son work is slightly different. Jesus Christ, the Son of God, came to do the Father's will and implement the Father's idea of the kingdom of God on earth (Luke 4:16–21). Again, Schumacher says, "The Son executes His Father's plan, he 'exteriorizes' it, he incarnates it within the bonds of matter, time and space."[13] He does this through self-emptying, not considering equality with God something to be used for his own advantage, and by taking the form of a servant (Phil 2:6). This means for those of us who follow Jesus, the pathway is one of downward mobility. The Son does this through self-giving, taking the form of a servant even to the laying down of his life for others (2:7). This means personal generosity and humility (2:8). Astonishingly, we have a humble God! Along with Israel's kings we are not to think of ourselves as better than anyone else.[14] And finally the Son does this through suffering (2:8), through his obedience even to death on a cross.

This last point deserves some explanation. "Taking up our cross," which Jesus says is a precondition of discipleship, means two things. First, it means identifying ourselves with the finished work of Christ on the cross. God needs to do nothing more to reconcile us to himself other than what he has accomplished on the cross. Second, it means sharing the passion of Christ. Paul spoke of filling up "what is still lacking in regard to Christ's afflictions" (Col 1:24). We do this by engaging the suffering of the world, by entering the affliction of the church, by experiencing the pain of other people, and the pain of the marketplace. My boss, then-president of Regent College, used to say to me frequently, when I served as Academic Dean, "You (and me) have to take the pain of the organization." So, Luther was right when he said there is a cross to be taken up in the marketplace.[15]

Christian Schumacher proposes that "the functions of planning, doing *and evaluating* within the world of work were analogous to the functions performed by the Father, the Son, and the Holy Spirit in the Godhead."[16] That means that to be deeply motivating, as some employment counsellors have affirmed, work needs to be planned, executed, and controlled (or evaluated and enjoyed) by the worker himself. As God delighted in his

---

13. Schumacher, *God in Work*, 74, 76.

14. See the qualifications for the Israelite king in Deut 17:20: "and not consider himself better than his fellow Israelites."

15. Kolden, "Luther on Vocation," 383, as expounded in chapter 5.

16. Schumacher, *God in Work*, 71, emphasis mine.

creation saying it was good (Gen 1:31), humans too find fulfilment when they see they have done good work. If the Father's and Son's work appeal to the mind, the Spirit's work is known through experience, prayer, and worship (the heart).

The Blessing of Working with the Holy Spirit

The Spirit works through empowerment, expressiveness, evaluation, and joy. It makes work a heart experience. The Spirit makes Jesus known. Jesus makes the Father known. So, the Spirit is the expressiveness of the Father and the Son. But the Spirit does not make God known in just church ministry but also in the workplace.

First, the Spirit confirms in our hearts that we belong to God wherever we are in the workplace. Romans 8:15–18 says that whenever we cry "Abba Father" it is the Spirit himself bearing witness. The Spirit hugs us inwardly as sons and daughters of God. In his monumental *Journal*, John Wesley tells how, before he experienced the Lord in his heart-warming encounter, he went to America to evangelize the native Indians. There he made the acquaintance of a devout and earnest German pastor, Mr. Spangberg. This good pastor plied the newcomer with a succession of penetrating and painful questions to Wesley. "Does the Spirit of God bear witness to your spirit that you are a child of God?" Utterly bewildered, Wesley did not know how to reply. This led to a second question. "Do you know Jesus Christ?" Wesley hemmed and hawed and mumbled something about hoping that Christ had died for him. Then Spangberg went a step back and asked, "Young man, do you know yourself?" Wesley replied that he did but confesses in his journal that his answer lacked sincerity and conviction.[17]

This Spirit confirmation, if we are truly children of God, means that we are walking and working sanctuaries. Wherever we go God is with us. And we are part of God's "filling the earth" with his glory (Gen 1:28; Eph 4:10). This means there is nowhere so demonized that we might not be called to serve there.

Second, the Spirit leads in vocational discernment, in making decisions, planning, and the execution of our plans. The apostle Paul knew himself to be constrained by the Spirit to do some things and was also restrained by the Spirit not to do other things even when he had an open door of opportunity. "Paul and his companions traveled throughout the region of Phrygia

---

17. Quoted in Boreham, *Prodigal*, 32–33.

and Galatia, having been *kept by the Holy Spirit from preaching the word in the province of Asia*. When they came to the border of Mysia, they tried to enter Bithynia, but *the Spirit of Jesus would not allow them to do*. So they passed by Mysia and went down to Troas" (Acts 16:6–8, emphasis mine). Frequently in my work as a carpenter and business owner I experienced the Spirit's leading. How do we know it is the Spirit speaking to us?

Teresa of Ávila, the medieval mystic, helpfully describes the various ways the God speaks to us. She called them "locutions" and draws on the *Medula Mystica* of Francisco de Santo. Teresa says that some of these messages or words come from *without*; they are corporeal and are heard in the hearing even if no one else is able to witness the sound. Some come from the inmost parts of the soul. They are *imaginary*, but not in the sense of fabricated. They are not heard in the ear but experienced as an impression received by the imaginative faculty. Some "locutions" are *intellectual and spiritual* as God imprints a message in the depth of the person's spirit and understanding. But we must ask a question. How might we know that these "locutions" are really from God and not from Satan, or a mere figment of our own misguided imagination?[18]

Teresa has a quiver full of wisdom on this subject. First, a message must agree with the Scriptures and therefore they have power and authority. "Unless it agrees strictly with the Scriptures, take no notice of it than you would if it came from the devil himself. The words may, in fact, come only from your weak imagination . . . and must invariably be resisted so that they may gradually cease; and cease they will, because they have little power of their own."[19]

Second is the sign that "a great tranquility dwells in the soul, which becomes peacefully and devoutly recollected, and ready to sing the praises of God." Saint Ignatius calls this "consolation" in contrast with "desolation," the negative sign that this is not from God.

The third sign is that "these words do not vanish from the memory for a very long time; some indeed never vanish at all." Teresa insists that even though others might conclude that these words are pure nonsense, and even though circumstances may militate against their fulfillment, "there still remains within it such a living spark of conviction that they will come true . . . though all other hopes may be dead, this spark of certainty could

---

18. Teresa of Ávila, *Interior Castle*, 139.
19. Teresa of Ávila, *Interior Castle*, 140–41.

not fail to remain alive, even if the soul wished it to die."[20] What does this mean? It means that our life is not a bundle of accidents; we are not subject to fate; we are led. We do not get guidance; we have a Guide.

Third, the Spirit anoints our creational talents and enables us to work with excellence. Here I must make a confession: I do not believe in spiritual gifts, at least in the sense of an organ or capacity transplant. I believe in Spirit gifts. What are called "spiritual gifts" or more accurately "Spirit gifts" in the New Testament are evidences of the Holy Spirit working through our lives. The three Greek words used in the New Testament for Spirit gifts are *ton pneumatikon* (1 Cor 12:1)—Spirit people or Spirit gifts; *charismata*—concrete expressions of grace; and *dorea* (Eph 4:7)—gifts. Spirit gifts may be exceptional ways of ministering to a brother or sister in the body of Christ such as tongues, a word of knowledge. But, usually these gifts are temporal and situational. Some of these gifts might occasionally be expressed in the work world, for example, prophecy, faith, healing. While other Spirit gifts mentioned in the ad hoc lists in the New Testament empower us for excellent service in the work world as well as the church, for example, faith, administration, prophecy, pastoring, helping. But the Spirit does something more.

The Spirit anoints the creational talents that we use in work, bringing them to a higher level of excellence and fruitfulness. Bezalel is the Old Testament example of this (Exod 31:3). Let me explain how this happens especially in relation to human talents which, like Spirit gifts, are also from God. Talents are creational aptitudes that are build into us by God when we were created. They are usually permanent and non-situational. If you are gifted in administration, for example, you can use this talent almost anywhere. Spirit gifts are endowments of the Holy Spirit that are not necessarily permanent and usually are contextualized or situational. One may exercise a Spirit gift in one group but not in another. But there is an overlap of talents and gifts. That is, while some Spirit gifts may emerge without any seeming connection to a talent the person has, normally the Spirit seems to anoint a person's capacities to ratchet it up a notch higher in effectiveness and bring with it the touch of God. Why do I affirm this?

I affirm this because of Rom 12:6-9 where Paul in speaking about Spirit gifts says:

> We have different gifts, according to the grace given to each of us.
> If your gift is prophesying, then prophesy in accordance with your

---

20. Teresa of Ávila, *Interior Castle*, 142–43.

> faith; if it is serving, then serve; if it is in teaching, then teach; if it is to encourage, then give encouragement [these statements seem to suggest that Spirit gifts are connected with these activities, but then Paul adds something significant]; *if it is in giving, then give generously; if it is to lead, do it diligently; if it is to show mercy, do it cheerfully."*

I have put the last phrases in italics because they indicate an anointing of a creational capacity with the Holy Spirit in generosity, in diligence, and in joy. What does this mean? *We do not have to work slavishly*, merely doing our duty. But we can flourish in the workplace. This is the Spirit's work and it is part of our witness. Jesus himself said, "So you also, when you have done everything you were told to do, should say, 'We are unworthy servants; we have only done our duty'" (Luke 17:10).

Fourth, the Spirit inspires creativity in the workplace. Through the Spirit's work we can make good and beautiful things as workers. The stunning Old Testament example of this is Bezalel.

> See I have chosen Bezalel son of Uri . . . and I have filled him with the Spirit of God [The only person in the Old Testament of whom this was said], with wisdom, with understanding, with knowledge and with all kinds of skill to make artistic designs for work in gold, silver and bronze . . . to work in wood, and to engage all kinds of crafts. (Exod 31:2–5)

How does this work? God the Spirit gives *wisdom*—practical intelligence and vision in seeing, designing, and figuring out how to do it. God the Spirit gives *discernment*—clarity in problem-solving. And God the Spirit gives *skill*—practical ability: hands and heart joined in doing. So, Spirit work glorifies God. It is a practical way of loving our neighbors. And Spirit work embellishes human life and creates beauty. God tells Moses to have sacred garments made for Aaron "for glory and for beauty" (28:2). Beauty is not just in music and graphic art, but a meal or a deal, a voice or an invoice, an operation or a cooperation, a community formed or an immunity created, a test or a quest, a swept floor or forgiven heart, a canvas painting or a computer program, a plaything or a work-thing, a toy or a tool. Is it possible that Christians could be the most creative people on earth? Edmund H. Oliver, a Canadian clergyperson, has tabulated the social achievements of the Christian church throughout history and notes that we have done our best work as a pioneer and not merely an ambulance.[21]

21. Oliver, *Social Achievements of the Christian Church*.

Fifth, the Holy Spirit brings joy even while we work. Joy is one aspect of the Spirit fruit in Gal 5:22–3 and a distinguishing mark of the Christian. Throughout the Acts of the Apostles people are filled with the Holy Spirit and joy. But not just joy in the gathered fellowship or even joy in ministry, but joy in working—getting into the work heart and soul, as Paul said to the Colossian slaves (Col 3:22–3)—using our gifts and talents. Cardinal Wyszynski affirms this "it is good" joy which God-imaging creatures experience.

> [Humankind] feels an almost divine joy when [they] contemplate the signs of [their] labor in material works. Just as God during the seven days of creation declared repeatedly that all He had made was very good, so [humankind] in [their] work sees a reflection of [their] own image.[22]

Even though there is no perfect "fit" this side of heaven, there is the joy of working for love, realizing for whom we are working: family, children, loved ones, neighbors (near and far), and ultimately God (Matt 25:40—"you did it to me"). Again, Wyszynski speaks to this: "There is the joy that flows from the feeling of having completed some task that will be useful for one's neighbours."[23] Further, there is the joy of working with and for God. Again, Wyszynski says,

> Work becomes for the man [generic] the source of great new joy ... from the knowledge that he is acting "hand in hand" with the Creator, from the graces of his state flowing over all his works, and from the actual grace given like a good spirit to all his efforts, labors and works.[24]

But ultimately through the Spirit we experience the joy of working *in* God. God is not a deadpan autocrat but is the most joyous being in the universe and we enter now, partly, and in the final evaluation fully, into the Master's joy (Matt 25:23). Scripture is full of it: "Do not grieve, for the joy of the LORD is your strength" said Nehemiah to the returned exiles (Neh 8:10). Ps 16:11 says of God: "You fill me with joy in your presence" (Ps 16:11). Then there is the joy of God in creation (Prov 8:27, 30), in redemption, in consummation. The prophet Isaiah said, "You will find your joy in the LORD" (Isa 58:13–4). Such is the fruit of the Spirit.

---

22. Wyszynski, *All You Who Labor*, 186.
23. Wyszynski, *All You Who Labor*, 185.
24. Wyszynski, *All You Who Labor*, 186.

So, to summarize, the Father is the originating principle. Workers do the Father's work when they design and envision a task, when they are engaged in protection and provision. Workers do the Son's work when they "incarnate" the plan, execute it, and serve in humility and with downward mobility (Phil 2; John 20:21). The Son provides a model of *how* we are to work. And workers do the Spirit's work when they evaluate, express the creativity inspired by the Spirit, and enjoy their work (Exod 31; Isa 58:14). It is a blessing to work with the Triune God. And for the Triune God to work through us. But there is further blessing in working with God. We can grow spiritually.

7

Growing Spiritually through Work

Someone asked Abba Antony [the founder of Eastern monasticism], "What must one do in order to please God?" The old man replied, "Pay attention to [these three things]: whoever you may be, always have God before your eyes; whatever you do, do it according to the testimony of the holy Scriptures; in whatever place you live, do not easily leave it."

ABBA ANTONY[1]

The spirit of persistence [in prayer] springs from an inward conviction that life is but one single way that leads to the kingdom of God.

MATTHEW THE POOR[2]

IMAGINE THAT YOU HAD so much money, either through winning the lottery or through a vast inheritance, that you did not have to work at all. You could enlist servants, mechanical as well as human, to do everything for you. Then you could spend your time doing anything you wish: travelling, watching TV and videos, eating and drinking, spending your time, like the landed gentry in England so well pictured in vintage films, going from one "society" party to another. Would it be good for you spiritually?

It would be terrible, possibly devastating. William Perkins, the seventeenth-century Puritan, said it would be "damnable." Why? And why would

---

1. Ward, *Sayings of the Desert Fathers*, 2.
2. Matthew the Poor, *Orthodox Prayer Life*, 164.

Eugene Peterson, pastor to pastors, write "I'm prepared to contend that the primary location for spiritual formation is the workplace"[3] Really? Not the church service; not the retreat center; not the personal quiet time daily (as good as all these things are). Why the rough and tumble of the workplace, where money is passed from person to person, or company to company; where there are seasons of intense pressure when you wonder if you will make it; where there are awkward and even difficult people to work with; where you have to spend the vast majority of your waking hours oiling the machine, or making thingmajigs, or designing a new advertisement for some product that will be out of date almost as soon as it is made? Why?

Your Soul Is Revealed through Your Work

Because you are really there—head, heart and hands. God is really there. And the pressures and joys, the downs and ups of the workplace, and your response to these situations reveals who you are on the inside, your need for security, for intimacy, status, or control, and ultimately your need for God. And every discovery of a crack in your armor, every test you encounter, every time you fail, every moment when you are out of your depth and you need to pray for help, every one of these occasions is a silent and unspoken prayer to God to reveal his wisdom, his grace, and the fruit of God's Spirit. How do I know this? My boss told me. And I experienced it. "In this job," he said, "you will have to deal with yourself."

I am impressed with the Roman Catholic Church's writings about work and the workplace, especially since Pope John Paul II called Vatican II. I have a picture of John Paul as a young man working on a construction site, as I have done for seven years. He knew what it was like to work in the world. That is surely one of the sources of his inspiration. But behind John Paul was his Polish mentor, Cardinal Stefan Wyszynski, who wrote a book entitled in English *All You Who Labor: Work and the Sanctification of Daily Life*. In this fine volume Wyszynski says,

> Without external work we could not know ourselves fully, for only in daily work do we have a perfect opportunity to observe ourselves; it is then indeed that we discover the good and evil in ourselves and see our merits and faults . . . What external work does for our interior life is shown in the fact that this work by the

---

3. Peterson, *Christ Plays*, 127.

sweat of our brow lays bare the image of our soul and unveils its real expression.[4]

Take some workplace situations for example. How many of these are your questions that arise in the workplace?

> Why am I so sensitive to criticism?
> Why do I fill up the gaps in my date book or on my smartphone?
> Why do I find it hard to give up places, positions, and ministries?
> Why am I so competitive?
> Why is it so important for me to succeed?
> Why am I unable to let go of the pain of others?
> Why am I afraid to be alone, always seeming to need people?
> Why am I so discontent?
> Here is some good news.

Your Arenas of Conflict Become Agents of Spiritual Growth

The "works of the flesh" (Gal 5:19–21) are somewhat related to the Seven Deadly Sins[5] of the church enumerated by the early church fathers and mothers. These happen in the workplace, certainly as much as anywhere else, if not more. Consider each of these "works" as it relates to work: "sexual immorality," "impurity," "debauchery"—think sexual exploitation, harassment, and discrimination; "idolatry"—think drivenness, workaholism, greed, and materialism; "witchcraft"—think power-brokering; "hatred," "discord," "jealousy," "fits of rage"—think relational manipulation; "selfish ambition," "dissensions," "factions," "envy"—think predatory competition, and creating envy or covetousness; "drunkenness," "orgies"—think using alcohol to manipulate or anesthetize, using sex to sell or accommodate customers.

Most people think of human beings as having a higher and lower nature, the higher being spiritual and the lower being physical. But that is not the case and surely not what Paul means when he says that "the flesh desires what is contrary to the Spirit, and the Spirit what is contrary to the flesh. They are in conflict with each other, so that you are not to do whatever you want" (5:17). Understanding flesh as body is the anthropological view, namely, that human nature has a lower, fleshly, and bodily inclination to do

---

4. Wyszynski, *All You Who Labor*, 113.
5. See Stevens and Ung, *Taking Your Soul to Work*.

evil and a higher spiritual inclination to do what is right. But how many of the "works of the flesh" listed here are physical? Not many.[6] In fact, Paul is taking an eschatological (end-times) viewpoint, namely that since Christ has come, we are living in the new age but the old age is still with us.

Consequently, until Christ comes again and consummates the kingdom of God, we are living and working now in the messy middle, in the overlap of the old and new. In that messy middle we are in conflict, not between the body and the soul but in our *persons as a whole* as they are influenced by the old way of living, without Christ, "according to the flesh" and being simultaneously influenced by the new way of living, with the Spirit, "according to the Spirit." There are a few places where Paul uses "flesh" to mean the physical body but normally it is his code word to say, "life lived as though Christ had not come," "a person turned in on herself," or as the NIV puts it in a footnote, "flesh (*sarx*) refers to the sinful state of human beings."[7]

Sin does not reside in our physical flesh which is mostly good, but in our persons. And this becomes evident to us in the workplace. But that is not all we are confronted with in the workplace. We are also experiencing the fallen and mostly invisible principalities and powers, such as images, institutions, structures, Mammon, ideologies, and even the demonic. These powers, though substantially defeated by Christ on the cross (Col 2:15), still trouble us. But we no longer need to live defeated lives before these inner and outer enemies of the person (the soul). How come?

In Col 2:15 Paul announces that Christ "having disarmed the powers and authorities, made a public spectacle of them, triumphing over them by the cross." Three things Christ did on the cross about these external enemies. First, he took away their weapons so that believers are puncture-proof. Second, he publicly shamed them. And third, he actually triumphed over them. The title placed over the cross was in three languages: Latin, the language of government, Greek, the language of culture, and Hebrew or Aramaic, the language of religion. Christ was crucified by government, culture, and religion, but he more than survived triumphing over these

---

6. To this Gordon Fee in his commentary notes, "This is not a list of sins of the *flesh* per se, that is, having to do with the physical body or bodily appetites. The only items that fit this category are the three sexual aberrations . . . Rather, this list basically describes human behavior, which is essentially very visible and identifiable—'Works' that people do who live in keeping with the basic fallenness and that of the world around them." Fee, *Galatians*, 215–16.

7. Footnote on Gal 5:13.

forces and powers by his resurrection. Government can attempt to control us, viewing our kingdom work as a threat of an alternative kingdom; culture can entice us to see our work as valuable only extrinsically by secular standards; religion can assert that only work directly related to the church or work where the name of God is used, can qualify as pleasing to God. But we are not helpless before these internal and external forces. God helps us through his Spirit.

The Provision of the Fruit of the Spirit

In writing *Taking Your Soul to Work*, Alvin Ung and I discovered an extraordinary thing: for every sin and "work of the flesh" in the workplace there is a Spirit fruit available: love, joy, peace, patience, kindness, goodness, faithfulness, gentleness, and self-control (Gal 5:22–23). It is as though every struggle is a silent prayer and heart cry for God to reveal his Spirit fruit. For example, for greed there is goodness, for lust there is love, for gluttony (even for work!) there is self-control, for envy there is kindness. What does this mean? The Spirit changes our character, developing increasing Christlikeness (the fruit of the Spirit) and giving us a godly motivation for our work in the world. We grow spiritually in the workplace, possibly mainly there. Evelyn Underhill, a twentieth century Christian mystic, says that fruit of the Spirit are "ways of thinking, speaking and acting, which are brought forth in us, gradually but inevitably, by the pressure of Divine Love in our souls."[8] So we grow spiritually right there in the workplace. How?

Paul says "the fruit of the Spirit is love, joy, peace" [these focus on our relationship with God], "forbearance [patience], kindness and goodness" [in our relationships with others in the workplace], and "faithfulness, gentleness and self-control" [in our internal personhood].[9] Looking at each of these leads us to say Hallelujah, there is help; there is growth! Paul then says something wonderful in Galatians 5:23: "Against such things there is no law." In other words, you can never have too much patience, never too much joy, never too much self-control!

Starting with the internal personhood we explore the triad "faithfulness, gentleness, and self-control." "Faithfulness" means you become reliable; your word is your bond. "Gentleness" means not that you are weak

---

8. Underhill, *Fruits of the Spirit*, 13.

9. I acknowledge my indebtedness to Dr. James Houston, founding principal of Regent College, for this breakdown of God, other, and self.

but that you become meek, that is, not demanding control, not insisting on your own agenda, being a velvet brick. And "self-control" means that you are not controlled by the media and that you can distinguish between the urgent and the important. Self-controlled people are not workaholics, not driven by internal unmet needs. Self-control is the opposite of "drivenness" something which makes work into an idolatry.[10]

I remember saying to my wife years ago, "I think I may be a little bit of a workaholic." She replied, "That is like being a little bit pregnant!" Not only my wife but an elder of the church said to me, "Paul, I do not know why you are such a driven person but I think it would be a good thing for you to find out why." These comments incited me to set me out on a journey of discovery and personal spiritual growth. I had really good parents and I honour them, but I discovered that in my youthful years I longed for parental approval, though, I seldom gained it. At least that is my perception. I sought this approval through my academic achievements and learned to love the praise of human beings more than the praise of God (John 5:44; 12:43). In a word, I became a Pharisee. I wish I could say I am completely healed, but I can say I am substantially healed.

The second triad deals with our relationship with others in the workplace and the work itself. "Patience" or "forbearance" means that you can stick with a project, stay with the work in a particular location, not always keeping your eye out for a more enticing assignment. There is an old English word for this: "longanimity." Cardinal Stefan Wyszynski says that this is one of the things we can grow in the workplace. "The prime virtue gained through our daily work is patience—a necessary virtue (Heb 10:6; Rom 5:3–5). Here is a ladder, as it were, by which we go ever higher in all our ordinary, daily work."[11]

"Kindness" is not soft-headedness but being soft-hearted, compassionate, like the Good Samaritan who saw the man who had fallen among thieves and, unlike the priest and the Levite, he did not pass by on the other side but stopped, poured wine and oil into his wounds, and placed him on his horse to take him to an inn where he could recover (Luke 10:25–37). Van Gogh composed an amazing painting of this scene with the Samaritan man, truly an outsider, placing the wounded person on his horse and feeling his weight, almost being crushed by it, as he lifted him on to his horse. He is almost crushed by the burden. The kind person is essentially positive

---

10. See Stevens, "Drivenness."
11. Wyszynski, *All You Who Labor*, 133.

towards people especially those in need. "Goodness" is not treating the world and people as junk. It means having God's view of creation and the creature. God declared and declares that "It is good," indeed "very good" (Gen 1:21). Good people appreciate beauty. So the affirmation "It is good" means aesthetic goodness as well as moral goodness.

The final triad concerns our relationship with God and, of course, people. "Love" is caring loyalty to people, places, and structures, seeing the best in people and meeting needs, not regarding people as an "unlovely person project" but expressing their true value and dignity—their lovableness. We get this love from God "because God's love has been poured out into our hearts through the Holy Spirit, who has been given to us" (Rom 5:5).

"Joy" is more than circumstantial happiness. It is an infusion of God's own Spirit bringing an exhilaration in life and work. Joy provides equilibrium even in difficult and untoward circumstances. It means not letting your situation determine your well-being, finding your delight mainly in God, and allowing the joy of the Holy Spirit to infect and infuse us as an artesian well. So, United Kingdom Canon Stanley Evans once described the Christian as a "controlled drunk purposively intoxicated with the joy of the life which is perpetually created by God himself."[12]

Peace is the threefold rest of God, humankind, and creation. It means living sabbatically. It is positive, not merely the negative absence of conflict. It means wholeness, completeness. It breeds vocational contentment as William Perkins, the seventeenth-century Puritan, gives some practical counsel in this matter: (1) We must labor to see our particular situation as a providence of God no matter how difficult; (2) We must resolve in our conscience that God is our portion (Ps 16:6); (3) We must resolve not to seek more in this world than we actually need—we have no warrant to pray for abundance.[13] This last issue we overcome by persistent thanksgiving which John Calvin said is the basic posture of the Christian person (Phil 4:6). So, how do we appropriate the fruit of the Spirit and deal with the works of the flesh?

On Being an Overcomer

We do it by crucifixion and aspiration. Paul says, "Those who belong to Christ Jesus have crucified the flesh with its passions and desires. Since we

---

12. Quoted in Leech, *Experiencing God*, 103.
13. Perkins, *Works of That Famous and Worthy Minister*, 770C.

live by the Spirit, let us keep in step with the Spirit" (Gal 5:24–5). First, we must not run away from the conflict situation we are in, seeking peace in another assignment, or dissolving the pain of it in alcohol, drugs, or the drug of overwork. Paul said to the Corinthians (1 Cor 7:17, 20), "Remain where you are." Do not think, Paul assures the Corinthians, that there is spiritual advantage in changing the location of your service—being freed from your spouse or your work situation, for example.

You discover that your present situation is exactly the soil needed for nurturing the virtuous life. "These useless desires usurp the place of virtues I ought to have—patience, resignation, mortification, obedience, and meekness under suffering. They are what God wishes me to practice at this time," says the seventeenth-century spiritual director Francis de Sales.[14] The early monks had a saying: Stay with your cell; your cell will teach you everything. But staying involves dealing with the "work of the flesh."

First, dealing with the flesh is a kind of death, mortification, agreeing with the death of Christ in our hearts and nailing our wrong desires to the cross. But second, Gal 5 says we appropriate the fruit of the Spirit in "living by the Spirit" and by "keeping in step with the Spirit" (5:25), lining ourselves up with God and God's leading, which is surely the same as remaining in God's love (as Jesus said) and keeping the commandments of Jesus—which is simply to love. Mortification and Aspiration are the two ways we deal with conflict in ourselves and in our workplaces. And how do we do that? It is through prayer.

I became a Christian through prayer, actually through non-prayer, from the attempt to have an hour of prayer without any light, books, Bible, or friends. I felt like my words were bouncing off an invisible glass ceiling. I realized that I was separated from God. I needed and wanted God wholeheartedly. The kingdom, Jesus said, is not for the mildly interested but for the desperate (Luke 16:16) and I was desperate. That night God came into my life in what I can only call waves and waves of liquid love. That was ten days before I entered university. When I did move into a men's residence at McMaster University in Hamilton, Ontario, someone in the residence heard that I was a new Christian and invited me to a Bible reading and prayer group every night after supper.

It was there that they gave me my first Christian book, a copy of Brother Lawrence's *The Practice of the Presence of God*. I devoured it. Lawrence, a kitchen chef in a medieval monastery, said that the prayer times were

---

14. De Sales, *Introduction to the Devout Life*, 205.

no different from the time of work. He said that he simply went to God through everything he did. His greatest business did not divert him from God. Before he would engage in a new task he would say to God that he could not do this without God's help. This simple, largely uneducated "lay" brother was my first mentor in a life of prayer. Since then, I have discovered a little-known book by my favorite theologian, Peter T. Forsyth, an English early twentieth-century congregational theologian.

In *The Soul of Prayer*, Forsyth in his typically pithy way reflects on prayer. I have selected a few quotations.

> The worst sin is prayerlessness. Overt sin, or crime, or the glaring inconsistencies which often surprise us in Christian people are the effect of this, or its punishment. We are left by God by lack of seeking him.[15]

> Not to want to pray, then, is the sin behind sin. And it ends in not being able to pray.[16]

> The prayer within all prayer is "Thy will be done."[17]

> We seek only because He found; we beseech Him because he first besought us (2 Cor 5:20).[18]

> For it is Christ at prayer who lives in us, and we are conduits of the Eternal Intercession.[19]

> A chief object of all prayer is to bring us to God. But we may attain His presence and come closer to Him by the way we ask Him for other things, concrete things, or things of the Kingdom, than by direct prayer for union with Him.[20]

Then Forsyth make a reference to praying before and while we work.

> Our prayer prepares for our work and sacrifice, but all our work and sacrifice still more prepare for prayer.[21]

---

15. Forsyth, *Soul of Prayer*, 11.
16. Forsyth, *Soul of Prayer*, 12.
17. Forsyth, *Soul of Prayer*, 13.
18. Forsyth, *Soul of Prayer*, 14.
19. Forsyth, *Soul of Prayer*, 16.
20. Forsyth, *Soul of Prayer*, 16.
21. Forsyth, *Soul of Prayer*, 16.

To make prayer our great end . . . in this sense to pray without ceasing . . . is a slow matter"[22]

Indeed, it is a slow journey to attain prayer without ceasing as we shall see later. But there is not just one way of praying without ceasing. In addition to constantly communing with God, we can be like Nehemiah who was cupbearer to a pagan king. He was asked why he was so sad and what he wanted to do about it. He shot a prayer to God, the so-called "arrow prayer," and answered the king (Neh 2:4–5). Not ceasing to pray even in the stress of a workplace situation.

We can pray before starting a new task, pray before meeting a client, pray in an interview, pray when things go wrong, pray when things go right, pray for our colleagues, pray for the corporation, pray for our boss, and pray for our subordinates. In parental work we have hundreds of occasions for prayer each day. There is no situation where we cannot consciously pray. And even if we do not get the answer we have requested, we gain God, we gain life in God, we gain the fruit of the Spirit. As Forsyth continues, "Nothing would do more to cure us of a belief in our own wisdom than the granting of some of our eager prayers."[23] But there is one circumstance when prayer is especially needed and sometimes action.

The Blessing of the Testing of Our Vocation

We are tested vocationally, not directly by God—though God apparently allows it—but by Satan and the world. Testing is not exactly the same thing as temptation. But the Greek word used in the New Testament (*peirazo*) can be translated both ways. Usually in English, *peirazo* (temptation) has a negative meaning—something that is going to trip you up. But the more common meaning of the original is to test and thus *rise or fall*. This helps me understand how Scripture says it was the Holy Spirit that led Jesus into the wilderness to be tested by Satan (Matt 4:1). The Holy Spirit would not lead Jesus into sin. But, you may ask, why is testing important?

Testing is essential to growth, especially spiritual growth. Take Adam and Eve in the garden with the test of the tree of the knowledge of good and evil. They failed! Take Jesus in the wilderness after being baptized and being affirmed by the Father as the Son of God and the Suffering Servant

---

22. Forsyth, *Soul of Prayer*, 16.
23. Forsyth, *Soul of Prayer*, 28.

(Matt 4:1–11).²⁴ He succeeded and grew. Take the average follower of Jesus referred to in 1 John 2:16 who experiences "the lust of the flesh, the lust of the eyes, and the pride of life." And what will we do when faced with these three tests that come either directly from Satan or the world?²⁵ And the tests are vocational.

The vocation of vocations is to follow Jesus. I remember praying beside the bed of a PhD student at the local university as he invited Christ to be his lord. I turned to him in the prayer and said, "As a follower of Jesus you have a calling on your life greater than becoming the prime minister of India."

He said, "How did you know?"

I said, "Know what?"

"That was my ambition in life," he confessed.

Jesus was tested vocationally in the areas of provision, pleasure, and power. These three are roughly equivalent to the issues which most people face in the workplace: money, sex, and power.²⁶

Money and the lack of it or, unusually, the abundance of it, is a test we often face in the workplace. When I was in business for myself I always felt I was one job away from poverty. But God provided. And even now that I am so-called retired (but still working) I lie in bed sometimes and go over my finances to see if we are going to "make it." So, this sacred window we have into what was going on in the mind and heart of Jesus centred around his identity. But it tells us that we too are tested in everyday life especially in the area of provision. Can we trust God that God will provide for us?

Pleasure was the second test which Jesus faced when he was tested by Satan in his identity as the Son of God and the Suffering Servant. We may not be tempted to jump off the temple wall and be miraculously rescued, but we are surely tested in the workplace in the sexual area. So, the ordinary Christian is tested with the "lust of the eyes" in the parallel passage in 1 John 2:16. Lust means an extraordinarily strong passion or desire. The Roman Catholic Church defines lust as "disordered desire for the inordinate enjoyment of sexual pleasure. Sexual pleasure is morally disordered when sought

---

24. I take the word of the Father to Jesus when he was baptized to be a combination of two Scriptures, Ps 2 ("You are my Son") and Isa 42:1 ("in whom I delight") a unique combination of the royal Son and the suffering servant.

25. 1 John 2:17.

26. For an extensive reflection on the temptations and testing of Jesus and how we enter into these see chs. 16–18 in Stevens, *Seven Days of Faith*, 139–60.

for itself, isolated from its procreative and unitive purposes."²⁷ Sexual lust is not mere arousal at the sight of an attractive person. This is perfectly normal. Martin Luther is credited as saying about arousal, "It is one thing for a bird to land on your head; one can hardly prevent this from happening. But it is quite another thing to allow the bird to build a nest there."

Arousal becomes lust when one fanaticizes a sexual embrace with someone who is not your marriage partner. The lust of the eyes is what we are seeing inwardly, a fantasy, or a vision. Augustine put it this way, speaking of acting on the lust in a peak experience:

> This lust assumes power not only over the whole body, and not only from the outside, *but also internally*; it disturbs the whole man, when the mental emotion combines and mingles with the physical craving, resulting in a pleasure surpassing all physical delights. So intense is the pleasure that when it reaches its climax there is an almost total extinction of mental alertness; the intellectual sentries, as it were, are overwhelmed [read the French saying for sexual orgasm as a "petite morte"].²⁸

So don't even think about jumping off a cliff physically, emotionally, relationally, vocationally, or sexually, and expect God to provide a miraculous rescue! But the third test was perhaps the most common in the money, sex, and power trio.

Power of course is not in itself wrong or evil. And everyone has power. Even infants have power to sway their mothers to provide food! But power tends to incline people away from trust in God and God's kingdom especially when it is expressed with brute force, or when dehumanizing demands are made. Often this caters to self-interest, the desire for control, and the perks that go with it. It makes a person think they are a god, which is why Friedrich Nietzsche is credited with saying, "But that I may reveal my heart entirely unto you, my friends; IF there were gods, how could I endure it to be no God! THEREFORE there are no Gods."²⁹

And what did Jesus do when tested with power? He worshipped the Father (Deut 6:13). But what are we to do with what power we have? Do with it what Jesus did: he empowered others (Matt 28:18–19; John 20:22–23). Jesus responded to his own test by going the way of the cross, laying

---

27. *Catechism of the Catholic Church*, no. 2351, p. 564, Quoted in Reed, *C. S. Lewis Explores*, 57.
28. Quoted in Lyman, *Seven Deadly Sins and Evil*, 55, emphasis mine.
29. Nietzsche, *Thus Spoke Zarathustra*, book 24.

down his life for the benefit of everyone. He took us with him, absorbing sin, alienation, and brokenness in his own person and winning a victory over sin, Satan, and death through resurrection. And for us wanderers in the wilderness we win true kingdom power by giving it away.

The deepest answer for testing is to turn to God, for there is no temptation that has overtaken us that is not common to humanity (1 Cor 10:13). But he will provide a way of escape. Sometimes our prayer will be simply a cry for help. Sometimes, like Joseph, we need to run away. Sometimes we need to answer our test with Scripture, as Jesus did. Jesus was tempted at all points as we are yet without sin (Heb 4:15). He can deliver us. So pray. But testing produces spiritual growth, a blessing.

The monks deal with the first—money—by embracing poverty. We can deal with it by trusting God for provision. The monastic community deals with the second, sex, by chastity. But there is an important insight here. Chastity is not only required outside of marriage but inside; and not just in the sexual area. Chastity is the ordering of our desires and directing them ultimately to God. Finally, the test of power in the history of the monastic tradition is challenged with the vow of obedience. And for those who are not monks it is submission and accountability. I once heard a famous preacher say that no Christian leader has fallen in North America who had an accountability group. They had followers but no peers who could ask them hard questions. So now I need to summarize practically how we can be blessed while we work.

So How Shall We Then Grow Spirituality While We Work?

There are eight ways to realize the blessing of God.

1. Develop disciplines of responsiveness to God before and after work.[30]
2. Use every work opportunity and every challenge to seek God in prayer.
3. Look for signs of God's presence and the kingdom in the context of your work.
4. Be reflective about what you learn of yourself by the way you work and treasure the feedback and criticisms of others. These are opportunities for spiritual growth.

---

30. Jonathan Wilson tells how he once got a friend to write a prayer each day about the temptations he would face at work, before he went and after he finished work. Email correspondence on November 15, 2022.

Growing Spiritually through Work

5. Recognize the presence of the Seven Deadly sins (works of the flesh) in yourself when they appear (first of all as a simple thought), and go to God seeking the "matching" fruit of the Spirit. Do this before the thought becomes rooted in your heart and becomes an obsession or passion. (Scripturally this is "mortifying the sinful nature" and "walking in the Spirit.")

6. Welcome testing in the workplace as an arena for growth (Jas 1) but do not seek it. God may allow you to be tested, as Jesus was, in the workplace.

7. Ask at least one person to be your accountability group. Ask them to inquire regularly about your struggles and joys, and to pray regularly for you.

8. Keep Sabbath, and let Sabbath keep you focussed on the really Real as the center for your life.

But we are not the only ones blessed by God through our work. Our work, if it is good work, or mainly so, blesses others. To that we now turn.

BLESSING OTHERS

8

Blessing Your Neighbor

> The only thing that counts is faith expressing itself through love.
> THE APOSTLE PAUL (GAL 5:6)

> Blessing is a central theme in the Bible, second only to its emphasis on deliverance... At its root, a blessing refers to God's friendly approach to those who are open to receiving divine generosity.
> ROBERT BANKS[1]

PEOPLE WHO ARE SELF-EMPLOYED, like me, are especially tempted to think that they are really working for their own survival, to pursue their passions, pay off their mortgage, or to build up a nest egg to leave to their children. This chapter will show how work is one of the primary ways that we love our neighbors and even love the world (in a good sense), leaving the world a little better than when we came. In other words, we bless our neighbor through our work. Think of all the ways that your work blesses someone, even if you cannot see them. We do this by obeying the second great commandment, the great commission, the greater commission, and the greatest commission.

The context is that of adapting William Perkins's definition of theology to define marketplace theology as "the science of working blessedly forever." And the word "blessing" hints that God has something to do with

---

1. Banks, "Blessing," 72.

this. His intention in making the man and woman in the garden was, in part, to bless them in and through their work. Blessing is the actual transmission of a positive and spiritual good, generally to a person but also to inanimate creation, and even workplaces.

God made work, as we saw in chapters 3–5, as a blessing. In chapters 6 and 7 we explored how the worker herself is blessed by God in the process of her daily work, how God—Father, Son, and Spirit—blesses us, enabling us to work and work well. We discovered that one of the blessings God gives us as workers is spiritual growth. But now we are considering the blessing that work brings to our neighbor and to the world. Of course, not all work is a blessing to our neighbor and the world, or even to ourselves. But essentially this is God's design. In this context we need to ask a preliminary question. Is this one of the things Jesus could have meant when he gave us the second great commandment?

Through the Second Great Commandment

Sitting outside an ice cream store I was talking with the owner as we watched people passing by. He turned to me and said, "Paul, I really don't know what the purpose of my life is." I had noticed how he spoke with many of the passersby by name and was encouraging them. He knew them and loved them. I said, "Jesus said that the purpose of our lives is to love God and to love our neighbor and you are certainly doing the latter, and possibly the former. You truly love these neighbors and your store sells a fine product that is very good."

Jesus said that our purpose is love, love for God wholeheartedly, whole-mindedly, and with a whole-bodied love. And the Second Great Commandment, he said, is like the first, but is taken from Lev 19:18, "Love your neighbor as yourself" (Matt 22:39). On these, Jesus said, hang all the law and the prophets; that is, they sum up what God wants of the human race. So it should not surprise us that Jesus said to his disciples, love one another (John 13:34). Jesus proposes that the major apologetic for the kingdom and the King will be the mutual love of believers. "By this everyone will know that you are my disciples, if you love one another" (13:35; 17:23). So, it also should not surprise us that love is the "greatest of these" three virtues that will last: faith, hope, and love (1 Cor 13:13). Paul, in writing to the church in Thessalonica, starts with thanksgiving for "your labor prompted by love" (1 Thess 1:3).

As John Taylor notes in his chapter on "Labor of Love: The Theology of Work in First and Second Thessalonians," Paul's "argument against idleness is made on moral and missional grounds,"[2] not on the view that the end of human history was imminent. Taylor argues persuasively from the text that "work as an act of love, for one another and for all, should be seen as an instruction to the church so as to be self-supporting, in the manner that Paul was, so as not to be a burden on others."[3] So working, not yielding to idleness, prevents our being a burden on others. That is a negative love-reason. But is there a positive love-reason for work?

Admittedly, not all of us work for love of the neighbor consciously. And certainly not all of us love the work that we do. For many people work is a mere means of survival. And for most, to be out of work is a personal catastrophe—not because we are unable to love through our work, blessing others, but because we are not able to support ourselves. And in some of the work we may hear echoes of Studs Terkel in the work stories of some people. "This book, being about work, is, by its very nature, about violence—to the spirit as well as to the body. It is about ulcers as well as accidents, about shouting matches as well as fistfights, about nervous breakdowns as well as kicking the dog around. It is, above all (or beneath all), about daily humiliations."[4]

If that were not enough there is the economic system that we must deal with. Does that system not cater to greed rather than love? Here I quote the early economist Adam Smith who wrote,

> Every individual is continually exerting himself to find out the most advantageous employment of whatever capital he can command. It is his own advantage, indeed, and not that of society which he has in view. But the study of his own advantage naturally, or rather necessarily, leads him to prefer that employment which is most advantageous to the society . . . He neither intends to promote the public interest, nor knows how much he is promoting it. . . . He intends only his own security; and by directing that industry in such a manner as its produce may be of the greatest value, he intends only his own gain, and he is in this, as in many other cases, led by an invisible hand to promote an end which was not part of his intention . . . By pursuing his own interest, he frequently

---

2. Taylor, "Labor of Love," 51.
3. Taylor, "Labor of Love," 57.
4. Terkel, *Working*, xiii.

promotes that of the society more effectively than when he really intends to promote it.[5]

Smith's mysterious reference to the "invisible hand" is not a reference to the hand of God, though it is tempting so to attribute it, but rather it is a metaphor for the fact that allowing people to pursue their own self-interest (and for Thomas Aquinas, the medieval theologian, there is a reasonable love of self) does in fact produce possibly unintended but beneficial good consequences for others. And what unintended consequences does the market and the current economic system actually produce, in addition to goods and services, that help people to flourish?

In fact each of us is unique and has unique gifts and talents. This means that we are necessarily interdependent: I have what you need, and you have what I need. And the exchange is called business. But let's not stop with just the goods, whether food or computers, and services, whether teaching, garbage collection, or health care, all of which are direct ways of serving and loving our neighbor. Let's consider the indirect ways we love and bless our neighbor, indeed the world, that come from marketplace activity.

One such way is trust. Samuel Gregg in his article on "The Marketplace as Common Ground for Serving Others" comments, "The trust required in free markets extends to faith in people as well as a confidence that certain rules will always, save in exceptional circumstances, be followed and that certain institutions such as courts will follow consistent patterns of behavior."[6] Gregg names civility as another indirect result of trade since, as Smith says, every person in a market economy becomes a merchant and civility is no longer associated with an inherited social caste.[7] Ptolemy of Lucca, one of Aquinas's disciples, said that "business affairs in cities needed to be conducted with politeness, gentility, and 'a certain civility.'"[8] Other mostly unintended benefits of commerce have been freedom and the growth of private property. So even the unintended results of our work can make it a labor of love. But Studs Terkel does not treat work as mere violence and frustration, as true as this sometimes is.

> It is about a search, too, for daily meaning as well as daily bread, for recognition as well as cash, for astonishment rather than torpor;

5. Smith, *Inquiry into the Nature*, quoted in Stackhouse et al., *On Moral Business*, 11.
6. Gregg, "Marketplace as Common Ground," 232.
7. Gregg, "Marketplace as Common Ground," 234.
8. Ptolemy of Lucca, *De Regimine Principum*, bks II-IV, quoted in Gregg, "Marketplace as Common Ground," 227.

in short, for a sort of life rather than a Monday through Friday sort of dying. Perhaps immortality, too, is part of the quest. To be remembered was the wish, spoken and unspoken, of the heroes and heroines of this book.[9]

So, the Great Commandment to love our neighbor finds at least partial fulfilment in our daily work. But what about the next, the Great Commission?

Through the Great Commission

The last words of a person are vitally important. The last words of my wife as she was dying were words of blessing for each and every member of our family, all twenty-two of them in groups of two. And these are the last words of Jesus before he ascended to heaven. "Therefore go [or "as you go"] and make disciples of all nations, baptizing them in the name of the Father and of the Son and of the Holy Spirit, and teaching them to obey everything I have commanded you" (Matt 29:19–20). This key missional commission is bracketed by the words of Jesus beforehand, "All authority in heaven and on earth has been given to me," and afterwards, "And surely I am with you always, to the very end of the age." And just what does this Great Commission have to do with working blessedly?

There is no question that we are in the beginning of a global movement of faith and work integration. And sometimes people want to name the founders. But one name in the Western world that is not often mentioned but who truly is a founder is Pete Hammond. In the middle of the twentieth century, Pete tirelessly taught and advocated for marketplace mission through InterVarsity Christian Fellowship and much more widely. He persuaded a wealthy benefactor to endow the movement, and in that context supported financially a professor of theology, Dr. John Davis, to research the history of the interpretation of the Great Commission as it relates to marketplace ministry. What he found was almost unbelievable.

Surveying the Interpretation of the Great Commission

"This survey of some sixteen centuries of Christian interpretation of Matthew's 'Great Commission' passage has shown how profoundly the *ecclesiastical* controversies and concerns of the day have dominated the church's

---

9. Terkel, *Working*, xiii.

understanding of the text." Further, Davis notes that "Interpreters tended to assume that Christ's mandate was fulfilled *by the apostles*, and read the text in terms of controversies about the Trinity and the proper subjects of and form of words for baptism."[10] While some recovery of the missional implications of the text came with the publication of William Carey's *Enquiry* (1792), Davis continues: "In the late 1990s initial signs of a "marketplace hermeneutic" began to appear, with such voices being raised from the contexts of parachurch ministries.[11] Davis concludes,

> Taking seriously Christ's mandate to make disciples by teaching them "to *observe all* that I have commanded" implies concrete, practical training for all the people of God to be "salt and light" in every sphere of service in the culture. The *horizontal extension* of the Kingdom through foreign missions and evangelism must be accompanied by the *vertical penetration* of the Kingdom in every dimension of life if the Great Commission is to be truly fulfilled in our or any other generation.[12]

So, what does this mean for loving others through work? Very simply it means that the theology of work, rightly understood, has huge missiological implications: we will reach the world with the good news of the kingdom of God partly through work. Further it means that the most neglected part of the Great Commission—"teaching them to obey everything I have commanded you"—means that it is not information that our neighbor needs but *whole-life discipleship* including their work life. Obedience comes from the heart not just the mind.

As Greg Forster says, "The primary mission of the church is to help people to become students ("disciples") of Jesus Christ through the gospel, even as they continue to participate in the life of their nation . . . Discipleship tends to become identified with the consumption of religious goods

---

10. Davis, "'Teaching Them to Observe,'" emphasis mine.

11. I.e., in the *Christian Growth Study Bible* (1997) [Youth With a Mission] and the *Promise Keeper Men's Study Bible* (1997) [Promise Keepers]. For historical perspective on the emergence of a "theology of the laity" since the Second World War, see Banks, "Appendix A." Neill and Weber, *Layman in Christian History*, is a standard reference on the subject indicated by the title. Diehl, *Monday Connection*, is a fine discussion of the problem of the "disconnect" between much of the church's preaching and teaching and the concerns of the workplace. It could be plausibly argued that the church's less-than-adequate equipping of the laity to practice Christian discipleship in the workplace has contributed to the secularization of Western culture that has been increasingly evident since the end of the Second World War.

12. Davis, "Teaching Them to Observe," 80.

and services . . . We were made to work as well as worship; we were made to worship in large part by working . . . The gospel restores us to worshipful work."[13] It also restores us to loving our neighbor through our work. For evidence of this we turn to a surprising source.

The Corporal and Spiritual Almsdeeds of Aquinas

Thomas Aquinas was a medieval theologian who wrote about corporal (bodily) and spiritual almsdeeds, or ways of loving our neighbor near and far. He summarized these love-works in the following way:

Seven Corporal (bodily) Almsdeeds:

- To feed the hungry
- To give drink to the thirsty
- To clothe the naked
- To give hospitality to strangers
- To visit the sick
- To ransom prisoners
- To bury the dead

Seven Spiritual Almsdeeds:

- To instruct the ignorant
- To give advice to those in doubt
- To comfort the sorrowful
- To reprove sinners
- To forgive offences
- To put up with people who are burdensome and hard to get along with
- To pray for all[14]

Taken together they represent almost completely the ministry of every member of the people of God in the world, not of course that any individual can do it all! But let us think about what the bodily almsdeeds mean in the world of work:

13. Forster, "Being God's People," 155–56.
14. Aquinas, *Summa Theologica*, Part II of second part, Q 32, art 2 (p. 241).

- To feed the hungry (think food industry)
- To give drink to the thirsty (think beverage industry)
- To clothe the naked (think clothing, design industry)
- To give hospitality to strangers (think hospitality industry)
- To visit the sick (think medicine, counselling)
- To ransom prisoners (think police, military)
- To bury the dead (think funeral business)

Then in the same way we may consider some of the spiritual dimensions of our love for our neighbor in the workplace:

- To instruct the ignorant (teaching and empowering others, even informally)
- To counsel the doubtful (encouraging those who have little confidence in what they are doing and in who they are)
- To comfort the sorrowful (helping people deal with failure and loss)
- To reprove the sinner (warning people who are on the wrong track and helping them to get on the right track)
- To forgive injuries (truly forgiving the hurts that we receive in the workplace)
- To bear with those who trouble and annoy us (not disconnecting ourselves from people we find difficult to be near)
- To pray for all (hold our neighbor workers up in prayer to God both for their work and their relationship to God).

If the Great Commission invites us to love our neighbors through our work, the *Greater* Commission, as I call it, found in Luke 4, does the same thing.

Through the Greater Commission

When Jesus returned to his home synagogue, the prophet Isaiah was read for him.

> The Spirit of the Sovereign LORD is on me, because the LORD has anointed me to proclaim good news to the poor. He has sent me to bind up the broken hearted. To proclaim freedom for the captives and release from darkness for the prisoners, to proclaim the year of the LORD's favor. (Isa 61:1–2)

Jesus simply said after the reading a one-sentence sermon, "Today this scripture is fulfilled in your hearing" (Luke 4:21). This was a breathtaking moment in which Jesus announced that the kingdom of God had truly come in his own person and through his teaching and deeds. In so announcing the kingdom he also stated how, again, we can love our neighbor and bless them, as well as the world, through our work.

Simply put, the coming of the kingdom of God brings human and creational flourishing. It has many dimensions: economic flourishing ("good news for the poor" [Isa 61:1]), emotional flourishing ("binding up the broken hearted" [61:1]), personal flourishing ("freedom for the captives" [61:1]), mental and physical flourishing ("recovery of sight to the blind" in the Greek version [61:1]), spiritual flourishing ("the year of the LORD's favor" [61:2]), workplace flourishing ("They will rebuild the ancient ruins and restore the places long devastated; they will renew the ruined cities that have been devastated for generations" [Isa 61:4]), and finally, ministerial flourishing for everyone ("And you will be called priests of the LORD, you will be named ministers of our God" [61:6]).

Taken together these are not only a handy summary of Jesus's ministry but they also spell out what God wants us to do as we work with God in bringing in his kingdom of human and creational flourishing on earth, partially now, and completely when Christ returns a second time. These dimensions of human flourishing are outlined more fully in my most recent book, *The Kingdom of God in Working Clothes: The Marketplace and the Reign of God*, from which I am here abstracting only one section from Isa 61 concerning work.

Rebuilding Society through Our Work

"They will rebuild the ancient ruins and restore the places long devastated; they will renew the ruined cities that have been devastated for generations" (Isa 61:4). We will flourish in the kingdom of God in our work. That means that work will be redemptive—restoring things that have been broken or debased, and work will be worshipful. In a fascinating and unique new book, Matthew Kaemingk and Cory B. Willson reconnect our work with liturgy, both within the corporate worship of the people of God and in the workplace itself.[15] This is totally in line with Rom 12:1–2 where we are exhorted, in view of God's mercy, to present our whole bodily life to God as

---

15. See Kaemingk and Willson, *Work and Worship*.

spiritual worship, including our work. So reconnecting faith and work, now a global movement, must include seeing our work as worship, as prophesied by Isaiah in which the flourishing people are clothed in "a garment of praise" and these oak trees, as they are called, would be a "display of [God's] splendor" (Isa 61:3). But to whom does the "they" refer as rebuilding the devastated ruins?

"They" refers to the people brought together by the anointed one, people obliquely mentioned as the "strangers [who] will shepherd your flocks" and the "foreigners [who] will work your fields and vineyards." The messiah will bring together people who normally would have nothing to do with each other. From the New Testament we learn that the wall separating Jews and gentiles, and any other groups of people that have nothing to do with each other, has been broken down by the cross of Jesus, thus making peace (Eph 2:14–18). So now there is neither Jew nor Greek, male or female, bond or free because (and this next verse is important) "for you are all one in Christ Jesus" (Gal 3:28). To this Mar Osthathios said, "The theological foundation of a classless society is the classless Godhead himself as a classless Nuclear family."[16] And here is where Jesus got into trouble in his home church after his one-sentence sermon.

Jesus almost got killed on the occasion for noting that the prophets Elijah and Elisha both were sent to people outside the Jewish community and brought flourishing to them, anticipating the rich diversity of people in the kingdom of God who form unity *through*, and not in spite of, diversity. This was so offensive that they took Jesus out to the brow of a hill and were about to toss him over, while he walked right through the angry crowd.

These once alienated people, now that the breakdown is mended, will work together to rebuild society. And they do this through their work. We can do this provisionally now in the marketplace. Is this also a picture of the new heaven and new earth, the kingdom fully come, when "the renewal of all things" (Matt 19:28) will be taking place? Perhaps all heaven is growth, healing, and renewal.[17] But this is only one of the facets of the Greater Commission. There are others.

---

16. Osthathios, *Thy Kingdom Come*, 43, quoted in Leech, *Experiencing God*, 379.

17. For a complete statement of the Jubilee and kingdom of God as it relates to work see ch. 1 in Stevens, *Kingdom of God in Working Clothes*.

Further Dimensions of the Greater Commission and Our Work

For each of the named dimensions of the coming kingdom I can think of human occupations and ways we have of loving our neighbors and the world. For *economic flourishing*, think micro- and medium-sized economic development, financial advisors, bankers, investment companies, the World Economic Forum, The World Bank, and charitable organizations dedicated to relieving poverty.

For *personal flourishing*, think advocates and agencies working for justice, those working to recover people working in the sex trade, those working in the drug scene, administrators, lawyers seeking justice for wounded people or people suffering from racial or sexual discrimination, and doctors and nurses, police people and the military, those working in government, parents and homemakers, along with social workers and charitable agencies.

For *mental flourishing*, think authors, teachers, educators, journalists, media workers, parents, and grandparents.

For *spiritual flourishing*, think pastors, mental health professionals, chaplains, and spiritual directors.

For *ministerial flourishing*, with the emphasis on universal priesthood, think about the ordinary church member in the workplace, home, and neighborhood, with teachers, doctors, nurses, cleaning persons, garbage collectors, politicians, broadcasters, writers, artists, and musicians.

All of these are ways we love and bless our neighbor and the world through our work. So, I have daringly called Luke 4 the "Greater Commission." But, in my opinion, there is a "Greatest Commission."

Through the Greatest Commission

In two places in the Gospel of John Jesus commissions his followers to participate in his coming kingdom: In John 17:18 Jesus prays, "As you sent me into the world, I have sent them into the world," and in John 20:21 when the resurrected Jesus passes through the locked door where the disciples were meeting he gives his last words to them: "As the Father has sent me, I am sending you."

Why am I calling this the Greatest Commission, which I note includes the "Great" and the "Greater"? Because this commission deals with the source of our mission and the style and pattern of it. The source is the Triune

God ("as the Father has sent me"). Jesus sends us out into the workplace and into the world with all the resources of the Triune God, all the love of the Father, the grace of the Lord Jesus and the empowerment of the Holy Spirit. But the style and pattern of our work and mission is incarnational.

Think of it: God sent his Son into the world becoming like us in every respect. "The Word became flesh and made his dwelling among us" (John 1:14), literally pitched his tent among us or moved into our neighborhood. He incarnated God, God's mission, and our humanity. He was with us physically (bodily), emotionally (with a human heart), occupationally (was a carpenter), socially (was middle class), culturally (he spoke with a Galilean twang), and above all spiritually (was tested as we are and knew the favor of the Father). His identification with us was complete, so much so that "God made him who had no sin to be sin [or a sin offering] for us, so that in him we might become the righteousness of God" (2 Cor 5:21). What does this mean for us who follow Jesus?

We cannot love our neighbor by keeping a safe comfortable distance from them, or by adopting postures that prevent our actually engaging them in their work situation. Love requires more. To reach them and to love them we have be with them. With them in their life. Such is the incarnational mission with which the Lord engages us. There are obviously limits to our engagement. We cannot live with everyone. We cannot even eat with everyone, let along work with them all.

We can, however, be a little Christ with a few people, and through mediating agencies to a broader population. We can even engage and grapple with the principalities and powers that affect our neighbor and his or her work.[18] We can engage the world, the flesh, and the devil, that trilogy of resistances named in the *Anglican Prayer Book*. This handy outline of the three dimensions of resistance to the regal claims of God is found in the Anglican/Episcopal prayer book. One of the Collects (gathering prayers) is "Lord, we beseech thee, grant thy people grace to withstand the temptations of the world, the flesh and the devil, and with pure hearts and minds to follow thee, the only God; through Jesus Christ our Lord."[19] But there is an extreme limit to our identification.

---

18. For a fuller treatment of the principalities and powers see Stevens, *Other Six Days*, 215–39.

19. Collect, 18th Sunday after Trinity, in General Synod of the Anglican Church of Canada, *Book of Common Prayer*, 247.

We certainly cannot become a sin offering for others, but we can enter into their lives and feel the weight of their sin and direct them to Jesus who has accomplished the one and final sacrifice for all the sins of humankind. We can lay down our life for our neighbor. But, as mentioned in an earlier chapter, the "entering into" the pain of others and the pain of the organization will constitute the mysterious reference in Paul's correspondence where Paul says, "I fill up in my flesh what is still lacking in regard to Christ's afflictions, for the sake of his body, which is the church" (Col 1:24). This is the cross that we take up in the workplace. We cannot save our neighbors but we can identity with them, feeling their pain and their joys, understanding their need of God, empathizing with them, and walking in their shoes, at least partly, in our wholistic down-to-earth, incarnational mission to them and the world. Of this our work is at least a part.

In all these ways—the Great Commandment (love of the neighbor), the Great Commission (including the vertical and horizontal dimensions of whole-life disciple-making), the Greater Commission (bringing Jubilee and flourishing to our neighbor), and the Greatest Commission (with the help of the Triune God doing this as much as we can through identification with our neighbor)—we bless our neighbor and the world through our work.

Now we wish to explore blessing the workplace itself.

9

Blessing the Workplace

The workplace will now be wherever work happens, and the workweek will be whenever work happens best for each person.

DREW HOUSTON, CEO OF DROPBOX[1]

Can we *entirely* alter what we do, so that here and now we practice the occupations of heaven? Of course not. Can we *somewhat* alter what we do, so that our occupations come closer to becoming our God-issued vocation? Usually, yes."

NICHOLAS WOLTERSTORFF[2]

WOLTERSTORFF'S QUESTION RAISES A related one: Can we practice our God-issued vocation in a toxic workplace? Or what if the workplace is our home with children clutching at our legs while we work on the computer? Or does practicing our God-given vocation require a flourishing and empowering workplace? This chapter is about the workplace, and we are approaching it, as we have "work" and "worker," through the tripartite lens we are using to do marketplace theology: head (thinking), heart (prayer), and hands (practice). We have previously explored work and worker but

---

1. Quoted in Elliott et al., *How the Future Works*, 11.
2. Wolterstorff, "More on Vocation," 20–23, quoted in Preece, *Changing Work Values*, 196–97.

now we are considering the workplace and asking what it means to work "blessedly" there.

The workplace may well be the home, factory, office, school, hospital, field, and retail stores. Place is important. One of the priestly tasks of the kingdom worker is to turn raw space into a place. I well remember my fourth-grade teacher, not because of anything she taught me, but because she turned raw school space into a place of joy and learning, pasting pictures on the walls, bringing in planted flowers to tend, and enhancing the learning environment. Miss Dickson made a place from raw space. And the place spoke deeply about what she wanted to do and wanted us to do. And to be. She was a priest in the workplace.

For many people during the pandemic all but essential workers have worked at home amidst the clutter of family and domestic realities. And many will never come back to the office, or if they do, they may meet occasionally in a shared office space, or in "phone booth offices" which provide noiseless privacy for meetings. Some massive office buildings may become ghost workplaces and may need to be repurposed for downtown housing. For many millions the workplace is currently their delivery van. Factories are being retooled, many with more robots and AI. Colleges will employ increasingly AI avatars and AI instructors, or use flipped courses with students taking lectures at home through videos and then students coming to the college to discuss the subject in small groups and to meet the professor. Tenured professors will become more scarce and most post-secondary schools will thrive on sessional or adjunct faculty who come into the building to teach or go to a recording studio and then go home. But these are workplaces.

In *How the Future Works*, the authors, dealing mainly with knowledge workers, argue that the future workplace will be not only flexible in *location*—home and office or school—but flexible in *schedule* as they propose how flexible teams of people working in different time zones can find the overlapping times when teams can meet. They use the terms *hybrid, remote, virtual, distributed* to describe what they mean by "flexible work,"[3] with the emphasis being put on virtual first. "Digital-First means making the switch from a mode of operations where digital technologies supplemented in-person communication as a way of getting work done, to one where in-person supplements the digital in order to build a more connected and

---

3. Elliott et al., *How the Future Works*, 15.

inclusive way of working for everyone."[4] It is already happening and to a large extent it is here to stay. And it affects what we mean by workplace.

In truth the workplace is simply where work is done.

But there is a culture in that workplace even if it is digital, home-based, office-based, a factory, a school, or a hospital. And these places can even be virtuous workplaces, holy places where there are hints of God's presence. Earlier we noted that when Adam and Eve were called by God to "fill the earth" (Gen 1:28) they were called to extend the sanctuary garden into the world. The sanctuary garden was a place of safety, prosperity, and beauty, a place where God was especially present where they worked and rested. That is the perennial human calling. It came before the fall. So, to experience this in the new workplace we must understand how the organizational culture of the workplace affects the worker.

Understanding Organizational Culture[5]

Culture is an important, even a crucial, dimension not only in the life of ethnic groups but also in organizations. Every organization has a corporate "feeling" or environment that communicates to new and old members what is important and what is permitted. This is true equally of businesses and not-for-profit organizations. The minute a person walks into the meeting room, a store, an office, or a church sanctuary, they pick up a nonverbal message that is more powerful than such mottoes as "The customer is number one"; "We exist to give extraordinary service"; "This is a friendly, family church." Attend a team meeting on the internet and you get the same feeling. Culture turns out to be profoundly influential in determining behavior, expressing values, and enabling or preventing change in individuals.

People are sometimes frustrated, without understanding why, when they try to bring about change in an organization. My wife Gail and I remember, sadly, trying to join a badminton club in a local community center. We were novices and everyone there was virtually professional. We tried and tried to join. But in the end after a few weeks, we gave up. No one would play with us. Many people feel the same way about the church. They try to join but are frozen out. Further, some seemingly successful changes in direction of workers get reversed in a few months because they were not

---

4. Elliott et al., *How the Future Works*, 23.

5. Some of the following is abstracted from Stevens, "Organizational Culture and Change," as well as "Organization" and "Organizational Values."

congruent with the culture of the organization; other changes are made easily for reasons that are not apparent unless one understands the invisible but all-pervasive impact of organizational environment. It is the water we swim in.

To change the culture itself is possibly the most substantial change that can be made. Culture normally resists change. But, that being said, culture has a multiple impact on everything else when change takes place. There is an old story about change that goes like this. A man in a museum was looking at the colossal skeleton of a dinosaur that once triumphantly roamed the earth. He turned to the woman beside him and asked, "What happened? Why did they die out?" She said, "The climate changed." But usually if you try to change the culture quickly, the culture will change you (i.e., give you an exit visa).

Motivation is related to culture. We draw motivation out of people in a healthy, life-giving organization. It is inspired, not compelled. Motivation is at least partially a result of a process in a system and is not just generated exclusively from within the individual. The motivational switch is both inside and outside the person. So, motivation is only marginally increased by trying to get people motivated through incentives or threats. It needs to be considered culturally and systemically. What was it about the toxic culture of Potiphar's house in Egypt that caused Joseph to fail and be imprisoned, and what was it about the culture of the prison into which he was thrust, that Joseph thrived and came to be in charge of everything except the key?

The classic study on organizational culture is Edgar H. Schein's *Organizational Culture and Leadership*. His central thesis is that much of what is mysterious about leadership becomes clearer "if we . . . link leadership specifically to creating and changing culture."[6] According to Schein, culture includes each of the following but is deeper than any one of them: (1) the observed behavioral regularities in a group (for example, really good employees show up for work fifteen minutes early); (2) the dominant values of the group (for example, church attendance is the ultimate expression of spirituality in a local church); (3) the rules or "ropes" of the group (for example, the usual way to climb the hierarchy is to engage in leisure-time diversions with your superior); and (4) the feeling or climate that is conveyed (for example, while not formally prohibited, it is also not acceptable to bring forward negative comments in staff meetings). Schein says that

---

6. Schein, *Organizational Culture and Leadership*, xi.

culture concerns the underlying assumptions and beliefs that are shared by members of the organization and often operate unconsciously.[7]

The factors at work in an organizational culture can be pictured as three concentric circles. On the outside are the *symbols, artifacts, and visible signs of the culture*, which are often incarnated in logos, mottoes, the appearance of a building, the way people dress, and the titles by which people are addressed. These artifacts include the physical layout you are entering if it is a physical workplace. But the same applies to a virtual workplace which is often more personal with artifacts from your home in the background.

The middle circle represents *the values* that underlie the more visible processes. Values are simply what behaviors are cherished by the organization. Often these are unexpressed and unconscious. Sometimes the stated values are incongruent with the real values that inform the culture. For example, a business may claim that it cherishes strong family life for its employees but actually requires the sacrifice of family for the corporation.

The smallest circle (and the least visible) represents *the beliefs* that inform the values. For example, a church may believe that women should be under men in a hierarchical arrangement. That belief will fundamentally affect the values and visible "artifacts" of the congregation. Beliefs are expressed in values, and values are expressed in symbols, cues, and visible patterns of behavior. Actually, however, there is often cognitive incongruity between the beliefs and values, or between the values and the symbols. Let's apply Schein's insights into our matrix of head, heart, and hand, starting with hand, that is, the actual practice including the physical layout of the workplace.

Hand—Engaging the Workplace Physically

Earlier I mentioned that the minute a person walks into a store or a workplace they make a judgment about who and what is important here. So, I was ushered through a new research lab in Toronto, and I noticed that all the cubicles were exactly the same size, including the one occupied by the general manager. That said something. When I go to a furniture and household fittings store in Vancouver, I enter a maze of twisted lanes that take me through everything they have for sale, even though I am only looking for one thing. Churches traditionally have pews lined up facing the front (telling us to sit and listen) while a few churches provide seating in the round

---

7. Schein, *Organizational Culture and Leadership*, 6.

to exemplify that we are here for mutual edification, not to watch and listen to a performance. My wife ended her days on earth in a hospice beautifully designed like a hotel rather than a hospital. It had a sitting room and was beautifully furnished. The artifacts and symbols communicated rest and welcome. So, the physical layout of the organization speaks. But what it should communicate is the values of the organization.

Values are cherished ways of behaving. These values become rules, operational principles, and habits that are both personal and organizational. A great example of this is provided by Stephen Covey in his widely read *Principle-Centered Leadership*. He says that habits such as #5—"Seek first to understand, then to be understood"—is a principle for behavior that will lead to success. The problem with rules, is that once you try to regulate behavior by rules, policies, and principles you will not be able to stop because there will always be a situation that you have not adequately covered by your existing rules. The Jewish Mishnah is a classic case of this. Is it Sabbath-breaking, the Mishnah asks, to carry a wooden tooth in your mouth on the Sabbath day because you are carrying a burden, which is work?

Recently I was walking the streets of Montreal in the evening in an orthodox Jewish area and a young Jewish man, complete with sidelocks, caps, and a big black hat stopped me and asked if I could help as I was obviously a *goim*, a gentile, and I could work on the Sabbath day. Why? He wanted to plug an extension cord into a wall outlet but could not do it on the Sabbath.

Far better than guiding behavior by rules, which are like fences, is inspiration. I have been told that in the Australian outback where there are huge ranches, if you want to keep the animals close by you do not build a fence to keep the animals near you. You drill an artesian well.

Values have some worth in the workplace. While being modestly motivating they certainly change perception. But there is a problem: Without a transcendent reference point, selecting values becomes a subjective experience, or merely "what succeeds." In the postmodern culture, values language has largely replaced "right and wrong," and are much less than justice and righteousness—matters that are at the core of holy living. Or put differently, values have no opposites. You have your values and I have mine. Nevertheless, values are influential. Businesses seize on values as rallying cries: "Zero Defects" (a North American automobile company touted this value while an Asian company promoted their products with the value, "Perfection!"). "We exist to provide extraordinary service" is a motivating value in an automobile dealership chair I know. Largely through the work of humanistic psychologists such as May, Maslow, Perls, Erikson, Rogers, and others, values are back "in the picture," even in the school system where it is increasingly recognized that "value-free" education is really impossible. Values continually brood in, over, around, and within life. They are cherished behaviors, principles, and attitudes.

Often institutions and corporations are unaware of the *actual* values that shape their behavior. So, values clarification is a revealing and helpful exercise. Values are taught and learned every day in all the interactions and decisions made in a business context; they are embedded in rituals and traditions (the office Christmas party, for example, or the company fishing trip). Values should cover the full range of organizational life: how people are treated, especially when being hired or fired, how mistakes are dealt with, how resources are used, how people relate, how decisions are made, how power is handled, how purposes are clarified, and how work is performed.

But there is something deeper than values and principles.

Heart—Forming Character in the Workplace

While values have no opposites as mentioned above, virtues have opposites: *vices*. Virtues are deeper than values. Virtues are the qualities of a person's character or a corporate cultural character that indicate an appropriate awareness of what is right and commendable behavior. They can be compared with the seven deadly sins or vices. "Virtue" is a term that is being recovered from Greek philosophy to become part of contemporary discussions on, for example, in "virtue-based ethics." There is good reason for this: both in ancient literature and in its occasional use in the Bible, virtue is a fundamental dimension of ethical living and moral character development. It is a matter of the heart. While the concept of virtue predates Christianity it has been greatly influenced and deepened by the Christian faith. It is also true to say that the thinking of Christians, especially in the Western church, has been influenced by these Greek sources.[8]

---

8. I refer you to a fine article Benson, "Virtues."

Virtues in the Bible

There is no equivalent Hebrew word for the Greek *arete* (virtue) even though the so-called cardinal virtues of Greek philosophy are often mentioned as part of the righteous lifestyle of God's covenant people. Not surprisingly, in the Old Testament, the righteous do justice and live by wisdom. In the New Testament the term *arete* is used only once in the writings of Paul (Phil 4:8) and four times in Peter's letters (1 Pet 2:9; 2 Pet 1:3,5) though usually not translated in English as "virtue." Nevertheless, it is indisputable that early Christians were aware of the good qualities found outside the family of God and they interpreted the Christian life partly in the categories of Greek thought. The list of commendable virtues Paul gives in Philippians—true, noble, right, pure, lovely, admirable, excellent, praiseworthy—seems reminiscent of virtues commended by the Greek philosophers. This is no more surprising than the fact that Paul frequently uses the Greek concept of "conscience" to communicate our moral responsibility and accountability in the Greek world when no such word was given him from his Jewish and biblical heritage.

Biblical revelation, however, offers something substantially different that appears to be "foolishness" from the perspective of Greek philosophy (1 Cor 1:22–25). The gospel declares that God gives what he requires, that the grace of the new creation accomplishes what never can be obtained by reason or moral effort alone. Virtues are not obtained solely by "pulling ourselves up by our own bootstraps." They are gifts of God. But they are gifts that invite and even require human cooperation.[9] That is surely what is behind New Testament exhortations to "think about such things" (Phil 4:8) in the context of a list of commendable character qualities, "get rid of" vices like slandering (Eph 4:31), "make every effort to add to your faith goodness" (2 Pet 1:5), and "live a life of love" (Eph 5:2).

The virtuous life engages the whole person in what must be seen as *active prayer*. But it is not autonomous activity. Rather than simple human achievements, certainly not ones we might boast about having attained, Christian living is essentially responsive and always God-centered. Faith, hope, and love keep us focused on the source—the God of all true virtue. Peter says that God's divine power "has given us everything we need for

---

9. Jonathan Wilson suggests that Prov 2 enjoins the "son" to work hard to get wisdom and then finds that wisdom is a gift. We have to work hard, suggests Wilson, so that when we receive it we will have the proper disposition to use it and to do so in the fear of the Lord. Email correspondence on November 28, 2022.

life and godliness through our knowledge of him who called us by his own glory and goodness [*aretē*]" (2 Pet 1:3). Paul reminds the Colossians that it is as "God's beloved" that they are to clothe themselves with goodness and patience (Col 3:12). What Athens requires, Christ inspires.

So organizational culture is expressed in the outworking of values in the physical artifacts of the organizational culture (the hand). But organizational culture expresses the values embraced by workers in the culture (the heart). Now we must consider workplace beliefs (the head).

Head—Naming Fundamental Workplace Beliefs

The New Testament names the fundamental beliefs as faith, hope, and love, often mentioned singly and sometimes as a triad (1 Cor 13:13; 1 Thess 1:2–3; Col 1:5). These are sometimes called the "theological virtues" because they are gifts of God, are ingrained character qualities, and because they have God as their primary object.[10] Obviously in a church or Christian parachurch organization faith, hope, and love can be applied directly (though they often are not so applied!). But in a secular organization in which a statedly Christian message is not allowed these revealed values must be translated with loss of some of the original meaning. Emilie Griffin, a marketing executive, asks, "Is it possible. . . that for people of the marketplace, conversion would need its own vocabulary?"[11] A business consultant working with frontline workers in the food store industry says that in his many years as CEO he has never had anyone object to his repeated statement that "I believe your Creator made you with the capacity to give yourself helpfully to frontline workers in such a way that instead of going home and beating their children, they will go home and read stories to them." Or take another concrete attempt to remint faith, hope, and love. Visiting Flow Automotive Companies in the USA years ago, I discovered that the CEO, Don Flow, was trying to translate the fundamental beliefs of faith, hope, and love into terms which even not-yet-believers could embrace. Here is what I wrote, as follows.

---

10. Much of this section is abstracted from Stevens, "Organizational Values."
11. Griffin, *Reflective Executive*, 135.

Faith in a Workplace Context

In its original meaning, faith is the response of the whole person to the full revelation of God's person (Rom 10:14–17) and God's intentions for the created order (Heb 11:3). Faith is a revolt against living on the basis of appearances. It is not merely a "belief system" but a total life orientation involving trust and action in all kinds of life situations (11:4–16). *Personal faith* requires "seeing" people and situations the way God does, with potential for change, integration, and wholeness which God holds before each person and every human enterprise. While full communion with God is a possibility reserved for those who become children of God through faith (John 1:12), persons of faith working in organizations of various kinds are invited to translate their own faith in God into the possibility of growth, whole person growth in their neighbor workers. In the same way a person of faith expresses *organizational faith* when she acts upon structures and organizational culture. Normally this results in openness to the possibility of substantial, though limited, change and transformation of an organization. Faith will inspire creative action to make the structures (as well as the people in them) reflect divine values and purposes in a way that is attractive to others.

Hope in a Workplace Context

Hope for the believer is resting in the revealed and certain conclusion of the created order, allowing these to shape our response to the present gains and losses. It involves understanding and living in the present in view of the future. It allows the vision of God's kingdom to inspire our confidence in the future. We are "prisoners of hope" as the prophet Zechariah says (9:12). Hope equips us with courage to hold essential values in uncertain times and to take appropriate steps to plan for tomorrow. While there is some meaning-loss in this process, incorporating hope in an organization plants a pregnant hint that there is "something more" and invites people to move towards it. *Personal hope* means never giving up on people (confidence) and helping people deal with the reality of their lives (courage), both in terms of their need for change and the positive fruits that can be appropriated through a realignment of their lives. Even when we have to terminate someone's employment we will not give up on them but do all we can to help them find suitable employment. *Organizational hope* means never giving up on situations (confidence) and empowering the structures, values, and culture of an organization (courage) to live in harmony with kingdom values and realities, even if in the short haul we appear to be engaging in fruitless activity or experiencing reversals.

Love in a Workplace Context

For the believer in the Old Testament, covenant love (*hesed*) is love plus loyalty, or affectionate loyalty. It is the glue of the covenant between God and God's people. It also includes *ahabah*, the love that reaches out to and incorporates the outsider. Covenant love is more concerned with relationships than commodities. It is not merely a sentiment but involves active caring and creative loyalty. *Personal love* means our love should reflect, albeit in a limited way, the love of God as we show caring loyalty (love plus loyalty) to employees, members, clients, peers, and customers. This involves meeting true needs, going the extra mile in relationships, understanding empathetically the other person's situation, supporting another's integrity. Love makes us stay with people even when we find them unpleasant, when they "push our buttons," or when they do not meet our expectations for development. Love means we do not jump to conclusions about the motives of our customers. And even when we must deal with negative realities, we will communicate worth and create an opportunity for people to change and have a second chance. *Organizational love* inspires caring loyalty to the structures and values of the organizational system—loving the company systemically, structurally, and culturally. Emilie Griffin says, "But I have loved, perhaps foolishly, if not a corporation, then at least the way that corporation demanded of me my best efforts, my most creative solutions, my possibilities of excellence. I have loved, too, the network of goods and Good bestowed on the larger community by corporations."[12]

A being-redeemed-community can express God's kindness and so lead people to repentance for sin (Rom 2:4). An organizational culture can be the aroma of Christ. And a loving organization should evoke gratitude to God and gratitude is a good enough reason to return to the seeking Father. But these reflections on the outer and inner of the organizational culture invite the question of how to make changes in the organizational culture.

---

12. Griffin, *Reflective Executive*, 95.

Making Organizational Change

We are not in heaven yet, even though one book bears the evocative title "earth crammed with heaven."[13] Indeed, all human organizations including even the church are approximations. The best we can hope for in this life is substantial, not complete, redemption. Gaining that—and it is as part of our public discipleship—involves organizational change. And changing the culture is difficult.

A Cultural Approach to Change

When the leader and the culture collide, the culture will probably win! Changing the artifacts—to use Schein's phrase—might involve moving the Sunday service to the church hall, where the chairs can be arranged in circles to increase participation or having a staff meeting every Monday to improve communication. But unless the fundamental assumptions of the organization are understood, cultivated, and gradually changed, such equipping initiatives may be as effective as rearranging the deck chairs on the *Titanic* when the ship is going down.

Schein's research shows, however, that culture-change mechanisms are at work in every stage of a group's history—birth, midlife, and maturity (which he calls "maturity and/or stagnation, decline and/or rebirth").[14] He also shows that change becomes increasingly more difficult as a group becomes more established. I have often said to aspiring pastors that there are three situations in a church when change is relatively easy: first, if the church is desperate; second, if the church is a new church plant; but third, at a time of profound infusion of the Holy Spirit. But change itself is mysterious. While all change is motivated and does not happen randomly, "many changes do not go in the direction that the motivated persons wanted them to go"[15] because they were unaware of other forces in the culture that were simultaneously acting. So being the leader of this process is complex indeed.

Several strategies are useful here. First, understand the culture before you try to change anything. Give the culture its due. It influences everything. Second, recognize that the culture cannot be manipulated. While you can manage and control many parts of the environment of an organization

---

13. Dreyer, *Earth Crammed with Heaven*.
14. Schein, *Organizational Culture and Leadership*, 270.
15. Schein, *Organizational Culture and Leadership*, 300–301.

(the president keeps her office door open all the time), the culture itself with its taken-for-granted underlying assumptions cannot be manipulated. Third, good leadership articulates and reinforces the culture, especially those parts consistent with the vision of the organization. If this is not done, people are unlikely to accept any serious change. During a time of changing culture, leaders have to bear some of the pain and anxiety felt in the group at the same time that they seek to make the members feel secure. Fourth, sometimes direct change in a culture can be promoted by introducing new people in leadership, by promoting maverick individuals from within and, more especially, people from outside who hold slightly different assumptions. The appointment of a new assistant, a new board chairperson, a new president is an opportunity for cultural change. Finally, change takes time.[16]

A Systemic Approach to Change

A systems approach assumes that an organization as a whole is more than the sum of its parts, and that each member and each subsystem is influenced by and influences the others. It can be easily pictured as a mobile over the bed of a baby: movement in one element requires adjustment and movement in all the others.

Edwin Friedman, a family systems therapist and a rabbi, has some additional insights on how a leader can bring change to a system. He uses the concept of *homeostasis*, that marvelous capacity of human bodies and social systems to regain their balance after a trauma. Every system has a natural tendency to maintain the status quo (homeostasis), just as a keel keeps the sailboat upright after the wind has blown it at an extreme angle. The system does this when new response patterns are required through a threat, tragedy, or positive change. Thus, the system returns to the tried and tested rather than shifts to operate on a revised and improved basis (morphogenesis).

A negative biblical example of homeostasis is the return of converted Jews in the first few years to a less-than-full expression of Christian unity with gentile believers, a hypocrisy that Paul fervently challenged (Gal 2:11–21). A positive example of morphogenesis is the extraordinary resolution of the council of Jerusalem (Acts 15:1–29) in which the church changed the terms upon which Jews and gentiles could have fellowship together.

16. Schein, *Organizational Culture and Leadership*, 197–327.

To bring about systemic change, leaders must first join the system, becoming an integral part of the whole and negotiating their place within it. The director, pastor, or president must lead the way in this. In fact, this involves many stages of negotiation as the leader finds his or her place in the organization.[17] Then the leader might take an initiative that has a ripple effect throughout the system. Usually, a problem will surface without provocation. But if a problem does not surface, something as inconsequential as changing the location of the water cooler or removing it altogether will do. How he or she responds to the ripple is crucial because the response of the system will be a reflection of all the systemic factors that make it stable, including the multigenerational influences. The provoked or unprovoked crisis is an opportunity to explain what is going on and to appeal, as Barnabas, Paul, and Peter did in the Jerusalem council (Acts 15:1–35), to systemic values that can be expressed in a more constructive way. The Chinese word for *crisis* is composed of two characters, one of which means "danger" and the other "opportunity." The systemic leader welcomes the opportunity of every crisis and sometimes will provoke one.

Using family systems theory, Friedman says we bring the greatest change in a system by concentrating not on the dissenting or sick member but on the person or persons in the group who have the greatest capacity to bring change.[18] The equipping leader must always remember that the only person open to definite and immediate change is herself or himself! A systems view encourages us to see that changing ourselves can make a difference to the those with whom we are interdependently connected.

In the context of counseling families, Virginia Satir, an early family therapist, makes a remarkable statement about systems leadership that applies to all kinds of organizations. She says, "I consider myself the leader of the process in the interview but not the leader of the people." This, she continues, "is based on the fact that I am the one who knows what the process I am trying to produce is all about. I want to help people to become their own designers of their own choice-making."[19]

So organizational leadership is not simply leading individual people in an organization. Leaders must work with the whole—culture and systems included. Process leadership asks questions, clarifies goals, orients people to their mission, maintains and explains the culture, and helps people and

---

17. Pattison, *Pastor and People*.
18. Friedman, *Generation to Generation*, 22.
19. Satir, *Conjoint Family Therapy*, 251–52.

subsystems take responsibility for their own systemic life. In the end leaders are charged with the awesome task of creating an environment in which people change themselves.

Life Signs of Kingdom Culture

There are several life-signs in the organizational culture noted by Griffin: *Gratuitousness,* doing something for its intrinsic rather than extrinsic value. The righteous executive or worker is in the deepest sense a volunteer, not "in it" for "what she can get out of it." *Integrity,* personal and organizational, inner and outer in sync, is another life-sign. Can you forgive an organization? Love an organization? Yes! *Persistence* or longanimity is a further life-sign. Will people stick at their job, stay with their calling through thick and thin? One more life-sign is *transcendence or faith and vision.* Our need is "to return, by means of what the philosopher Paul Ricoeur calls a *second naivete,* to the fundamentals of an honorable dream," says Griffin.[20]

And finally there is *Sabbath rest and contemplation.* Griffin makes an astute observation on why contemplation is largely absent from the workplace.

> The believer in the marketplace is buffeted by cultural forces that discourage contemplation in at least these five ways: with a language and philosophy of achievement that appears to be godless; by a mentality of sophistication that sees faith as naive; by those who stereotype prayer as rote performance and lip service; by an "in crowd" prejudice against faith that makes the failures of institutional religion a satisfactory excuse for infidelity to God; by the failure of "successful people" to practice the inner life and their scorn of those who do; and by the lack of good and modest teachers and exemplars in the life of prayer. Serious prayer initiatives in worldly settings are often lacking.[21]

In closing I return to Wolterstorff's question raised in the first sentence above. "Can we *somewhat* alter what we do [in developing an empowering workplace], so that our occupations come closer to becoming our God-issued vocation? Usually, yes." Now we turn from blessing others to blessing God through our work. We will consider work as worship and, secondly, seeing God in the marketplace, what is commonly called the beatific vision.

20. Griffin, *Reflective Executive,* 88–89.
21. Griffin, *Reflective Executive,* 149.

BLESSING GOD

10

Work and Worship

Even their seemingly secular works are a worship of God and an obedience well pleasing to God.

MARTIN LUTHER[1]

Man was placed in Paradise . . . that he would till the land not in servile labor but with a spiritual pleasure befitting his dignity.

AUGUSTINE[2]

Monday work [is] an extension of Sunday worship. Sunday worship is not a "moment" of worship; it is the beginning of a whole week of worship.

KAEMINGK AND WILLSON[3]

TO ME THE MOST amazing thing about worship is that through it we *actually bless God*. That is, God is not the Unmoved Mover of Greek philosophy but a Moveable Mover, one who is *actually blessed*, moved, through our words and deeds. And, secondly, the most amazing thing about our work in the marketplace is this: through it we can bless God. God is *affected* by our work as Jesus noted in the Parable of the Sheep and Goats. In this passage Jesus receives our work (Matt 25:35–46), through our making a product,

1. Luther, *Luther's Works: Genesis*, 348.
2. Augustine, *Literal Meaning of Genesis*, 46.
3. Kaemingk and Willson, *Work and Worship*, 46.

offering a service, whether that service is a meal or a deal, a voice or an invoice, an operation or a cooperation.

In this chapter we are considering just how our work can be worship, as well as how our worship in the gathered life of the church can make the connection between Sunday and Monday. Previously we have considered what marketplace theology does and how it does it, through the head (thought), the heart (prayer), and the hand (practice), being together the ways that the Western church, Eastern church, and Asian church, respectively, mainly do theology. So, with respect to prayer, Nicholas Wolterstorff makes this seminal statement:

> Theologies of work matter, but they need to be sung and prayed. We need to find ways for our theologies of work to inhabit more than our brains—they need to enter our bones . . . An integrated life is not an intellectual achievement, an all-of-a-sudden eureka moment of theological discovery . . . The fabric of faith and work needs to be slowly and intentionally woven back together over a lifetime of prayer and worship.[4]

We have been insisting that a wholistic theology of the marketplace needs to be done "from above," that is from the revealed truths about God and God's purposes for life and applying them to work, worker, and workplace. But it also needs to be done "from below," starting with our concrete experiences of work, worker, and workplaces. Previously we have explored "work" using Perkins's definition. But in this chapter, we are expounding one aspect of the "working blessedly" phrase, here specifically *how we can bring blessing to God through our worship and work in the marketplace*. This is in contrast with the situation where we "worship our work, work at our play, and play at our worship," a nice turn of the phrase by Dahl.[5] We will see that through our work we bless God in the following ways:

- By serving as priests of creation
- By ruling as God's sons and daughters
- By doing God's work with God
- By gathering for worship and mutual edification

---

4. Quoted in Kaemingk and Willson, *Work and Worship*, xi.
5. Kaemingk and Willson, *Work and Worship*, 3.

Work and Worship

Blessing God as Priests of Creation

God placed Adam and Eve in a sanctuary garden with the intent of continuous 24/7 communion through every life activity, including their work. They were priests of creation. So, Alexander Schmemann, the Orthodox theologian, has succinctly written,

> "Homo sapiens," "homo faber" . . . yes, but first of all, "homo adorans." The first, the basic definition of man is that he is *the priest*. He stands in the center of the world and unifies it in his act of blessing God, of both receiving the world from God and offering it to God—and by filling the world with this eucharist, he transforms his life, the one he receives from the world into life in God, into communion with Him. The world was created as the "matter," the material of one all-embracing eucharist, and man was created as the priest of this cosmic sacrament.[6]

Priests are like two-way bridges between God and the world. They touch God (through intercession and worship) on behalf of people and places—the upward journey. And they touch people and places (through care, work, ministry, and prayer) on behalf of God—the downward journey. N.T. Wright says we are like mirrors, reflecting God into his creation and then reflecting the praises of creation back to God. I know a person in Montreal, Quebec, who runs a electronic vacuum tube repair shop for high fidelity audio equipment and lovers of fine recorded music. His shop on Park Avenue is a place with the touch of God in it. He says he speaks more about God in his shop than he does on Sunday when he serves as a tentmaking pastor.

Adam and Eve had three full-time jobs, the first being *communion with God*; the second was *community-building*, as he made them male and female in his image, built for community as God is a community of Father, Son, and Spirit in a communion of love. But the third full-time job was *co-creativity* (or sub-creativity) because like God the worker, the man and the woman were called to be workers.

So, when God said to Adam and Eve, "fill the earth" (Gen 1:28) he did not mean merely to populate the earth—something we have manifestly already done. But he meant humankind to fill the earth with his glory, to take the sanctuary garden into the whole world. The sanctuary was a place of safety, beauty, prosperity, and above all a place anointed with the

---

6. Schmemann, *For the Life of the World*, 15.

presence of God. Adam and Eve were forced to leave the garden by their expulsion—which was both judgment on their autonomous living and, at the same time, fulfillment of their calling. In the same way the people living on the plain of Shinar, building their Babel tower to reach the heavens were unwilling to fill the earth, hugging together as they did. Their confusion of language and their dispersion into the earth was, once again, both judgment and fulfillment.

So, in Genesis the *sanctuary* garden was in Eden, not as in Ezekiel where it is called "the garden *of* Eden." Eden was a larger reality, the *home* of humankind. But there is a still larger circle and it is the *world*, where there were other nations like Havilah where the gold is good (2:11). So, without saying these actual words Adam and Eve and their successors were commissioned to *take the sanctuary into the world*. And how were they to do it?

They were to accomplish this filling of the earth through their presence and their work. They were to lift up their whole lives as an offering to God, as Paul said in Rom 12:1–2 where he exhorts us to present our whole bodily life as an offering to God which is our spiritual worship. Yes, Adam and Eve sinned. Yes, they were thrust out of the garden. But there is the beginning of redemption right there in the story in the provision of clothing to cover their nakedness with the bloodstained clothing from an animal, and the prophecy that the seed of woman would bruise the serpent's head. And therefore, those of us now living east of Eden, but having received substantial salvation through Christ, are offering ourselves in the totality of our lives in worship through unpacking the potential of creation, humanizing the earth, and serving as priests of creation. It is important to note that the Hebrew word *avodah* means both "to work" and "to worship." That word is used for both the horizontal dimension (human work) and the vertical (worship of God). Human being are priests of creation, cultic officiants. Why and how?

Images (*selamin*) of the god were installed in the precincts in the Ancient Near East temples. The garden was a temple sanctuary. But in this case the image of God was two living human beings, not merely a sacred object made of stone or precious metals.[7] Consequently as Alexander Schmemann cogently explains above, humankind is not merely *homo faber* but *homo adorans*. But there is another dimension of humankind's work-worship engagement.

---

7. Bergsma, "Creation Narratives," 14.

Work and Worship

Blessing God by Ruling as Royal Sons and Daughters

Think of work as a way of ruling as we unpack the potential of creation, as we serve our neighbors near and far! Genesis chapters one to three is critically important in this matter of work as worship. In the opening verse of these three chapters, we find that God is a worker. Then we discover that God made human beings, male and female *in his image* (Gen 1:26). As John Bergsma shows, the meaning of "in the image and likeness of God" is polyvalent, meaning it carries with it multiple meanings. It connotes kinship, kingship, and cult.[8] In the previous section we dealt with the cult, how humankind is to function as priests of creation. Here we see how Adam and Eve were *kins* of God, that is sons of God, as Luke 3:37 indicates. They were at the same time kings and queens as indicated by the use of the words "subdue" (*kabas*, 1:28) and "rule" (*rada*, 1:26, 28).

As royal sons and as vice-regents Adam and Eve were to imitate and even participate in the work of their Father God. As Bergsma says, "Human work is a royal work, not slavery to the gods [as in the mythology and religion of the Ancient Near East where the gods created human slaves to do their dirty work] or [slavery] to a divinized environment [as in Egyptian religion]."[9] It is often noted that in the text of Gen 2 where the creation story is restated, two words are used: to "work" (*abad*) the earth, and "guard" or "take care of" (*samar*) the earth (Gen 2:15). These are the exact words used of the Levites in Num 3:7 who were called to guard the congregation before the tent of meeting and to do the work of the tabernacle. In other words, there was to be no distinction between their work and worship. But the fall changed all that.

After Adam and Eve broke their covenant relationship with God[10] through disobedience Adam was told to "work the soil," no longer guarding the sanctuary, a task that was given to the cherubim. The first pair were driven out of the garden. Adam's mission was not secularized but desacralized. But a savior figure emerges in the narrative in Noah who "experiences the flood as an act of re-creation"[11] and who offers an acceptable sacrifice after the flood (Gen 8:20–22). God is on the move to redeem humankind and humankind's work. Then God makes his promise to Abraham, a

---

8. Bergsma, "Creation Narratives," 14.
9. Bergsma, "Creation Narratives," 15.
10. On the Adamic covenant see footnote 30 of Bergsma, "Creation Narratives," 27.
11. Bergsma, "Creation Narratives," 19.

promise that substantially fulfills the creation mandate in Genesis. This is followed by the Exodus.

As Bergsma notes, the "central theme of Exodus [is] the restoration to Israel of the priestly status, whereby their labor will no longer be the profane slavery to Pharaoh, but will be the divine service given to the Lord. The original unity of work and worship in the garden is restored to Israel along with the construction of the tabernacle as a portable Eden."[12]

In Leviticus the priestly duty, which was intended to be a whole people ministry, is taken over by the Levites rather than the whole of Israel though the whole people was in view. That is, the Levites were to equip the people for their corporate ministry as a "kingdom of priests and a holy nation" (Exod 19:6). Even in that, however, in Israel's subsequent history the nation was "largely unsuccessful in fulfilling a corporate priestly role."[13] This brings us to the New Testament.

Christ reunited the royal and the priestly roles. Every work of Jesus is holy and "like that of the priests, he and his disciples may work on the Sabbath as the priesthood does (Matt 12:1–8)."[14] Christ's Father is still working, as Jesus says in John 5:17 and Jesus says that he is still working. So, Paul in writing to the Colossian slaves and masters says that "it is the Lord Christ you are serving" (Col 3:24) thus commanding them to "reverence" (3:22) the Lord (read "worship") while they do even menial work. They were to work for the audience of one, the Lord, with all their hearts.

Thus work in Christ is now a way to bless God, a priestly and royal act. It is pleasing to God, exalting God as the owner of creation and the proper object of all we do in this world. We are to extend, with Adam and Eve, the sanctuary into the world and we do this through our priestly and royal roles. We do this not only by worshipping God in the formal sanctuary but also in the sanctuary of the world, creation being the Creator's temple. But in this partially redeemed life we do so with worship mixed with deconstruction and defamation. Essentially work is a sacrament through which men and women in the workplace are offering their work-service to God and neighbor as a sweet and pleasing gift.

There is no such thing as secular work for the Christian. They either view their work as a sacrament with themselves as royal priests offering up their work to God or they are defaming their work. For the Christian,

---

12. Bergsma, "Creation Narratives," 21.
13. Bergsma, "Creation Narratives," 22.
14. Bergsma, "Creation Narratives," 23.

secular work is impossible. So, dualism, namely that some work, such as the work of pastors and missionaries is holy and other work, such as what we do in the marketplace or home, is secular—this is patently, terribly wrong. It may be the worst heresy around in the global church today. Why? Because God's people as a whole are doing the work of the Lord, not only as royal priests or priestly royalty but also because they amazingly are working *with* God.

Blessing God by Doing God's Work with God

Years ago, Robert Banks crafted a book on *God the Worker* in which he shows that the work God does, as revealed in Scripture is all-encompassing, from creating the world to bringing new creation into it. But in a recent book, Banks expands his earlier treatment of the work of the Lord to show how human beings enter into God's ongoing work, not merely copying God, or using God as a model, but actually participating in God's ongoing work. Banks does this by outlining the characteristics of God's work, the dimensions, descriptions, and purposes of the divine worker.[15]

This does not mean that the work God performs and work we do are exactly the same. God acts in ways that are both qualitatively and quantitatively larger, deeper, and more complex than anything we can do. However, our categories of work are built on what he does, restricted by our human limitations and flawed by our ingrained sinfulness. So, what we do is not simply an indirect reflection of what God does but one of the ways through which God actually accomplishes his work. He draws us in as participants in his ongoing creative, providential, judicial, revelatory, and redemptive work in the world. He makes us collaborators in fulfilling his everyday and ultimate purposes.[16]

For example, in Ps 127 the psalmist says, "unless the LORD builds the house, the builders labour in vain" (127:1). I have built a few houses in my carpentry days. But, I confess, I only partly realized that I was building them *with* God, that God was showing us how to lay out the foundation, how to arrange the floor joists, how to erect the walls and the roof trusses. One of my students owns a business in Asia that is quite large. In his reflection for our "Money Matters" course at Regent College he wrote the following:

---

15. Banks, *Transforming Daily Work*, 10.
16. Banks, *Transforming Daily Work*, 14.

> I have been contemplating selling my "worldly secular business" and going into more "sacred and holy" calling of ministry for years and have almost succeeded twice. By the intervention of God, it did not go through. I thank God for that, for now I understand my work is my ministry! I have thousands of direct and indirect employees to take care of, I have millions of customers to satisfy. I have so many problems when running the business that I need to come to God and pray for his power and guidance daily. God has put me into this position of relying on him to bring out blessings to so many lives and making changes to the industries that I have never thought of...
>
> First, I am working with God and for his great pleasure and not for myself. Before I realized that, I had rarely come to God for his guidance for my work, for I have been relying on my own strength. I thought he is not really interested in what I do for a living, but more interested in my spiritual health. Now I learned to come to Him for guidance for all my decisions because he is the Lord of all aspects of my life!
>
> Second, I need to work diligently and let my work glorify his name! I will continue to innovate and set the standards in the bento industry in Taiwan. I will continue to pay my employees with fair and decent salaries to honor their work and take care of their families. I will provide training and entrepreneurial opportunities for them to own their own shops to further improve their living standards and personal dignity. I will use the highest standard ingredients possible and provide the best bento in Taiwan for my customers with reasonable price. I will set up shops in those places that are less well-served in rural Taiwan to serve more customers.[17]

Frank is worshipping God through his work!

Scripture frequently speaks of working with God, not just in ministry situations but in daily work. In Gen 4:1 Eve says, "with the help of the LORD I have brought forth a man." Take, for example, the situation with Bezalel, the craftsman who worked on the tabernacle. He was filled with the Spirit to work in metal and fabrics (Exod 31:1–11). Daniel, in his political career in Babylon, frequently spoke of how God gave him the answer for occupational riddles, such as the dream of King Nebuchadnezzar (Dan 2) and the writing on the wall which left the later King Belshazzar pale and worried (Dan 5).

---

17. Lin, "Reflection Paper for Money Matters Course."

Then there is Joseph in Egypt who interpreted Pharaoh's dreams and became vice regent for all of Egypt during the seven years of plenty to be followed by the seven years of famine (Gen 41). Jacob, his father, tells his wives that God gave him a dream that enabled him to breed multicolored animals on his father-in-law's ranch, and to do so in a big way (Gen 31:10–13). Yes, some of these were crisis situations, which believers in Jesus would face and for which Jesus said, "when they arrest you, do not worry what you say or how you are to say it. At that time, you will be given what to say, for it will not be you speaking, but the Spirit of your Father speaking through you" (Matt 10:19–20).

Then there was the crisis faced by the apostle Paul on his way to Rome to be tried by Caesar, when he was given a message from God in the middle of a life-threatening storm, that while the ship would be wrecked, not a life will be lost (Acts 27:23–5).[18] But what about the humdrum work of making tents, which Paul, Aquila, and Priscilla did, or selling fabric in Europe which Lydia did, or making clothing as Dorcas did, or fishing as some of the disciples did?

God does chores. He keeps gravity running. He keeps the earth circling the sun. Therefore Jesus, in responding to the criticism that he had healed a man on the Sabbath, said, "My Father is always at his work to this very day, and I too am working" (John 5:17). Does God only work in spectacular healings? Does God only work in saving souls? Does not God work in creation, in sustaining people and systems, in transformation and consumption, as God tells Job when he finally speaks to him (Job 38–41)?

As Leon Morris says in his commentary on the John passage, "Jesus repudiates the thought that the divine rest from Creation took the form

---

18. Other references in Scripture that suggest that God is involved in our work, or rather we are involved in his work, include: Deut 28:12 ("The LORD... will bless the work of your hands"); Ps 90:17 ("May the favor of the LORD our God rest on us; establish the work of our hands for us—yes, establish the work of our hands"); Eccl 11:5 ("As you do not know the path of the wind, or how the body is formed in the mother's womb, so you cannot understand the work of God, the Maker of all things"); Isa 64:8 ("Yet you, LORD, are our Father. We are the clay, you are the potter; we are all the work of your hand"); 1 Cor 12:11 ("All these [various Spirit services] are the work of one and the same Spirit, and he distributes them to each one, just as he determines"); 1 Cor 15:58 ("Always give yourselves fully to the work of the Lord, because you know that your labor in the Lord is not in vain"); Col 1:28 ("To this end I strenuously contend with all the energy Christ so powerfully works in me"); Col 3:23–4 ("Whatever you do, work at it with all your heart, as working for the Lord, not for human masters"); Heb 13:21 ("May [God] work in us what is pleasing to him, through Jesus Christ, to whom be glory for ever and ever. Amen").

of idleness."[19] C. H. Dodd, quoting a Hermetic saying, notes that "God is not idle, else all things would be idle, for all things are full of God."[20] So the intertestamental book Ecclesiasticus says that we earthbound workers "tend to the fabric of this world, and their prayer is the practice of their trade" (38:34). Yes, doing our work *for* God is a great thing. But doing our work *with* God is even greater for it affirms that, bidden or not, God is with us and is working with us. As we saw in an earlier chapter,

- God as *creator* invites people to invent new things, start new businesses, design new computer programs, and write new music with him!
- God the *sustainer* invites people to make meals with him, to sweep floors with him, to put out the garbage with him, to make a home with him, and to work in politics providing infrastructure so a nation or a city might thrive.
- God the *redeemer* invites us to fix things, transform things, and people not just in imitation of what he does—as though we could—but with him, fixing cars, setting broken bones, and preaching.
- God the *consummator* invites educators, pastors, and journalists to show where things are going.

Working with God is a way of worshipping him. But why then do we need to gather as believers?

Blessing God by Gathering for Worship and Mutual Edification

Why does Paul not mention that Christians are to gather specifically *to worship*? My friend Robert Banks offers an answer:

> One of the most puzzling features of Paul's understanding of *ekklesia* for his contemporaries, whether Jews or Gentiles, must have been his failure to say that a person went to church primarily to "worship." Not once in all his writings does he suggest that this is the case. Indeed it could not be, for he held a view of "worship" that prevented him from doing so.[21]

19. Morris, *Gospel according to John*, 309.

20. Dodd, *Interpretation of the Fourth Gospel*, 20, quoted in Morris, *Gospel according to John*, 309.

21. Banks, *Paul's Idea of Community*, 88.

Banks continues to note that, drawing on Rom 12:1–2,

> the spiritual or rational 'worship' (*latreia*) that Christians are called upon to make requires them to offer (*parastesai*) their whole selves, bodies included, as a living sacrifice (*thusia*), dedicated (*hagia*) and acceptable to him ... Since all places and times have now become the venue for worship, Paul cannot speak of Christians assembling in church *distinctively* for this purpose. They are already worshipping God, acceptably or unacceptably, in whatever they are doing. While this means that when they are in church they are worshipping as well, it is not worship but something else that marks off their coming together from everything else that they are doing.[22]

So, asks Banks, what is the purpose of the gathered life? "The purpose of the [gathered] church is the growth and edification of its members into Christ and into a common life through their God-given ministry to one another (1 Cor 14:12, 19, 26) ... The most general form of meeting, however, centred around the eating of a meal and the exercise of ministry to each other's benefit."[23] So, in 1 Thessalonians Paul says, "Therefore encourage one another and build each other up, just as in fact you are doing" (5:11). Hebrews says the same thing. "Let us consider how we may spur one another on toward love and good deeds, not giving up meeting together, as some are in the habit of doing, but encouraging one another—and all the more as you see the Day approaching" (10:24–5; cf 3:13). This is mutual edification. And one important area with which we need to mutually edify one another is where and how we spend most of our waking hours.

Sadly, I observe that most gathered-life worship has become abstracted from the dispersed life of the church. The actual service is often a performance from the front. Actual mutual edification takes place, if at all, before the service starts in the narthex or foyer, as people talk, and sometimes afterwards, where people share their lives, pray for one another, and encourage each other. Why not design the gathered life community around mutual edification in the context of worship? That is precisely the proposal made by a recent book by Matthew Kaemingk and Cory B. Willson, entitled *Work and Worship: Reconnecting our Work and Liturgy*.

Their vision is the integration of faith and work through a *lifetime* of prayer and worship. Note the emphasis on "lifetime." They envision

---

22. Banks, *Paul's Idea of Community*, 89.
23. Banks. *Paul's Idea of Community*, 90.

awakening people to their integral role in the mission of God through their daily vocation. But they see Sunday as "worship starters," launching people into a week of worship.[24] They unearth the real meaning of liturgy, which is the "work of service on behalf of the people" and, quoting another author, they note that "liturgy [is] work for the common good [and is thus] a form of participation in the mission of God."[25] They note that the Israelites "did not think their way into an integrated life; they worshipped their way into it."[26] But they offer that the well-meaning and increasingly popular phrase, "your work is worship" is "vulnerable to a dangerous misinterpretation."

The misinterpretation goes something like this: if all my work is worship then why do I need to gather for corporate worship? Kaemingk and Willson offer a cogent response. What if, in corporate worship, such as that provided by Ps 73, "we are able to peer through the cluttered economy of the world to see the deeper—and truer—economy of God?"[27] Then, quoting Walter Brueggemann, they affirm that corporate "worship models an alternative world of sanity that prevents Israel from succumbing to the seductive insanities of a world raging against the holiness of Yahweh."[28] So these two authors offer in closing a number of practices that connect the world of work with the world of worship.

One practice is the Lord's Table where we bring the fruit of our hands and even the fruits of the industrial process to the Lord in an act of thanksgiving.[29] To this point Alexander Schmemann offers a salient remark: "Just as Christianity can—and must—be considered the end of religion, so the Christian liturgy in general, and the eucharist in particular, are indeed the end of cult, of the 'sacred' religious act isolated from, and opposed to, the 'profane' life of the community."[30] Schmemann continues: "We offered the bread in remembrance of Christ because we know that Christ is Life, and all food, therefore, must lead us to Him. And now when we receive this bread from His hands, we know that he has taken up all of life, filled it

---

24. Kaemingk and Willson, *Work and Worship*, 46.
25. Kaemingk and Willson, *Work and Worship*, 166–67.
26. Kaemingk and Willson, *Work and Worship*, 64, 102.
27. Kaemingk and Willson, *Work and Worship*, 110.
28. Brueggemann, *Theology of the Old Testament*, 665, quoted in Kaemingk and Wilkson, *Work and Worship*, 111.
29. Kaemingk and Willson, *Work and Worship*, 193–208.
30. Schmemann, *For the Life of the World*, 25–26.

with Himself, and made it what it was meant to be: communion with God, sacrament of His presence and love."[31]

Another integrating practice is preparing worship that *gathers* workers, through such things as workers's testimonies.[32] But they also brilliantly propose corporate worship that *scatters* workers, through placing photos of members in their workplace setting, mapping where people work, asking where they will be and what they will be doing tomorrow at ten o'clock. Most controversially but strategically, they suggest commissioning workers for their scattered life occupations and not just pastors, missionaries, and people going on short-term mission trips.[33] The Institute for Marketplace Transformation offers a free "Pastor's Toolbox" for developing the scattered life ministry of church members when they are gathered.[34]

So go to work to worship God. And join in the gathered life of the congregation to continue to worship, but also to be mutually edified in the integration of faith and work. I conclude with the summary of Kaemingk and Willson:

> *Through worship*, these workers are reminded that profit, joy, and nourishment are part of God's design for human work. *Through worship*, these workers are reminded that the purpose of work is to bless not simply themselves but all humanity *and God as well*. *Through worship*, these workers are reminded that God is intimately present with them in the fields and markets actively "perfecting" their work with his "Word."[35]

Or as Kaemingk and Willson say above, "Monday work [is] an extension of Sunday worship. Sunday worship is not a 'moment' of worship; it is the beginning of a whole week of worship."[36] And God is blessed by it. But can we see God in the marketplace?

---

31. Schmemann, *For the Life of the World*, 43.

32. Kaemingk and Willson, *Work and Worship*, 209–39.

33. Kaemingk and Willson, *Work and Worship*, 241–60. For commissioning people other than stated Christian workers, see also Stockhard, "Commissioning Ministries of the Laity."

34. See https://imtglobal.org/pastors-toolbox for tools to help pastors and church leaders equip their congregation in a life-giving theology of work and to affirm that their Monday to Saturday work is valued by God.

35. Kaemingk and Willson, *Work and Worship*, 175, emphasis mine.

36. Kaemingk and Willson, *Work and Worship*, 46.

11

The Beatific Vision and the Marketplace

> God could easily give you grain and fruit without your plowing and planting. But He does not want to do so... What else is all our work to God—whether in the fields, in the garden, in the city, in the house, in war, or in government—but just such a child's performance, by which He wants to give His gifts in the fields, at home, and everywhere else? *These are the masks of God, behind which He wants to remain concealed and do all things.*
>
> MARTIN LUTHER, EXPOSITION OF PS 147[1]

> The glory of God is a living human being, and the life of man consists in beholding God.
>
> IRENAEUS OF LYONS 182–88 AD[2]

> Blessed are the pure in heart for they shall see God.
>
> JESUS, MATT 5:8

WE CAN SEE GOD in the church, in our quiet times, or in a retreat centre. But can we behold God while we work in the marketplace? I want to take up Darrell Cosden's intriguing reference to the beatific vision. This term speaks of the vision of God, seeing God, or knowing God mystically. And

---

1. See Martin Luther's "Exposition of Psalm 147," quoted in Greear, "Martin Luther on the Masks," emphasis mine.

2. Irenaeus of Lyons, *Haer.* 4.20.7 (p. 490).

that elusive term "mystical" simply means having direct contact with reality. And I, for one, join those wanting direct contact with God and to be able to say with the theologian Karl Barth, "God is beautiful," or as Cosden says to be taken "into the centre of what some have called the beatific vision," here quoted.

> Importantly, this theology of work is neither a spin off nor a marginal doctrine within theology. Nor is it relegated simply to an application of "real" doctrine. Rather, it takes us to the heart of what Christians have always and everywhere believed and proclaimed about who God is and what God is doing. It takes us to the heart of the doctrine of the Trinity as expressed in the creeds. *It takes us into the centre of what some have called the beatific vision.*[3]

Irenaeus, quoted famously above for his statement that the glory of God is a human being fully alive, said, "For if the manifestation of God which is made by means of the creation, affords life to all living in the earth, much more does that revelation of the Father which comes through the Word [Jesus], give life to those who see God."[4] He further noted that the Lord Jesus Christ "became what we are, that he might bring us to be even what he is himself,"[5] and "where the Spirit of the Father is, there is a living man."[6] Writing as a bishop in the late second century Irenaeus had grasped how Jesus Christ destroyed the dualism of the sacred versus the secular, the dualism of regarding the devoted charismatic living somewhere in a cave as a saint and the simple believer working in the world as less than holy. Really?

Seeing with a Single Eye

Then there is Jesus who, in the Beatitudes said, "Blessed are the pure in heart for they shall see God" (Matt 5:8). The monastic movement has taken this word "pure" to mean sinless. But the Greek word actually used here, *katharoi*, communicates not so much sinlessness but being fully consecrated to God, being full of integrity, not being double-minded, being unfeigned, or rather being single eyed (see Matt 6:22). In other words, if we are fully consecrated to God in our entire life, we will see God. The single-minded

---

3. Cosden, "Work and the New Creation," 176, emphasis mine.
4. Irenaeus of Lyons, *Haer.* 4.20.7 (p. 490).
5. Irenaeus of Lyons, *Haer.* 5, Preface (p. 526).
6. Irenaeus of Lyons, *Haer.* 5.9.3 (p. 535).

are unmixed, unadulterated, un-alloyed. The single-eyed are those who see. The double-minded are two-souled and blind. They are duplicitous. They do not see correctly. But with *katharoi* (single-minded consecration to God)[7] we can see God at work everywhere. Really?

Can we be single-minded—life orientated towards God, dedicated to God in all of its practical everyday dimensions—in a marketplace inclined to embrace short-term goals and where black-and-white ethics is often taken over by the color gray? Amid the tussle and sweat of the workplace, as well as the aha moments, are we able to see God in and through our work in the office, at home, in the factory, in the medical clinic, in the school or university, in government, or with media? Yes.

French theologian Jacques Ellul expressed it enigmatically in his extraordinary commentary on *Ecclesiastes*. If God is the "maker of all things" (Eccl 11:5), then why work? But the author of *Ecclesiastes* whom I am calling the Professor, says in effect, if you do not work you will not know that God is working! So Ellul reflects on this amazing truth, here repeated from chapter 3: "If you do nothing, if you fail to sow, if you keep staring at the clouds, you will not know the work of God who does everything. These words astonish: God does everything, yet I must do something! God will cause one thing or the other to succeed, or both things. But you and I must do them!"[8] In the same passage, chapter 11 of Ecclesiastes, the Professor says, "As you do not know how the body is formed in the mother's womb, so you cannot understand the work of God, the Maker of all things" (v. 5). So, God's work is a mystery, especially his wild work which only God can do.

Seeing God in Our Ordinary Work

It is relatively easy to see how God can be known in his extraordinary works, his wild works such as brought Job to repentance at the end of his African safari (chapters 38–41). But where is God in our day-to-day work? God is present in the fact that we are working at all. God is present in the work we do as a partial revelation of God's ongoing work. But our deeper

---

7. A parallel word used in Heb 12:14, *agiasmos*, is usually translated in English as "holiness" or "sanctification" in the exhortation, "without holiness no one will see the Lord." But as F.F. Bruce notes in his commentary on this verse "it is practical holiness of life that is meant . . . To see the Lord is the highest and most glorious blessing that mortals can enjoy, but this beatific vision is reserved for those who are holy in heart and life." Bruce, *Epistle to the Hebrew*, 364–65.

8. Ellul, *Reason for Being*, 226.

question is this: how can we see God in our daily work? God is the one who sees us. But can we say with Hagar, mother of Ishmael, son of Abraham, "I have now seen the one who sees me" (Gen 16:13)?

Jesus said that God is revealed in a woman looking for a lost coin in her home, in a father welcoming home his errant younger son and trying to persuade his younger son's self-righteous older brother to come into the grand reunion party. But God was also revealed in Dorcas's working in the home, making domestic things like aprons and clothing; in the fishermen casting their nets on the right side of their vessel to land a big catch. God was also with the apostle Paul's explanation to the philosophers on Mars Hill in Athens about the meaning of Christ's resurrection in terms they could understand. But these were extraordinary moments. God was also in his tent-making work daytime and evening, working with his hands and mind so as not to be a burden to anyone.

But how can we see him who sees us in the ordinary humdrum daily work? Is the beatific vision—the vision of God—possible in the Monday to Friday routine? Can life centered on God transform the ordinary into the extraordinary so we discover what Alfons Auer described as "the sense of transparency in worldly matters."[9]

Seeing God in the Dull, Drumming Repetition of Trivial Toil

Earlier I quoted Kathleen Norris in her little book *The Quotidian Mysteries*. The word "quotidian" really means "occurring every day" so she subtitled her book *Laundry, Liturgy and "Women's Work."* Her little book was a 1998 lecture on spirituality. In it she says that the true mystics, certainly in the sense of direct contact with ultimate reality, are those "who manage to find God in a life of noise, the demands of other people and relentless daily duties."[10] It sounds like a business executive, a laborer, or a homemaker. It also was the experience of a pope.

The medieval pope Gregory the Great (540–604) was "plucked from the haven of cloister and tossed into the tempest of the world's affairs" as pope.[11] He was forced to adjust his spirituality. Consequently, he would say

---

9. Auer, *Open to the World*, 230 (emphasis mine).

10. Norris, *Quotidian Mysteries*, 70.

11. Markus, *Gregory the Great*, 20. To a former bishop in Antioch he wrote, "I am being smashed by many waves of affairs and afflicted by the storms of a life of tumults, so

and write that the married cleaning woman might attain to the beatific vision, to greater spiritual heights than the cloistered monk or nun.

Unlike Augustine, who maintained that the contemplative life was greater than the active life, Gregory, through his own struggle with heavy administrative responsibilities as a pope, came to define the options not as first and foremost the contemplative life focused on eternal matters, and then, secondarily, the active life focused on worldly concerns. Gregory forged a synthesis of the two. He concluded that "activity precedes contemplation, but contemplation must be expressed in service to one's neighbour."[12] This synthesis, had it been heeded, would have virtually destroyed the sacred-secular dualism, that terrible split that has plagued the global church for nearly 2,000 years, namely that religious work is holy and pleasing to God while secular work is less than holy.

This is the false Mary and Martha distinction. Mary is seen as the contemplative sitting at the feet of Jesus and Martha is viewed as the active believer preparing a meal for Jesus and his friends. But in a parallel tradition of the church Mary and Martha have come to symbolize "the mixed life," a life when sometimes one is active, like Martha, and sometimes one withdraws from action to attend to God, like Mary. But Gregory went beyond the mixed life of action and reflection, says Chris Armstrong,

> to a kind of sacramental unity very unlike the sacred-secular divide that characterizes the church today. He insisted that when we commit and engage in our worldly vocations, everything in our experience can become an instrument of God's direct, special communication to us: the material goods that sustain us; our sometimes-stressful relationships with our co-workers; even the dull, drumming repetition of trivial toil.[13]

Speaking to the "dull drumming repetition of trivial toil" and "stressful relationships" Gregory argues that through these experiences, "the attentive layperson may develop the holy discernment, spiritual integrity, an unruffled tranquility that once was thought to belong only to the monks and nuns in their cloisters."[14] So Gregory defined what we might call being an "active contemplative" in the sacramental unity of life.

---

that many rightly say: *I am come into deep waters where the floods overflow me* [Ps 69:2], quoted in Moorhead, *Gregory the Great*, 3.

12. Straw, *Gregory the Great*, 20, quoted in Armstrong, "Problem of Meaning," 205.

13. Armstrong, "Problem of Meaning," 206.

14. Armstrong, "Problem of Meaning," 207.

The Beatific Vision and the Marketplace

Seeing God in Prayer as Work

I write this in a Benedictine monastery where the motto is *ora et labora* (prayer and work). But, having said this, there is also reason to change one word. Prayer *is* work (*ora est labora*) and work *is* prayer (*labora est ora*). I am not the first to do so. Thomas Carlyle famously made the change even though it is not a phrase found in Scripture.[15] But first, let me affirm that prayer *is* work. For many of us it is just this. It was even for Jesus whose sweat was like drops of blood when he prayed in the garden of Gethsemane (Luke 22:44). Theologian P. T. Forsyth asks,

> Does not Christ set more value upon importunity than on submission? . . . I would refer to the incident of the Syrophenician woman, where her wit, faith, and importunity together did actually change our Lord's intention and break his custom. Then there is Paul beseeching the Lord thrice for a boon; and urging us to be instant, insistent, continual in prayer. We have Jacob wrestling. We have Abraham pleading, yea haggling, with God for Sodom. We have Moses interceding for Israel and asking God to blot out his name out of the book of life, if that were needful to save Israel. We have Job facing God, withstanding him, almost bearding him and extracting revelation. We have Christ's own struggle with the Father in Gethsemene . . . Prayer is wrestling with God . . . So, the prayer which resists his dealings may be part of his will and its fulfilment.[16]

Prayer is work, working with God who prays with us and in us.

Prayer is simply contact and communication with God. It is for this reason that the theologian P. T. Forsyth says that "prayer is for the religious life what original research is to science—by it we get direct contact with reality."[17] He continues: "In prayer we do not think out God; we draw him out . . . God draws us out by breathing himself in."[18] "A chief object of all prayer is to bring us to God. But we may attain his presence and come closer to Him by the way we ask him for other things, concrete things, or things of the kingdom, than by direct prayer for union with him."[19] Prayer is needed to develop a marketplace theology, as we have previously shown

---

15. Carlyle, *Past and Present*, 193.
16. Forsyth, *Soul of Prayer*, 86–88.
17. Forsyth, *Soul of Prayer*, 78.
18. Forsyth, *Soul of Prayer*, 15.
19. Forsyth, *Soul of Prayer*, 16.

in the first and fourth chapters. It is part of our doing theology and part of our work-life.[20] Job, the besieged Old Testament character, is an example of this.

Job was affirmed by God as "speaking the truth about [God]" (Job 42:7), which is what a theologian must do, even though his blustering prayers were accusations that God was using him for target practice. Meanwhile the top-down theologians, Job's "miserable comforters," were rejected (42:6). We must ask why Job's friends were rejected when their speeches were orthodox and the kind of statements that come out of seminaries. Here is the reason. Simply, Job spoke *to* God in prayer about his troubles and suffering; the friends spoke *about* God to Job. So, says Forsyth, "the best theology is compressed prayer"[21] and here, as we do the theology of work, worker, and workplace, we are praying. But having considered how prayer can be work we must now consider how work can be prayer, and whether we can see God transparently through our work, the other half of Gregory's sacramental unity.

Seeing God in Work as Prayer

To explore this, I will expound the enigmatic and challenging verse in the New Testament in which Paul says, "pray without ceasing" or "pray continually" (1 Thess 5:17). Prayer is not just the words that we speak to God—words of petition, thanksgiving, or words of adoration and praise. Work itself can be a prayer. Basil the Great (fourth century) said, "Thus wilt thou pray without ceasing; if thou prayest not only in words, but unites thyself to God through all the course of life and so thy life be made one ceaseless and uninterrupted prayer."[22] How can this be?

To explain this, I must refer to the Hebraic understanding of words. The Hebrew view of communication is that it is not mere verbiage, wave forms, or digitalized data. In the Hebrew view of the human and divine word, the *person comes out of the mouth* and enacts what that person says.

---

20. In the first chapter, we noted that the Western church has concentrated on thought; the Eastern orthodox church has concentrated on prayer and mystery; and the Asian church has concentrated on practice. But a complete theology of the marketplace requires thought, prayer, and practice. And not necessarily in that order. We can do marketplace theology from below, starting with concrete situations in the workplace, or we can start with prayer.

21. Forsyth, *Soul of Prayer*, 44.

22. Basil the Great quoted in Schaff and Wace, *Select Library*, xix.

So, for example, when Jesus is tested by Satan to turn stones into bread, he quotes Deut 8:3 that "man shall not live on bread alone, but on every word that comes from the mouth of God."

That has led countless preachers to assert that Jesus is saying that we should live by Scripture, which, while true, is not the intent of the original quote. In Deuteronomy the children of Israel were in the wilderness and God provided or spoke manna, food, not just words, but enacted words through the mouth of God. So, God is saying, "I provided manna so you are not to live on bread alone, or bread of your own making, but the bread God provides." Jesus is hearing that Scripture as "God will provide."

So, there is much more to speaking than mouthing words. The person comes out of the mouth and gets revealed. That is why God's word does not return to him empty or void (Isa 55:11), because God is not an empty being. And Samuel's words did not fall to the ground (1 Sam 3:19) because Samuel was a person with integrity. So, it is impossible for a person not to be revealed when she opens her mouth. How does this relate to prayer and work as prayer?

Here I refer once again to Forsyth in his *Soul of Prayer*. "To pray without ceasing is not, of course, to engage in prayer without break. That is an impossible literalism . . . The only answer to God's eternity is an eternal attitude of prayer."[23] Even the Benedictines cannot do it. They live a fairly balanced life of eight hours of work, eight hours of prayer and eight hours of sleep. But if they tried to pray continuously, they would soon be sleep-deprived and the necessary work would not be done. They would have to hire non-monks to do the work. But work is part of their discipline. Rather than becoming inefficient and distracted at work by stopping as often as possible to pray, there is a better way.

Our prayer is the "constant bent and drift of the soul . . . the soul's habitual appetite and habitual food. Prayer is not identical with the occasional act of praying. Like the act of faith, it is a *whole life thought of as action* . . . For what is life's prayer but its ruling passions?"[24] Forsyth continues, "Pray without a break between your prayer and your life. Pray so that there is a real continuity between your prayer and your whole actual life."[25] In other words *what we need is not a prayer life but a life of prayer*, a life directed towards God, thanking God, speaking to God about our needs (yes, even

---

23. Forsyth, *Soul of Prayer*, 59.
24. Forsyth, *Soul of Prayer*, 60, emphasis mine.
25. Forsyth, *Soul of Prayer*, 64.

though he knows what we need before we ask him), presenting our whole bodily life to God as a living sacrifice which is our spiritual adoration of God (Rom 12:1–2)—including our work. So, with Forsyth again, "If you may not come to God with the occasions of your private life and affairs, then there is some unreality in the relation between you and him."[26] If we pray without ceasing in the manner outlined above what can we see of God? Can and should this be the purpose of the Christian life?

Medieval and Patristic theologians "regarded the beatific vision as the undisputed purpose of the Christian life," says Hans Boersma, former theologian at Regent College.[27] But as Boersma shows, this spiritual *telos* (goal) has often been thought to be reached *only* after death. Tragically, the beatific vision has been somewhat lost in contemporary theology, especially Western systematic theology which has largely become a rational enterprise. So, the doctrine has been neglected. It has been replaced largely by material flourishing as the goal of human existence. Boersma notes that there is a biblical promise that after death believers will see God face to face.[28] The burning question is whether we can, however darkly, even see God *in this life*, in the midst of our toil.[29] To explore this, Boersma turns to the writing of Gregory of Nyssa, a bishop of Nyssa, Cappadocia, from 372 to 376 AD and later.

For this Gregory—not to be confused with Gregory the Great previously mentioned—the aim of the spiritual journey on earth is identical with the seeking of God in the next life—to see the face of God, however dimly, in the here and now. "For Gregory this theological longing was grounded in his understanding of the beatific vision: the eschatological [end times] future of perpetual progress (*epektasis*) in the life of Christ meant that already in this life Gregory set his desire on seeking the face of God in Jesus Christ."[30]

So, continues Boersma, "for Gregory everyday spirituality—seeing what God is like by looking at the world around us and observing with the 'eye of the soul' the 'luminous outpoured rays of the divine nature'—is

---

26. Forsyth, *Soul of Prayer*, 66.

27. See Boersma, "Gregory of Nyssa," 146.

28. Job 19:26–7; Matt 5:8; John 17;24; 1 Cor 13:12; 2 Cor 5:6; 1 John 3:2

29. Boersma notes the discussions of theophanies (appearances of God) in Scripture: Abraham (Gen 18), Jacob (Gen 28, 32), Moses (Exod 33–34; Num 12:7–8; Heb 11:27), Micaiah (1 Kgs 22:19), Isaiah (Isa 6:1–5), Ezekiel (Ezek 1:4–28; 8:1–4), Peter, James, and John (Matt 17:1–8), Paul (Acts 9:3–9; 2 Cor 12:1–4), and John (Rev 1:12–16; 4–5)

30. Boersma, "Gregory of Nyssa," 149.

intrinsically linked to the beatific vision."[31] Through this "eye of the soul" we can see traces of God in the ways he works in this world. Then Boersma quotes Gregory directly, "This truly is the vision of God; never to be satisfied in the desire to see him."[32] And in directing our desires to God we human beings find our true identity and aim in life. Yes, I answer, knowing God should be the goal of the Christian life if that goal is to love God wholeheartedly and love our neighbor as we love ourselves. So, I now ask, how do we find "traces" of God in our work, worker, and workplaces, both now in the light of God's ultimate purpose for work in the new heaven and new earth?

Seeing God in Work, Worker, and Workplace

God is in our work. Yes, it is mixed with sin in this life but in the "now" of the kingdom of God. But with the eye of faith, we can see God. We are doing the work of the Lord, creating, sustaining, fixing and redeeming, judging, and consummating. If we can even for a moment stop and ask about a specific work we have undertaken, asking whether there was a compassionate dimension, a judging factor, a surge of creativity, a consummating dimension, or a providential-sustaining action, we can see God in our work. We can rejoice that we are "doing the work of the Lord." *Opus dei*, literally the work of God, is the work of worship in the monastic tradition. But *opus dei* is not only specific devotional words and actions directed to God's pleasure. *Opus dei* is the reality of our day-to-day labor directed to God. Yes, we see God, darkly and partially in our work. "For now we see only a reflection as in a mirror; then [when Christ comes again] we shall see face to face" (1 Cor 13:12).

God is in the way we work. As we put to death the fleshly ways of working—emotional manipulation, envy and greed, predatory competition, making our work an idol (all works "of the flesh [Gal 5:19–21])—and breathe in the Holy Spirit whose fruit brings life, joy, peace, self-control, kindness, peace, and patience, we see God at work in us in the way we work. It is only as we work with faith, hope, and love that our work will please God and will last. It is not the bare non-incarnated virtues of faith, hope, and love that last and "remain" (1 Cor 13:13). These virtues, however little of them we have kneaded into our labor like yeast in dough, will make

---

31. Boersma, "Gregory of Nyssa," 153.
32. Boersma, "Gregory of Nyssa," 159.

these human efforts last. But we can see God in this. "For now we see only a reflection as in a mirror; then [when we are resurrected into the new world] we shall see face to face" (1 Cor 13:12).

God is in us as workers. We are walking sanctuaries of God. Workplace spirituality is shoe-leather spirituality. The key is "Christ in you, the hope of glory" (Col 1:27), Paul's great assertion. This does not mean that our identity is lost when we come to Christ, as a drop of water is "lost" in the ocean. That has been called by the older New Testament scholar Gustav Adolf Deissmann "union" mysticism, something that is proclaimed in some religions even today. Instead, we have "communion" mysticism. It is Christ in me; I am in Christ. This is Paul's "I, yet not I."[33] So, the apostle Paul did not lose his personality when he was apprehended by Christ on the Damascus Road. Instead his personality was infused with the person of Christ, and he gained a magnificent obsession. "Christ in me" and "I in Christ," "in Christ," or "in the Lord" occurs 164 times in Paul's writings.[34] Of course, we are still being saved, still being sanctified, still being perfected, but with Christ and the Spirit of Christ within us, we have a vision, albeit dimly, of who he is. "For now we see only a reflection as in a mirror; then [when we see God as complete human beings in the new heaven and new earth] we shall see face to face" (1 Cor 13:12).

God is in our coworkers. Each human being is made in the image of God, made to reflect God, to suggest God, to hint at who God is. No one has sunk so low in sin and self-destruction that there is not at least a sign of the image. Every human being is an icon of God. Icons in computer usage are ways that let you into a massive amount of perspective, information, and data. And as icons of God our coworkers are holy images of God. Yes, they are "not yet" what they will be but they "are now" the holiest thing around next to the blessed sacrament, as C.S. Lewis says. Indeed, our neighbor worker is already a sacrament to us even if partially, if only we have eyes to see. "For now we see only a reflection as in a mirror; then [when with all God's people who have gone before us we meet God] we shall see face to face" (1 Cor 13:12).

---

33. 1 Cor 15:10; 7:10; Gal 2:20. See Deissmann, *Paul*. "The aim of mysticism is either *unio* or *communion*; either oneness with God, or fellowship with God; either loss of the human personality in God or sanctification of the personality through the presence of God; either transformation into the deity, or conformation of the human towards the divine; participation in the deity or prostration before the deity" (p. 150–51).

34. Deissmann, *Paul*, 140.

The Beatific Vision and the Marketplace

God is in the workplace itself. Our workplaces range from miserable workplaces to places of inspiration, empowerment, and community. Make no mistake about it, the workplace is important, whether it be the home, the office, the factory, the school, or the military. It matters for motivation. The motivational switch in workers is both on the inside and outside. By saying the motivational switch is both inside and outside I mean that there is something leaders can do in the organizational culture to unleash the motivation of workers, to encourage people to turn the motivational switch on. The culture speaks more loudly than the president about what is important, how people are treated, and what you have to do to join it. But God is there. There is no workplace so demonized that a Christian might not be called to work there. And those in leadership have the challenge of shaping and nurturing the organizational culture. God is there, even in hints of sanity and grace in a miserable workplace as well as in the virtues, values, and symbols of a healthy organizational culture.

Forsyth says, "If the kingdom of God not only got over the murder of Christ, but made it into its great lever, there is nothing that it cannot get over, and nothing that it cannot turn to eternal blessing and to the glory of his holy name."[35] Truly we are "not yet" but longing for the kingdom to come "on earth as it is [already] in heaven." In our final workplace, the new heaven and new earth, all work will be play and worship. But for now, we have a foretaste of that beatific work experience in the next life. "For now we see only a reflection as in a mirror; then [when in the new heaven and new earth work, play and worship will be completely one] we shall see face to face" (1 Cor 13:12).

And all of this comes through prayer, prayer without ceasing, prayer that is work and work that is prayer. And we pray because God is praying through us. Forsyth underscores the reality of this: "The real power of prayer in history is not a fusillade of praying units of whom Christ is the chief, but it is a corporate action of the Saviour-Intercessor and his community, a volume and energy of prayer organized in a Holy Spirit and in the Church the Spirit creates."[36] He draws us in. But it is not we who are praying. For, says Forsyth, "it is the Christ at prayer who lives in us, and we are conduits of the eternal Intercession."[37]

---

35. Forsyth, *Soul of Prayer*, 36.
36. Forsyth, *Soul of Prayer*, 55.
37. Forsyth, *Soul of Prayer*, 16.

Seeing God in the Sacrament of Everyday Work

I conclude with an article from the journal I read each month, *Initiatives* from the National Center for the Laity. It is capturing the ongoing fruit of Vatican II in the Roman Catholic Church especially with respect to work and faith. The editor, Bill Droel, and Kathy Hidy speak of *Catholic Sensibility* noting that many Catholics have lost it and many non-Catholics have it. What he calls Catholic sensibility is really the beatific vision.

> NCL believes that there is a unique treasure imprinted in each person's imagination ... The unique treasure is the suspicion that embedded in the ordinary lies the extraordinary, the miraculous, or the salvic. To have a Catholic sensibility is to appreciate the sacramental; it is to be aware, however, dimly, that an exchange of love between God and God's people is mediated through this grace-filled co-created world. The Catholic sensibility sees bread and wine, "works of human hands," as the body and blood of Christ. It sees the shopping mall, the school, the kitchen table, the factory, the courtroom, and the hospital as altars of sorts—places where the ordinary, mundane labors of life may be offered up, blessed, and transformed into things of beauty.
>
> Imagining toil and turmoil as sacramental moments is not easy. Yet a profoundly simple truth lies somewhere in the corporate layoffs, the boring factory routine, the gossipy neighbours, the crying children, the disgruntled client, plus in the curiosity of students, the gratefulness of patients, the solidarity of coworkers and the unearned love of a spouse. The truth is that God so loved the world that God became one of us. God became a baby in a trough, a common criminal on a cross, a fisherman, a co-worker in an office, a neighbour, a machinist, a customer, a middle-manager, a nurse, an accountant, a human being. This incarnate God is related to each of us, not just through baptism but many times a day, thousands of times in a lifetime, in every ordinary encounter.
>
> Entwined with the ordinary we know so well is the extraordinary we barely recognize. Yet as in a distant remembering, we deeply yearn for this extraordinary. It is a love so knowing and embracing in our circumstances that it redeems the very stuff of our work and our existence. Through that redemptive love, our very selves are made sacrament, are raised up, are blessed, and broken ... bread of and for lives we lead on the job, around the home and in the neighbourhood.
>
> To be clear, this sensibility is rarely explicit ... This sensibility is a profound yet accessible way of looking at the world and

appreciating each person's place in it. Are you interested in such a sensibility?[38]

The centre of Gregory the Great's faith, mentioned above, could be called "desiderium," a kind of yearning, the unsatisfied longing of the human heart. One historian of the monastic life has described Gregory the Great as the "doctor of desire" since the desire for God is never satisfied, at least in this life.[39] Turning to Scripture he cites Peter's comment that God is the one on whom "angels long to look" (1 Pet 1:12) and Jesus who said of children "their angels in heaven always behold the face of my father who is in heaven" (Matt 18:10). Both, he claimed, are true. Gregory says, "*Someone who longs for God with his whole soul certainly already possesses the one he loves.*"[40]

"For now we see only a reflection as in a mirror; then we shall see face to face" (1 Cor 13:12). But the "reflection in the mirror" is beautiful to behold.

We turn now to the final word in William Perkins's definition of theology, here amended, "Marketplace theology is the science of working blessedly *forever*." Can our work last? And will we work in heaven, or more accurately, in the new heaven and new earth?

---

38. Droel and Hidy, "Holy Work," 1, quoted with permission.

39. Leclercq, *Love of Learning*, quoted in Moorhead, *Gregory the Great*, 44.

40. Gregory the Great, *Homilaie xl in Evangelia* 30.1, quoted in Leclercq, *Love of Learning*, 44–45, emphasis mine.

WORKING BLESSEDLY FOREVER

12

Contributing to a Down-to-Earth Heaven

All who have committed their work in faithfulness to God will be by Him raised up to share in the new age, and will find that their labor was not lost, but that it has found its place in the completed kingdom.

LESSLIE NEWBIGIN[1]

Unless the LORD *builds the house, the builders labor in vain.*

SOLOMON, PS 127:1

MARKETPLACE THEOLOGY IS THE science of working blessedly *forever*. But is it really forever?

My wife died while I was writing this book. I miss her deeply but know she is with the Lord. In a strange way I still feel close to her as she has become part of the great cloud of witnesses, the communion of saints. Her work and my work continue. Indeed, I believe she is now freer to work in her gifted area of welcoming, inclusion, discipling, and mentoring. Perhaps she is offering hospitality and a listening ear to those joining the church triumphant. A prayer from George MacLeod, founder of the Iona Community, sums up what I feel and what I believe:

> Be You, triune God, in the midst of us as we give thanks for those who have gone from the sight of earthly eyes. They, in Your nearer presence, still worship with us in the mystery of the one family on

---

1. Newbigin, *Signs amid the Rubble*, 47, quoted in Sherman, *Kingdom Calling*, 236.

heaven and on earth . . . If it be Your holy will, tell them how we love them, and how we miss them, and how we long for the day when we shall meet with them again. God of all comfort, we lift into Your immediate care those recently bereaved, who sometimes in the night-time cry "Would God it were morning," and in the morning cry "Would God that it were night." Bereft of their dear ones, too often they are bereft also of the familiar scenes where happiness once reigned.

Lift from their eyes the too distant vision of the resurrection at the last day. Alert them to hear the voice of Jesus saying: "I AM Resurrection and I AM Life": that they may believe this. Strengthen them to go on in loving service of all Your children. *Thus shall they have communion with You and in You, with their beloved.* Thus shall they come to know, in themselves, that there is no death and that only a veil divides, thin as gossamer.[2]

So, we come to the end of this study in marketplace theology with two questions. First, will anything we do in this life survive the grave and take its place in the new heaven and new earth? Second, will we work in the new heaven and new earth? To explore this, we must return to Scripture and its overriding theme of the kingdom of God.[3]

The Kingdom of God Consummated

The kingdom is crucial for understanding and practising marketplace theology. Why? Because it gives meaning to our work in the world, whether it is remunerated or voluntary. It provides an ethical basis for our work.[4] It spells out the kind of community that a church, corporation, or a not-for-profit organization can become. "The Kingdom of God . . . is righteousness, peace and joy in the Holy Spirit" (Rom 14:17). The kingdom expounds the nature of God's mission in the marketplace.[5] It challenges us to ministry in the workplace.[6] It assures us that the workplace is the primary location for spiritual growth into kingdom spirituality. But finally, it promises that some

---

2. Excerpted from MacLeod, *Whole Earth Shall Cry Glory*, 88, emphasis mine.

3. For a more complete exposition of the kingdom of God see Stevens, *Kingdom of God in Working Clothes*.

4. See chapters 8 and 10, "Values" and "Virtues," in *Kingdom of God in Working Clothes*.

5. See chapter 10 in *Kingdom of God in Working Clothes*.

6. See chapter 9 in *Kingdom of God in Working Clothes*.

Contributing to a Down-to-Earth Heaven

of our work will last and be part of the new heaven and the new earth.[7] It is this last statement that I wish to develop here.

So, while the kingdom seems to be, from Scripture, mostly, and sometimes totally, the work of God, at the initiative of God, and through the power of God, we are left asking is there any part we can play in bringing in the kingdom—other than winning people to Christ. How does the kingdom actually come? Is it all God's work, God's gift? Or is there a symphony of wills and initiatives human and divine?

Often in Scripture the kingdom is something to be received and to be entered. George Eldon Ladd in his classic work on the subject says, "The kingdom of God is a miracle. It is the act of God . . . Men cannot build the kingdom . . . It is God's reign . . . The fruitage is produced not by human effort or skill but by the life of the Kingdom itself. It is God's deed." But, to balance his understanding of how the kingdom comes, he concludes later, drawing on Luke 10:9, 17, "Thus the kingdom of God was at work among men not only in the person of our Lord but also through his disciples as they brought the word and the signs of the kingdom to the cities of Galilee."[8] So, can we also *bring in* the kingdom, or work with God in so doing even now, not just in the afterlife? Did Augustine get it right when he said, "God without us will not, as we without God cannot."[9] So, let me return to the first question: Will anything we have done in this life last beyond the grave?

Paul's letter in 1 Cor 15:58 says *yes*. "Always give yourselves fully to the work of the Lord, because you know that your labor in the Lord is not in vain." Coming as this text does in the resurrection chapter it is certainly not limiting "the work of the Lord" to the work of pastors or missionaries. In Col 3 Paul tells the slaves in Colossae that they are "working for the Lord" (v. 23) and "It is the Lord Christ [they] are serving" (v. 24). Certainly, it is not the religious character of our work, the fact that the Bible is open, and God's name is spoken, which makes it "in the Lord." But what does it mean that we "labor in the Lord?"

Is it the Lord's work when the work was done with a different *motive*—out of love to God and neighbor? Or is it that the *method* of the work is in harmony with God's purposes and God's declared values—forgiveness, boundary-breaking behavior, transparency, extraordinary service, being

---

7. See chapter 14, "Working our Way to Heaven," in *Kingdom of God in Working Clothes*.

8. Ladd, *Gospel of the Kingdom*, 64, 115.

9. Quoted in Sherman, *Kingdom Calling*, 238.

just and fair, integrity of word and deed, and other salty values?[10] Or is it the *purpose* of the work that it confirms God's purpose of bringing human and creational flourishing that makes it the Lord's work? Or is it the *goal* of the work—formed by the vision of God's final restoration and renewal of everything, people, peoples, communities, and creation itself? Or is it the fact that the work was done with faith, hope, and love, that the work will not be in vain? Perhaps it is all of the above that makes it work "in the Lord." All good work done "in the Lord" is kingdom of God work, albeit mixed in with sin and deconstruction in this world. Kingdom work is not merely religious work; but nor is it secular work. Kingdom work means that dualism is dead. Kingdom work unifies everything we do in the home, marketplace, or educational institution into a sacrament, a means of bringing grace into the world and to people for the common good. Through down-to-earth work—the kingdom of God comes in working clothes. But, what does Paul mean when he says that your labor in the Lord is "not in vain"?

Is Paul reflecting the servant of the Lord in Isa 49 when that servant exclaims, "I have labored in vain, I have spent my strength for nothing at all. Yet what is due me is in the Lord's hand, and my reward is with my God" (v. 4)? Apparently from the Revelation "the kings of the earth will bring their splendor into [the New Jerusalem]" (21:24) and the "glory and honor of the nations will be brought into it" (21:26). Will there be a transfiguration of our work in the grand reappearing of the Lord Jesus at the end of history? Yes, some of our work for sure, and all kinds of work.

- *Service work*: Serving people directly—physically, emotionally, intellectually, socially, and spiritually; home care, public health care, counselling, teaching, barbering, caring professions, educators, homemaking—helping people flourish.

---

10. Salty kingdom values: *forgiveness and accountability*—giving people a second chance, going the second mile (Matt 18:21–35; 5:41); *integrity in word and deed*—letting your yes be yes, inner and outer life in sync, transparency (Matt 5:37); *fairness and justice*—doing the right thing in compensation, purity of product, handling of money; *extraordinary service*—going beyond duty (Col 4:1; Luke 17:7–10); *boundary-breaking behavior* (Luke 5:27–31); *stewardship*—treasuring the gifts of others, caring for creation, developing an empowering organizational culture (Matt 25:14–30); *empowerment*—releasing other people's gifts and talents, helping others to thrive in service (Eph 4:11–12); *shalom and being socially responsible*—neighbor love personally and socially (Matt 22:39); *joy*—experiencing a God-infusion of exuberance and well-being that is not dependent on circumstances—some have called this "fun" in the workplace (Phil 4:4). See Bakke, *Joy at Work*.

Contributing to a Down-to-Earth Heaven

- *Culture work*: art, music, images, information technology, communication, film, internet, media, system engineering.
- *Creational work*: earth keeping, farming, exploration.
- *Social work*: creating community; facilitating communication; listening; building homes, workplaces, hospitals, and schools; providing safety; and seeing justice is done.
- *Powers work*: dealing with unjust structures; grappling with the principalities and powers: political, ecclesiastical, judicial structures, images, institutions, angels and demons, death, the demonic.
- *Spiritual work*: intercessory prayer, proclamation, spiritual direction, pastoral care, spiritual leadership.

All ways of contributing to the kingdom of God . . . now and coming.

But we must live, work, and witness with the ambiguity of the presence of the kingdom—it is here and not yet here. It is something in which we can participate but we cannot bring it in by ourselves. John Bright, in his classic book *The Kingdom of God*, asks "Who will tell us that in escaping the tension of the kingdom we have betrayed ourselves." He continues:

> Yet in this plodding survival which lives at peace with the secular order, without tension and with no inkling of that Other Order which is ever intruding, less than that? Or is the kingdom so small a thing that we can just take it by the arm and usher it in on our own terms, if only we would set our minds to do it? No, we cannot put the awful immediacy and the radical challenge of the kingdom from our minds, nor turn it into a figure of speech, or perhaps a pale synonym for the sum total of human good, and remain the New Testament Church. For the New Testament Church is the people of the kingdom of God.[11]

So, there it is. God can do it without us. But mostly chooses to do it with us. But we cannot do it without godwardness, without dependence on God himself. Augustine had the right balance: "God without us will not, as we without God cannot."[12]

We gain a marketplace theology not just from its origin, from God's splendid purpose in creating humankind in God's image as a worker, but we gain the meaning of our work also from the future, from the eschatological vision of work, what work will be. We need to look forward as well

---

11. Bright, *Kingdom of God*, 242–43.
12. Quoted in Sherman, *Kingdom Calling*, 238.

as backwards. So, F.F. Bruce comments on Paul's statement in Romans 8:21 where Paul says,

> For the creation waits in eager expectation for the children of God to be revealed. For the creation was subjected to frustration, not by its own choice, but by the will of the one who subjected it, in hope that the creation itself will be liberated from its bondage to decay and brought into the freedom and glory of the children of God. (Rom 8:19–21)

About this text Bruce remarks, "if words mean anything, these words of Paul denote not the annihilation of the present material universe on the day of revelation, to be replaced by a universe completely new, but the transformation of the present universe so that it will fulfil the purpose for which God created it."[13]

So, as Miroslav Volf notes, this eschatological significance of human work means that our work in this life are the "building materials of a glorified world."[14] Volf suggests that the statement in Revelation that the resurrected saints "will rest from their labor, for their deeds will follow them" (Rev 14:13) could mean that their "earthly work will leave traces on resurrected personalities."[15] Volf takes a charismatic and eschatological perspective on work and carefully outlines why he thinks that the Holy Spirit is not just the "Spirit of religious experience but also the Spirit of worldly engagement."[16] So, looking forward to the consummation of the kingdom we gain a perspective on the meaning of work, especially as we read the last book of the New Testament.

There we are ushered in Rev 21 and 22 into a final vision not of Eden restored, as the NIV title, in my view, wrongly puts it, but the garden of Eden *transfigured* as the final living quarters and workplace of all the people of God. In what is arguably the best renewal verse in the Bible, Jesus, sitting on the throne of God says, "I am making everything new!" (21:5). Note that Jesus will not make new things. This is not a brand-new creation, as though

---

13. Bruce, *Epistle of Paul to the Romans*, 170, quoted in Volf, "Work as Cooperation with God," 89.

14. Volf, "Work as Cooperation with God," 90.

15. Volf, "Work as Cooperation with God," 91.

16. Volf, "Work as Cooperation with God," 95. Read pp. 99–101 where Volf expresses theologically what the charisms of the Spirit are not and are. It is not their addition of a new substance or quality that is added to the person, so moved, but rather the fruit of interaction between the Holy Spirit and the person at work with their God-given genetic heritage.

God will annihilate everything in the world when Christ returns, as some wrongly interpret the somewhat enigmatic words of the apostle Peter (2 Pet 3:10–13). Indeed, this passage ends with our looking forward to a new (really renewed) heaven *and a new (renewed) earth* (3:13). We dare not drop "the new earth" from the phrase. So, the two questions we ask about our work in this life and the next find their answer partly in this last strange book of the New Testament.

The Survival and Transfiguration of This Life's Work

First, will any of our work done in this life, if done for the Lord, survive and take their place in the renewed creation (perfected of course). We ask it in the contemporary context of the view of most Christians that only gospel work lasts. This has driven a generation into full-time ministry, as though anyone could be a part-time disciple of Jesus. But, contrary to this dualistic view of work, namely that work in the church lasts and work in the world goes up in a puff of smoke, there are biblical reasons why some work in this life, done with faith, hope, and love, will last and contribute to the new heaven and new earth. So it is good to ask, is what we are doing worthy of becoming the furniture of heaven? Here are nine biblical reasons to suggest that what we do in this life, what we have made with our hands, minds, or souls, will not only survive but be glorified. Otherwise "all things" will not be reconciled by Christ.

First, there is discontinuity between this life and the next but there is also continuity. The New Jerusalem is related to this world—a city and land (Rev 21–22).

Second, the resurrected body of Jesus bore scars from this life, but they are now transfigured and become a means of faith (John 20:27). Our violent acts against nature and culture may not be erased by the final Armageddon and the final renewal but may by God's grace be transfigured. This is part of our hope. Through transcendent reasoning we can imagine that the marks we leave in this life and in this world last: open pit mines, well-manicured gardens, cedar decks, and satellite receiving stations, the good and the bad of what we are doing in this world. But there will be a transfiguration. There will be a *new* heaven and a *new* earth, really. So, Jesus spoke about "the renewal of *all things*" (Matt 19:28, emphasis mine).[17]

---

17. For a fuller treatment of this thought see "Working with Hope" in Stevens, *Seven Days of Faith*, 43–51.

Third, in the final judgment Jesus personally receives our service done in this life. "You did it to me," he will say (Matt 25:31–46).

Fourth, the apostle Paul in his letter to the Corinthians suggests that if our work is built on Christ it, the work, will be saved at the end. If it is not saved the work will be burned up in the great fire at the end, though we, the worker might be saved.

> If anyone builds on this foundation [Christ] . . . their work will be shown for what it is, because the Day will bring it to light. It will be revealed with fire, and the fire will test the quality of each person's work. If what has been built survives, the builder will receive a reward. If it is burned up, the builder will suffer loss but yet will be saved—even though only as one escaping through flames. (1 Cor 3:12–15)

Fifth, the fire of judgment (2 Pet 3:7) does not mean annihilation but transformation (3:13). The image comprises putting raw ore into a cauldron and turning the heat up to burn out the dross. The next verse underscores that we wait for a new heaven and a new earth.

Sixth, the earth groans and waits for liberation (Rom 8:19–22). Our future is a heavenly earth or a down-to-earth heaven.

Seventh, faith, hope, and love last, according to 1 Cor 13:13 but not just as isolated virtues but *what is done* with faith, hope, and love. A Catholic scholar, Haughey, comments on this occurrence of the triad of marketplace virtues.

> It seems that it is not acts of faith, hope and love in themselves that last, but rather works done in faith, hope and love: it is not the pure intention alone, nor is it faith, hope and love residing unexercised as three infused theological virtues in a person that last. What lasts is the action taken on these virtues, the praxis that flows from the intention, the works the virtues shape. These last![18]

Eighth, the deeds of Christians follow them into the new heaven and new earth, according to Rev 14:13.

Ninth, as considered briefly above, Paul says that our "labor in the Lord" is not in vain (1 Cor 15:58). To this, N.T. Wright notes:

> In the Lord your labor is not in vain. You are following Jesus and shaping our world in the power of the Spirit; and when the final consummation comes, the work that you have done, whether

---

18. Haughey, *Converting Nine to Five*, 106.

in Bible study or biochemistry, whether in preaching or in pure mathematics, whether in digging ditches or in composing symphonies, will stand, will last (1 Cor 15:58).[19]

Yves Congar was the French theologian who did much of the advance theological work in preparation for Vatican II, that great opening for the whole people of God in the Catholic church. Congar puts the matter succinctly:

> Ontologically, this is the world that, transformed and renewed will pass into the kingdom; so . . . the dualist position is wrong; final salvation will be achieved by a wonderful refloating of our earthly vessel rather than the transfer of the survivors to another ship wholly built by God.[20]

So, I give a very promising and positive answer to the first question, whether any of our work in this life will find its way into a down-to-earth heaven even though our imaginations will be stretched in so envisaging how this could be. But the second question—whether we will work when we "get to heaven"—is only partly answered in the last book of the Bible.

Restful Work in the Next Life

Will we work when we get there? Or will we merely sit around playing our guitars and singing the same worship song a million times. Robert Farrar Capon sums up the usual thought about "going to heaven":

> For us, heaven is an unearthly, humanly irrelevant condition in which bed-sheeted, paper-winged spirits sit on clouds and play tinkly music until their pipe-cleaner halos drop off in boredom. As we envision it, it contains not one baby's bottom, not one woman's breast, not even one man's bare chest—much less a risen basketball game between glorified "shirts" and "skins." But in Scripture, it is a city with boys and girls playing in the streets; it is buildings put up by a Department of Public Works that uses amethysts for cinder blocks and pearls as big as the Ritz for gates; and indoors, it is a dinner party to end all dinner parties at the marriage supper of the Lamb. It is, in short, earth wedded. Not earth jilted. It is the world as the irremovable apple of God's eye.[21]

---

19. Wright, *Challenge of Jesus*, 180–81.
20. Congar, *Lay People in the Church*, 92.
21. Capon, *Parables of the Kingdom*, 92.

One thing for sure: we will not be disembodied souls floating in ether, but fully resurrected persons in a beautifully renewed creation in which the invisible heaven and the visible earth have come together in a glorious union called the Wedding Supper of the Lamb.

There are two approaches to dealing with this question. The first approach is theological in the sense of a logical, rational understanding. The second is a textual approach.

First, the Theological Answer

We will be fully human (including glorified bodies) in the new heaven and new earth, rather than mere immortal souls (the Greek view of the future). In the Hebrew and biblical view of the person, the body is not an evil shell for the precious and holy soul. We do not *have* souls and bodies. We *are* bodies, *are* souls, *are* spirits. We are psycho-pneuma-somatic wholes. So, contrary to the Greek view that you get saved by getting the soul out of the body, which happens when we die, the biblical future of the human person is a glorified ensouled body or embodied soul. As fully human beings made even more into the image of God than we were in our earth-life, we will work because this is part of what it means to be made in the image of God. God is a worker and he made us in his image (Gen 1:27–28). We will be put in charge, another word for "serve" (Rev 22:3) or "reign" (22:5). There will be no curse to deal with, no sin, no cantankerous customers, and no sleepless nights worrying about the bottom line. Indeed, George MacDonald in his children's books envisages exchange taking place in heaven without money. Each of us will be unique and have unique gifts to bring to the community of heaven. That means we are dependent on one another and must exchange. And exchange is business. Two marketing professors postulate that marketing people will be needed to help people make choices! So, to be human—and we will be more human than ever—is to work, yes work in the new heaven and new earth.

Second, the Textual Answer

Here we look specifically at the text of Revelation. "The kings of the earth will bring their splendor into [the holy city]" (21:24). This is the best of the culture of every nation on earth—its technology, art, literature, service, and products. Human creativity will be expressed fully and beautifully. "The glory and honour of the nations will be brought into it" (21:26). So, there will be culture creation and world-making. But more than culture there is the activity of the people of the consummated kingdom.

These people will work. "They will reign (read "work") with him age after age after age" (Rev 22:5 *The Message*). And "the leaves of the tree [of life] are for the healing of the nations" (Rev 22:2). On each side of the river of life are not just the solitary tree of life, reminiscent of the garden of Eden, but the *trees* of life. And the leaves of the tree are for the healing of the nations. Sometimes doctors say to me there will be no work for them in heaven. Here is what I answer. Whatever gifts, talents, and personality you have now will be present and exalted in the new heaven and new earth. Indeed, your calling, which I assume is to help people, does not end with death, or worse still with formal retirement. It continues into eternity. And what if all heaven is healing, renewal, and growth? And what if your gifts and talents find new expression in the context of the presence of God and the love community of the Lamb?

Yes, there will be judgment and discrimination. "The cowardly, the unbelieving, the vile, the murderers, the sexually immoral, those who practice magic arts, the idolaters and all liars" will be outside (21:8). We will work without troublemakers and without resistance from the pacified principalities and powers.[22] There will be unmixed joy at work.

And who would not want to be there? Speaking many years ago at a course at Regent College, the late Dr. Clark Pinnock read from 1 Corinthians: "What no eye has seen, what no ear has heard, and what no human mind has conceived—the things God has prepared for those who love him—these are the things God has revealed to us by the Spirit" (2:9–10). Then Pinnock, through his tears, said: "It is like this. A little girl wants a baby doll for her Christmas present. But what she is given is a living baby sister."

W. H. Auden, while introducing Charles Williams's novel, *The Descent of the Dove*, put it starkly:

> Charles Williams succeeds, where even Dante, I think, fails, in showing us that nobody is ever *sent* to Hell; he, or she, insists on going there. If, as Christians believe, God is love, then, in one sense, he is not omnipotent, for he cannot compel his creatures to

---

22. See Stevens, *Other Six Days*, 235–39.

accept his Love without ceasing to be himself. The wrath of God is not *his* wrath but the way in which those feel his love who refuse it, and the right of refusal is a privilege which not even their Creator can take from them.[23]

No one is ever sent to hell. I take this to be a fairly good translation of the statement of Jesus in the Gospel of John 3:19: "This is the verdict [judgement]: Light has come into the world, but people loved darkness instead of light because their deeds were evil." In other words, people judge themselves in the presence of the light of the kingdom and the King. They insist on going. Why is this so? Because heaven is permeated with the presence of God whom we will see face to face and know as we are known. They do not want that presence.

Yes, creativity will be there. Yes, humanity will be there. Yes, work will be there. But best of all, God and the people of God from every race culture and background will be there. And also, as we have seen, some of the things we have done and made in this life will be there. Relational, instrumental, medical, domestic, service, construction work will have eternity kneaded into it. Lesslie Newbigin concludes,

> We commit ourselves without reserve to all the secular work our shared humanity requires of us, knowing that nothing we do in itself is good enough to form part of that city's building ... and yet knowing that as we offer it up to the Father in the name of Jesus and in the power of the Spirit, it is safe with him and—purged in fire—it will find its place in the holy city at the end.[24]

So, to return to my opening question concerning my wife: Will some of the hundreds of cherry pies my wife made during our sixty years together when we had group after group in our home, will some of them survive and after being transfigured find their place in the new heaven and new earth. I do not know. But I do know that she did it "in the Lord" with faith, hope, and love, lots of love. But I would not be surprised to find them there. And I suspect that many of the people she has included, welcomed, and mentored will be there and they, in their resurrected and transfigured state, will attest to her work lasting. And with regard to her work in the new heaven and new earth, she will be *herself*, more truly herself, with her old gifts and even her old calling. She will always be a welcomer, a mentor, and

---

23. Williams, *Descent of the Dove*, viii.
24. Newbigin, *Foolishness to the Greeks*, 136.

a people lover. I can envision her welcoming people to the wedding supper of the Lamb (Rev 19:7). So, I put on her gravestone the text of Rev 14:13: "Blessed are the dead who die in the Lord... They will rest from their labor, for their deeds will follow them."

Epilogue

A Summary

In contrast to saying that inner work (work on oneself) is the indispensable condition of doing the outer work (work to earn a living) rightly, outer work is "a precondition of that purification without which no real progress in inner work can be made . . . outer and inner complement each other."

ERIC STEVEN DALE,
QUOTING ST. NIKODIMOS FROM THE *PHILOKALIA*[1]

Unless the encounter with transcendence [God] infiltrates work—transforms its aims, outcomes and possibilities—we are not really integrating presence but more compensating for its disintegration.

JOHN DALLA COSTA[2]

1. Marketplace theology concerns *the integration of faith and work in the world*. The assumption is that none of the work, worker, and the workplace is the center of the universe, that we need a transcendent reference point outside of ourselves in order to see, hear, and know properly what we are doing and why. The Big Me or Selfie culture of the West, and to a large extent globally, resists this transcendent orientation. The result is that we put too much or too little into our work: too much for the

---

1. Palmer et al., "Introduction," 14, quoted in Dale, *Bringing Heaven Down to Earth*, 32.
2. Costa, *Magnificent at Work*, 34.

workaholic who makes an idol of her work, or too little for the slave, or its modern equivalent, who is tempted to put as little as possible into his or her work.³

In *The Road to Character,* David Brooks proposes that we have two sets of virtues: *resume* virtues and *eulogy* virtues. He draws on the work of Rabbi Joseph Soloveitchik who noted that the two accounts of the creation of humankind in Genesis represent two sides of our nature. Adam I, the resume side, promotes our energetic career, and Adam II, the eulogy side through which we want to embody certain moral and spiritual attributes as we obey our calling to serve the world and our Creator.⁴ So we are fragmented persons, largely because of pervasive sin, and we long to be one whole person. Jesus alludes to this in his parable of the eye and the body (Luke 11:33–36). For the light entering the eye, a metaphor for faith, to illuminate everything in our bodily life requires integration. Indeed it *is* integration. But integration of faith and work is comprehensive.

2. Marketplace theology actually involves *four arenas of integration* (and I am adapting this from a matrix originally proposed by David Miller). The four arenas, each starting with an "m," are *meaning* (our understanding of God and God's purpose in our work—in other words theology), *mission* (our practice of work especially engaging the mission of God to bring transformation to people and the whole world), *mysticism* (or spirituality, which is our responsiveness to the seeking God who loves us and wants us to commune with him even in our work and workplace), and finally, *morality* (or ethics which is finding the pathway to be as shrewd as serpents but as innocent as doves in the complicated grey areas of life and human enterprise). Most organizations, institutes, and seminaries concentrate on only one of these areas when the full integration of faith and work requires all four. And all four comprise a marketplace theology. For example, Business as Mission, while a blessed global movement, does nevertheless require the constant definition of what we mean by it. Do we mean that business is simply a context for evangelism, a platform that gives us access to restricted countries, or do we mean that business is part of the mission of God in the world? Or both?

---

3. Someone working in Hong Kong in a 7:00 a.m. to 9:00 p.m. job recently asked "What is the hope for modern slavery?"

4. Brooks, *Road to Character*, xi–xii.

Epilogue

So, all four arenas of integration are needed. Meaning without mission is sterile—theory without practice. Mission without mysticism is inert—without soul. Mysticism without morality is disembodied spirituality—without righteousness. Morality without meaning leads to phariseeism—without humility. Missing the integral wholistic nature of all theology, and marketplace theology in particular, there is lacking the beauty and empowerment that comes from head, heart, and hands in lockstep together. Paul wrote to the Galatians "The only thing that counts is faith active in love" (Gal 5:6).

3. Marketplace theology is an example of faith active in love. It *combines God-love with neighbor-love, covering the vertical and the horizontal.* The *vertical* is the way we bless, worship, and love God through our work, even though our good work in this world is mixed with bad in this messy middle period that is the overlap of the old age in creation and the new age in Christ. In the vertical we discover God's intention for our work as God-imaging creatures to work as cocreators or sub-creators with him, whether making a meal or a deal. But in the *horizontal,* our work is a means of blessing our neighbor, the world, and even the workplace itself since all good work is a means of embellishing and improving human life on the planet.

   So, since we are not the center of the universe, marketplace theology should inspire humility, the primary virtue, in contrast to pride, the primary vice. While the combination of God-love and neighbor-love inspires humility it also inspires initiative since we are coworkers (1 Cor 3:9) with the most beautiful and creative person in all reality. But this does not happen all of a sudden like the instant communication we experience so ubiquitously today. The character of the marketplace theologian will be formed slowly. And because marketplace theology derives in part from our practice, and practice reflects our character, we are always on the way.

4. Marketplace theology *takes time, indeed a lifetime.* The character of the theological worker is formed in part in the hammer and heat of life, especially in the work life. As Cardinal Wyzysynski says, the prime virtue gained through daily work is patience or persistence: "Here is a ladder, as it were, by which we go ever higher in our ordinary, daily work."[5] So work itself becomes an arena for character formation and, as well, our

---

5. Wyszynski, *All You Who Labor,* 123.

character is reflected in our work. Earlier I said that if you ponder, pray, and practice your work you are a marketplace theologian—but only a beginning one. Indeed, do we ever get beyond the constant beginnings we make east of Eden, sinful, stumbling, stubborn creatures that we are?

Perhaps like the Christian life itself marketplace theology is a series of new starts. We never in this life fully arrive. And perhaps not even in the next life if, as I believe, the new heaven and new earth is continuous growth, healing, transformation, and discovery. Paul wrote to the Colossians that his goal in ministry was to "present everyone fully mature in Christ. To this end," Paul continues, "I strenuously contend with all the energy Christ so powerfully works in me" (Col 1:28–29). I, for example, am not there yet. I am still struggling with pride and some drivenness, still longing for the full integration of head, heart, and hand, still learning and growing. But what matters is that we are on the journey and progressing towards maturity of character, what David Brooks calls Adam II character or what we would like to be said at our funeral. But this progress calls for a conversion, indeed *continuous* conversion.

5. Marketplace theology is *not something we get convinced about but something we get converted to*, and continuously. Being convinced intellectually can be obtained through study, research, and investigation but it can leave one with abundant information not acted upon, the empty shell of informational "knowledge." In contrast the Hebrew word "know" suggests intercourse. True knowledge affects the soul, heart, mind, and body. So, when we invite people to take a course on marketplace theology we are inviting them to have intercourse with the truth, to embody it, to love it into action. This requires being converted to God's perspective, God's kingdom.

Conversion means making a right about-face in life, turning around directionally, and renouncing the dark life lived and the dark work done, "under the sun," to quote Professor Ecclesiastes in his hands-on research. In turn it means embracing the light and transparent work "under heaven." And what do we experience through this conversion?

Mystery! We discover that the ways of God are inscrutable, past our finding out, as the Old Testament character Job discovered: "And these are but the outer fringe of his works; how faint the whisper we hear of him! Who then can understand the thunder of his power?" (Job 26:14). But in this long obedience in the same direction, we discover contentment with where we are placed in life, not dashing about looking

Epilogue

for greener fields further away. And we are converted to joy, truly en-joying our work regardless of the circumstances, or rather en-joying God in the context of our work. And in the process we meet and know God day by day, not completely "through and through" but as a "reflection . . . in a mirror" (1 Cor 13:12).

So Paul started to write in Gal 4:9 "Now that you know God" but then he corrected himself and wrote "or rather are known by God."[6] Truly through this continuing conversion we come to know that we are known by God; we accept our acceptance with God; we cherish the God who cherishes us; we are assured that his hold on us is stronger than our hold on him; we are comforted in our souls, no matter whether we work in a toxic workplace or with demonized people beside us. But that suggests that we are not only being converted to Christ and to the world but to our brothers and sisters.

6. Marketplace theology *should never be prayed, performed, and pondered alone*. Edwin Friedman, psychoanalyst and rabbi lecturing at the University of British Columbia, mentioned in chapter 5, said that we have two needs: the need to be me and the need to be we.[7] The West has emphasized the first—the need to be *me*; the East and Africa have emphasized the second—the need to be *we*. But we need both. So many people, largely unnamed, have contributed to this volume. And volumes 2 and 3 will be written mostly by thoughtful practitioners, but *together*. We are built for community as children of the great Lover, Beloved, and Love itself, as Augustine described the Triune God. We were created in love and for love. We are all "love children" born in the love of God no matter what the circumstances of our conception. And the world (and the marketplace for that matter) runs on love. "The earth is filled with your love, Lord" says the psalmist in the acrostic poem Ps 119:64. So, made in the image of God, and made male and female in his image, we are built for community, for teams,[8] of which the people of God is a model.

---

6. See Ps 139.

7. I heard this psychoanalyst and rabbi at a lecture at Vancouver School of Theology, UBC, in the late 1970s. His book, *Generation to Generation*, is a classic of understanding how systems thinking (togetherness thinking) affects the church, synagogue, and the family.

8. See Elliott et al., *How the Future Works*.

The church gathers not primarily to worship—which according to Paul we can do all week long (Rom 12:1–2) but for mutual edification. The body of Christ is not a body of Christians, a kind of Christian club. Nor is the body the corpse of Christ because Jesus is not dead. The community of God's people is the body of Christ. The Head is intimately connected with the entire body, articulating, and directing. So, Paul coined a whole new set of words to describe our life together: raised up with Christ together, embodied together, joined together, "members together, sharers together in the promise of Christ Jesus" (Eph 3:6). It is impossible to be in Christ alone. Theologian Ernest Best once put it starkly, "It is impossible to conceive of a Christian who is not a member of the Church, which is related to Christ as in him and as his body . . . Individual Christians consequently do not exist."[9]

We have emphasized Paul's great word that it is only "together with all the Lord's holy people" that we can grasp "how wide and long and high and deep is the love of Christ" (Eph 3:18) whether Western, Eastern, Asian, African, Indigenous, or Latin American. And this includes the saints that have gone before us, of whom William Perkins is one, as well as Martin Luther and Brother Lawrence, mentioned earlier, my late wife Gail, and unnamed believers who as that great cloud of witnesses, the communion of saints, continue to influence us whether through their writing while on earth or through their mysterious presence. Death is as thin as gossamer separating us from those gone before. Why? Because marketplace theology is vocational, and our vocation does not end with this life.

7. *Marketplace theology is not only* about *our vocation but is part of our vocation.* We are summoned by God through the way we were created as God-imaging creatures to find the meaning and purpose of our lives and to undertake that meaning, as distinct from animals.[10] But our calling[11] is larger than the meaning and practice of our occupations or even

---

9. Best, *One Body in Christ*, 190.

10. I take this from the creation narrative in Genesis in which God speaks to Adam and Eve about what they are to do and be, from Ecclesiastes and Job where these latter two biblical characters actively search out the meaning and purpose of their lives on earth, and finally from the Great Commandment to love God and neighbor (Matt 22:34–40).

11. I prefer the term "calling" to the term "vocation" even though as translations from the Latin they are identical. I do this because "vocation" has become a synonym for "occupation" and because the term "calling" invites the question of who is calling.

our avocational hobbies and private passions. Robert Frost, the American poet, wrote in his poem "Two Tramps in Mud Time" how just as his two eyes make one in sight so he would unite his vocation and his avocation.[12] But even more importantly, calling—or vocation—is salvic. It concerns our salvation through the lovely summons of God to have "fellowship with his Son, Jesus Christ our Lord" (1 Cor 1:9), to belong to God as a son or daughter all made possible through the finished work of Christ on the cross and his resurrection. But that calling includes our daily work and the context of that work, including the institutions and mediating communities which are part of God's purpose for humankind. So not just pastors, missionaries, monks, and nuns have a calling but also plumbers and farmers, doctors, professors, and homemakers, lest we perish in a swamp of meaninglessness.

Calling tells us why we work, for whom we work, how we are to work, and what our work should be. It informs us that we are doing God's work in the world. It invites us to do God's work God's way. It suggests that we are in this life building something which, in some way beyond our wildest imagination, will last beyond the grave. Our work in the Lord will not be in vain (1 Cor 15:58). Calling is central to our external missional life and work in the world. But it is also central for our interior life as we navigate through the gray areas of life in this messy age of busyness, compromise, and politics, by providing meaning and motivation. The meaning is simply that we are doing God's work for God, with God and in God, and for our neighbor. And the motivation for vocational life comes from the hug of the Holy Spirit (Rom 8:14–17), from the creativity inspired by the Spirit, from the anointing of our creational talents by that same Spirit. So, in this way we are called to invest in the kingdom of God.

8. Marketplace theology is *based on the coming of the kingdom of God*. Because of the irruption of the kingdom of God in Jesus, who embodied the kingdom in its preliminary phase on earth, dualism is dead. Dualism says that some work is spiritual and God-pleasing and other work is secular and not pleasing to God, that pastoral work is holy and in-the-world work is unholy. The lowliest woman going about, as Luther said so cogently, is as holy as the priest and nun, however arduous are their practices. The good news is not the gospel of soul-salvation that gives us

---

12. Frost, "Two Tramps in Mud Time," 41–42.

a ticket to heaven. It is, as Jesus said, the gospel of the kingdom of God (Matt 4:17), that lovely life-giving rule of God.

The kingdom is beautiful. It brings human flourishing, transformation, and hope for our life and work in this world and the next. And our work, our workplaces, and we ourselves as workers are being transformed both in spite of ourselves and because of our efforts, as Augustine pointed out, "God without us will not, as we without God cannot."[13] The only dualism we now experience is between this life and the next life. Even so-called secular work done in the Lord is part of the new creation that God has inaugurated through the coming of Jesus. Through faith provisioned by prayer and imagination we may see some of the work we have done in this life in the new heaven and new earth. But we are not there yet, and we are not even the theologian we wish to be.

9. *Marketplace theology is never finished*, always provisional, always in process, ever being learned and practiced however imperfectly. I offer this volume as a starting point for other beginners, knowing that others, and not merely those writing in volumes 2 and 3, will expand, amplify, critique, and modify what I have written and done in my life. They will expand on William Perkins's definition (modified) that "marketplace theology is the science of working blessedly forever." That word "forever" suggests the need to finish well and to persist in doing marketplace theology. For this purpose I offer the Institute for Marketplace Transformation rule more easily remembered by the acronym "persist," which is one of the things we gain partly through work.

PERSIST
P-People **I will maintain a whole-person orientation and seek community.**
E-Empowerment **I will help others to flourish.**
R-Regeneration **I will daily grow and be renewed.**
S-Satisfying Work **I will find meaning in what I am doing today.**
I-Integrity **I will cultivate consistency and wholeheartedness.**
S-Staying **I will remain within my divine calling wholeheartedly.**
T-Time **I will seek God's presence and purpose all day and undertake a daily time of contemplation.**

---

13. Quoted in Sherman, *Kingdom Calling*, 238.

10. Why keep a rule? Simply because *we need help and the help we need is transcendent help*. As David Brooks says, "everybody needs redemptive help from outside."[14] We need help from God supremely and from other strugglers because we live and work in a distracting culture. Matthew Crawford in his second book, *The World beyond Your Head*, writes, "We are living through a crisis of attention . . . As our mental lives become more fragmented, what is at stake often seems to be nothing less than the question of whether one can maintain a coherent self."[15] Crawford continues, "what we really have is an attentional economy, if the term 'economy' applies to what is scarce and therefore valuable."[16] He speaks of the "colonization of life by hassle" and the "intensification of nervous stimulation," this last comment being made by the German sociologist Georg Simmel one hundred years ago.[17] Crawford quotes Christian philosopher Simone Weil and psychologist William James in their suggestion that "the struggle to pay attention trains the faculty of attention; it is a habit built up through practice." And this habit of attention is, according to Weil, "the substance of prayer."[18] So how do we gain a coherent self?

Partly by keeping a rule. By working wholeheartedly for God. By reflecting on the meaning of our life and work. By conspiring with other human beings to integrate one's whole life through the mutual edification of God's people. And, supremely, we gain a coherent self from God by prayer. And in prayer we attend to God. An old distinction between meditation and contemplation is simply this, that in meditating we turn our attention from the "things" of the world to attend to the "things" of God (including God's mercy, love, and justice). But in contemplation we turn our attention from the "things" of God *to attend to God himself*. May we become active contemplatives as we undertake "the science of working blessedly forever."

---

14. Brooks, *Road to Character*, 264.
15. Crawford, *World beyond Your Head*, ix.
16. Crawford, *World beyond Your Head*, 4.
17. Crawford, *World beyond Your Head*, 7, 5.
18. Crawford, *World beyond Your Head*, 15.

Bibliography

Alexander, Irene, and Charles Ringma, eds. *Pub Theology: Where Potato Wedges and a Beer are a Eucharistic Experience*. Great Britain: Piquant, 2021.
Anderson, R. S. *The Praxis of Pentecost: Revisioning the Church's Life and Mission*. Downers Grove, IL: InterVarsity, 1993.
Aquinas, Thomas. *Summa Theologica*. London: Eyre & Spottiswoode, 1975.
Armstrong, Chris R. "The Problem of Meaning and Related Problems: Four Voices in a Pastoral Theology of Work." In *Work: Theological Foundations and Practical Implications*, edited by R. Keith Loftin and Trey Dimsdale, 202–23. London: SCM, 2018.
Auer, Alfons. *Open to the World: An Analysis of Lay Spirituality*. Translated by Dennis Doherty and Carmel Callaghan. Baltimore: Helicon, 1966.
Augustine. *The Literal Meaning of Genesis*. Vol. 2. Translated by John Hammond Taylor. Ancient Christian Writers 42. New York: Newman, 1982.
Bakke, Dennis W. *Joy at Work: A Revolutionary Approach to Fun on the Job*. Seattle: PVG, 2005.
Banks, Robert. "Appendix A: Lay Theology and Education since 1945." In *Redeeming the Routines: Bringing Theology to Life*, 153–74. Wheaton, IL: Victor, 1993.
———. "Blessing." In *The Complete Book of Everyday Christianity*, edited by Robert Banks and R. Paul Stevens, 72–74. Downers Grove, IL: InterVarsity, 1997.
———. *God the Worker: Journeys into the Mind, Heart and Imagination of God*. Sutherland, Australia: Albatross, 1992.
———. *Paul's Idea of Community: The Early House Churches in Their Historical Setting*. Rev. ed. Peabody, MA: Hendricksen, 1994.
———. *Transforming Daily Work into a Divine Vocation*. Eugene, OR: Cascade, 2022.
Barkman, Dale. "Dualism and Work: The Greek Contribution." *Marketplace Theology* (blog), 2022. https://imtglobal.org/marketplace-theology/dualism-and-work.
Benson, Iain. "Virtues." In *The Complete Book of Everyday Christianity*, edited by Robert Banks and R. Paul Stevens, 1069–72. Downers Grove, IL: InterVarsity, 1997.
Bergsma, John. "The Creation Narratives and the Original Unity of Work and Worship in the Human Vocation." In *Work: Theological Foundations and Practical Implications*, edited by R. Keith Loftin and Trey Dimsdale, 11–29. London: SCM, 2018.
Bernstein, Peter L. *Against the Gods: The Remarkable Story of Risk*. New York: Wiley, 1996.
Best, Ernest. *One Body in Christ: A Study in the Relationship of the Church to Christ in the Epistles of the Apostle Paul*. London: SPCK, 1955.

Bibliography

Boersma, Hans. "Gregory of Nyssa: Becoming Human in the Face of God." In *Sources of the Christian Self; A Cultural History of Christian Identity*, edited by James M. Houston and Jens Zimmerman, 146–67. Grand Rapids: Eerdmans, 2018.

Bonhoeffer, Dietrich. *No Rusty Swords: Letters, Lectures and Notes 1928–1936*. In *The Collected Works of Dietrich Bonhoeffer*, edited by Edwin H. Robertson, 1:186–200. Translated by Edwin H. Robertson and John Bowden. New York: Harper & Row, 1965.

Boreham, Frank W. *The Prodigal: Sidelights on an Immortal Story*. London: Epworth, 1941.

Breuninger, Christian Beck. "The Usefulness of Søren Kierkegaard's Strategy of Edification for Homiletics." MCS thesis, Regent College, 1988.

Bright, John. *The Kingdom of God: The Biblical Concept and Its Meaning for the Church*. Nashville: Abingdon, 1953.

Brooks, David. *The Road to Character*. New York: Random House, 2015.

Bruce, A.B. *The Training of the Twelve*. Grand Rapids: Eerdmans, 1871.

Bruce, F.F. *The Epistle of Paul to the Romans: An Introduction and Commentary*. Grand Rapids: Eerdmans, 1963.

———. *The Epistle to the Hebrews*. Grand Rapids: Eerdmans, 1964.

Brueggemann, Walter. *Theology of the Old Testament: Testimony, Dispute, Advocacy*. Minneapolis: Fortress, 1997.

Calvin, John. *Commentary on the Psalms*. 5 vols. Translated by James Anderson. Grand Rapids: Baker, 1996.

Capon, Robert Farrar. *The Parables of the Kingdom*. Grand Rapids: Eerdmans, 1985.

Carlyle, Thomas. *Past and Present*. London: Dent, 1960.

The Catechism of the Catholic Church. Boston: St. Paul Books and Media, 1994.

Chan, Simon. *Grassroots Asian Theology: Thinking the Faith from the Group Up*. Downers Grove, IL: InterVarsity, 2014.

———. *Spiritual Theology: A Systematic Study of the Christian Life*. Downers Grove, IL: InterVarsity, 1998.

Charles, J. Daryl. "Interpretive Strategy in Ecclesiastes." In *Wisdom and Work: Theological Reflections on Human Labor from Ecclesiastes*, 48–60. Eugene, OR: Cascade Books, 2021.

———. *Wisdom and Work: Theological Reflections on Human Labor from Ecclesiastes*. Eugene, OR: Cascade Books, 2021.

———. "Wisdom Literature and the Wisdom Perspective." In *Wisdom and Work: Theological Reflections on Human Labor from Ecclesiastes*, 17–47. Eugene, OR: Cascade Books, 2021.

Charry, Ellen T. *By the Renewing of Your Minds: The Pastoral Function of Christian Doctrine*. New York: Oxford University Press, 1997.

Collier, Winn. *A Burning in My Bones: The Authorized Biography of Eugene Peterson*. Colorado Springs: WaterBrook, 2021.

Collins, Phil, and R. Paul Stevens. *The Equipping Pastor: A Systems Approach to Congregational Leadership*. New York: Alban Institute, 1993.

Congar, Yves. *Lay People in the Church: A Study for the Theology of the Laity*. Translated by D. Attwater. Westminster, MD: Newman, 1957.

Cosden, Darrell. *A Theology of Work: Work and the New Creation*. Carlisle, UK: Paternoster, 2004.

Bibliography

———. "Work and the New Creation." In *Work: Theological Foundations and Practical Implications*, edited by R. Keith Loftin and Trey Dimsdale, 165–77. London: SCM, 2018.

Costa, John Dalla. *Magnificence at Work: Living Faith in Business*. Ottawa: Novalis, 2005.

Crawford, Matthew B. *Shop Class as Soulcraft: An Inquiry into the Value of Work*. New York: Penguin, 2009.

———. *The World beyond Your Head: On Becoming an Individual in an Age of Distraction*. New York: Penguin, 2015.

Dale, Eric Steven. *Bringing Heaven Down to Earth: A Practical Spirituality of Work*. American University Studies. Series VII: Theology and Religon 83. New York: Lang, 1991.

Davis, John Jefferson. "'Teaching Them to Observe All That I Have Commanded You': The History of the Interpretation of the 'Great Commission' and Implications for Marketplace Ministries." *Evangelical Review of Theology* 25 (2001) 65–80.

Deissmann, Adolf. *Paul: A Study in Social and Religious History*. London: Hodder & Stoughton, 1926.

De Sales, Francis. *Introduction to the Devout Life*. Translated and edited by John K. Ryan. New York: Image, 2003.

Diddams, Margaret. "Good Work, Done Well for the Right Reasons and with an End in Mind: Playing at Work." *Christian Scholar's Review* 50 (2021) 423–33.

Diehl, William. *The Monday Connection: On Being an Authentic Christian in a Weekday World*. San Francisco: HarperSanFrancisco, 1993.

Dodd, C.H. *The Interpretation of the Fourth Gospel*. Cambridge: Cambridge University Press, 1953.

Droel, Bill, and Kathy Hidy. "Holy Work." *Initiatives: In Support of Christians in the World* 263 (2022).

Dreyer, Elizabeth A. *Earth Crammed with Heaven: A Spirituality of Everyday Life*. New York: Paulist, 1994.

Dumbrell, William J. "Creation, Covenant and Work." *Crux* 24 (1988) 14–24.

Dykstra, Craig. "Reconceiving Practice." In *Shifting Boundaries: Contextual Approaches to the Structure of Theological Education*, edited by Barbara Wheeler and Edward Farley, 35–66. Louisville: Westminster John Knox, 1991.

Eastwood, Cyril. *The Priesthood of All Believers: An Examination of the Doctrine from the Reformation to the Present Day*. Minneapolis: Augsburg, 1962.

Elliott, Brian, et al. *How the Future Works: Leading Flexible Teams to Do the Best Work of Their Lives*. Hoboken, NJ: Wiley, 2022.

Ellul, Jacques. "Meditation on Inutility." In *The Politics of God and the Politics of Man*, translated by Geoffrey W. Bromiley, 190–99. 1972. Reprint, Eugene, OR: Wipf & Stock, 2012.

———. *Reason for Being: A Meditation on Ecclesiastes*. Translated by Joyce Main Hanks. Grand Rapids: Eerdmans, 1990.

Farley, Edward. "Interpreting Situations: An Inquiry into the Nature of Practical Theology." In *Formation and Reflection: The Promise of Practical Theology*, edited by Lewis S. Mudge and James N. Poling, 1–26. Philadelphia: Fortress, 1987.

Fee, Gordon D. *Galatians*. Pentecostal Commentary. Dorset, UK: Deo, 2007.

Forster, Greg. "Being God's People by Working on God's Mission." In *Work: Theological Foundations and Practical Implications*, edited by R. Keith Loftin and Trey Dimsdale, 144–64. London: SCM, 2018.

Bibliography

Forsyth, Peter T. *The Soul of Prayer*. London: Independent Press, 1954.

Friedman, E. H. *Generation to Generation: Family Process in Church and Synagogue*. New York: Guilford, 1985.

Frost, Robert. "Two Tramps in Mud Time." In *The Poems of Robert Frost*, 41–42. New York: Random House, 1946.

The General Synod of the Anglican Church of Canada. *The Book of Common Prayer*. Toronto.: Anglican Book Centre, 1962.

Graham, Elaine, et al. *Theological Reflection: Methods*. 2nd ed. London: SCM, 2005.

Greear, J.D. "Martin Luther on the Masks of God." *J. D. Greear Ministries* (blog), August 5, 2013. https://jdgreear.com/martin-luther-on-gods-masks/.

Gregg, Samuel. "The Marketplace as Common Ground for Serving Others." In *Work: Theological Foundations and Practical Implications*, edited by R. Keith Loftin and Trey Dimsdale, 224–39. London: SCM, 2018.

Grenz, Stanley J. "Star Trek and the Next Generation: Postmodernism and the Future of Evangelical Theology Today." *Crux* 30 (1994) 24–32.

Griffin, Emilie. *The Reflective Executive: A Spirituality of Business and Enterprise*. New York: Crossroad, 1993.

Griffiths, Brian. *The Creation of Wealth: A Christian's Case for Capitalism*. Downers Grove, IL: InterVarsity, 1984.

Gutiérrez, Gustavo. *On Job: God-Talk and the Suffering of the Innocent*. Translated by Matthew J. O'Connell. Maryknoll, NY: Orbis, 1988.

Haughey, John. *Converting Nine to Five: A Spirituality of Daily Work*. New York: Crossroads, 1989.

Heschel, Abraham. "Anthropopathy." In *The Prophets*, 2:48–58. New York: Harper & Row, 1962.

Houston, James. *I Believe in the Creator*. Grand Rapids: Eerdmans, 1980.

Irenaeus of Lyons. *Against Heresies*. In *The Ante-Nicene Fathers*, 1:487–92. Grand Rapids: Eerdmans, 1979.

Kaemingk, Matthew, and Cory B. Willson. *Work and Worship: Reconnecting Our Labor and Liturgy*. Grand Rapids: Baker Academic, 2020.

Kidner, Derek. *A Time to Mourn and a Time to Dance: Ecclesiastes and the Way of the World*. Downers Grove, IL: InterVarsity, 1976.

Kierkegaard, Søren. *Journals and Papers*. 6 vols. Translated by Howard Hong and Edna Hong. Bloomington, IN: Indiana University Press, 1978.

———. *The Point of View for My Life as an Author*. Translated by Walter Lowrie. New York: Harper & Row, 1962.

Kolden, Marc. "Luther on Vocation." *Word and World* 3 (1988) 382–90.

Ladd, George Eldon. *The Gospel of the Kingdom: Popular Expositions on the Kingdom of God*. Grand Rapids: Eerdmans, 1959.

Lawrence, Brother. *The Practice of the Presence of God*. Grand Rapids: Spire, 1967.

Leclercq, Jean. *The Love of Learning and the Desire for God*. New York: Fordham University Press, 1974.

Leech, Kenneth. *Experiencing God: An Invitation to Christian Spirituality*. San Francisco: Harper & Row, 1980.

Lin, Frank. "Reflection Paper for Money Matters Course." Regent College, Vancouver, BC, 2021.

Loftin, R. Keith, and Trey Dimsdale, eds. *Work: Theological Foundations and Practical Implication*. London: SCM, 2018.

Bibliography

Luther, Martin. *Luthers Werke. Kritische Gesamtausgabe.* 65 vols. Weimer: Bohlaus, 1983–66.

———. *Luther's Works.* American ed. 55 vols. Edited by Jaroslav Pelikan and Helmut T. Lehmann. Philadelphia: Fortress, 1958–86.

———. *Luther's Works.* Vol. 2, *Genesis.* Edited by Jaroslav Pelikan and Daniel E. Poellet. Saint Louis, MO: Concordia, 2000.

———. "Treatise on Good Works." In *Luther's Works*, edited by Jaroslav Pelikan, 44:21–141. 55 vols. Minneapolis: Fortress, 1966.

Lyman, Stanford M. *The Seven Deadly Sins and Evil.* Dix Hills, NY: General Hall, 1989.

MacDonald, George. *The Curate's Awakening.* Minneapolis: Bethany House, 1985.

MacLeod, George. *The Whole Earth Shall Cry Glory: Iona Prayers.* Glasgow: Wild Goose, 2007.

Maddox, R. L. "The Recovery of Theology as a Practical Discipline." *Theological Studies* 51 (1990) 650–72.

Markus, R. A. *Gregory the Great and His World.* Cambridge: Cambridge University Press, 1997.

Marshall, I. Howard. "Son of Man." In *Dictionary of Jesus and the Gospels*, edited by Joel B. Green et al., 776. Downers Grove, IL: InterVarsity, 1992.

Matthew the Poor. *Orthodox Prayer Life.* Crestwood, NY: St Vladimir's Seminary Press, 2003.

McGrath, Alister E. *Luther's Theology of the Cross: Martin Luther's Theological Breakthrough.* 2nd ed. Oxford: Wiley-Blackwell, 2011.

Miller, David. *God at Work: The History and Promise of the Faith at Work Movement.* New York: Oxford University Press, 2007.

Moorhead, John. *Gregory the Great.* Early Church Fathers. London: Routledge, 2005.

Morris, Leon. *The Gospel according to John.* Grand Rapids: Eerdmans, 1971.

Morrison, Melanie. "As One Stands Convicted." *Sojourners*, May 1979, 15.

Mudge, Lewis S., and James N. Poling. *Formation and Reflection: The Promise of Practical Theology.* Philadelphia: Fortress, 1987.

Neill, Stephen Charles, and Hans-Ruedi Weber, eds. *The Layman in Christian History.* Philadelphia: Westminster, 1963.

Newbigin, Lesslie. *Foolishness to the Greeks: The Gospel and Western Culture.* Grand Rapids: Eerdmans, 1988.

———. *Signs amid the Rubble: The Purpose of God in Human History.* Grand Rapids: Eerdmans, 2003.

Nietzsche, Friedrich. *Thus Spoke Zarathustra.* Translated by Thomas Common. https://www.gutenberg.org/files/1998/1998-h/1998-h.htm.

Norris, Kathleen. *The Quotidian Mysteries: Laundry, Liturgy and "Women's Work."* New York: Paulist, 1998.

O'Connell Killen, Patricia, and John de Beer. *The Art of Theological Reflection.* New York: Crossroads, 2019.

Oliver, Edmund H. *The Social Achievements of the Christian Church.* Vancouver, BC: Regent College Publishing, 1930.

Osthathios, Mar. *Thy Kingdom Come: Mission Perspectives.* World Council of Churches, 1980.

Palmer, G. E. M., et al. "Introduction." In *The Philokalia*, translated and edited by G. E. M. Palmer et al., 1:11–18. London: Faber & Faber, 1979.

Bibliography

"Pastor's Toolbox." Institute for Marketplace Transformation. https://imtglobal.org/pastors-toolbox.

Pattison, M. E. *Pastor and Parish: A Systems Approach.* Philadelphia: Fortress, 1977.

Perkins, William. *A Golden Chain* (1592). In *The Courtenay Library of Reformational Classics: The Work of William Perkins,* edited by I. Breward, 3:169–259. Appleford, UK: Sutton Courtenay, 1970.

———. *The Works of That Famous and Worthy Minister of Christ in the University of Cambridge.* London: Legatt, 1626.

Peterson, Eugene H. *Christ Plays in Ten Thousand Places: A Conversation in Spiritual Theology.* Grand Rapids: Eerdmans, 2005.

Pink, Daniel. *A Whole New Mind: Why Right-Brainers Will Rule the Future.* New York: Riverhead, 2005.

Preece, Gordon. *Changing Work Values.* Brunswick, VIC: Acorn, 1995.

———. "Work." In *The Complete Book of Everyday Christianity: An A-to-Z Guide to Following Christ in Every Aspect of Life,* edited by Robert Banks and R. Paul Stevens, 1123–29. Downers Grove, IL: InterVarsity, 1997.

Reed, Gerard. *C. S. Lewis Explores Vice and Virtue.* Kansas City: Beacon Hill, 2001.

Satir, Virginia. *Conjoint Family Therapy.* Rev. ed. Palo Alto, CA: Science & Behavior, 1983.

Sayers, Dorothy L. *The Mind of the Maker.* London: Methuen, 1952.

———. "Why Work?" In *Creed or Chaos? Why Christians Must Choose Either Dogma or Disaster (Or, Why It Really Does Matter What You Believe),* 89–116. Manchester, NH: Sophia Institute Press, 1974.

Schaff, Philip, and Henry Wace, eds. *A Select Library of Nicene and Post-Nicene Fathers of the Christian Church.* 14 vols. New York: Christian Literature, 1895.

Schein, Edgar H. *Organizational Culture and Leadership: A Dynamic View.* 2nd ed. Jossey-Bass Social and Behavioral Science Series. San Francisco: Jossey-Bass, 1992.

Schmemann, Alexander. *For the Life of the World.* Crestwood, NY: St Vladimir's Seminary Press, 1988.

Schumacher, Christian. *God in Work: Discovering the Divine Pattern for Work in the New Millennium.* Oxford: Lion, 1998.

Sherman, Amy L. *Kingdom Calling: Vocational Stewardship for the Common Good.* Downers Grove, IL: InterVarsity, 2011.

Singh, Sadhu Sundar. *With and without Christ.* London: Cassell, 1929.

Smith, Adam. *An Inquiry into the Nature and Causes of the Wealth of Nations.* New York: Modern Library, 1985.

Spidlik, Tomas. *The Spirituality of the Christian East: A Systematic Handbook.* Kalamazoo, MI: Cistercian, 1986.

Stackhouse, Max L., et al. *On Moral Business: Classical and Contemporary Resources for Ethics in Economic Life.* Grand Rapids: Eerdmans, 1995.

Stevens, R. Paul. *The Abolition of the Laity: Vocation, Work and Ministry in a Biblical Perspective.* Carlisle, UK: Paternoster, 1999.

———. "The Anti-Kingdom in the Marketplace." In *The Kingdom of God in Working Clothes: The Marketplace and the Reign of God,* 139–51. Eugene, OR: Wipf & Stock, 2022.

———. "Drivenness." In *The Complete Book of Everyday Christianity: An A-to-Z Guide to Following Christ in Every Aspect of Life,* edited by Robert Banks and R. Paul Stevens, 312–18. Downers Grove, IL: InterVarsity, 1999.

Bibliography

———. *The Kingdom of God in Working Clothes: The Marketplace and the Reign of God.* Eugene, OR: Cascade Books, 2022.

———. "Living Theologically." In *The Other Six Days: Vocation Work and Ministry in Biblical Perspective*, 243–55. Grand Rapids, MI: Eerdmans, 1999.

———. "On Being a Biblical Servant Leader: Insights from the Global Church." *Marketplace Theology* (blog), n.d. https://imtglobal.org/marketplace-theology/biblical-servant-leadership.

———. "Organization." In *The Complete Book of Everyday Christianity: An A-to-Z Guide to Following Christ in Every Aspect of Life*, edited by Robert Banks and R. Paul Stevens, 707–13. Downers Grove, IL: InterVarsity, 1999.

———. "Organizational Culture and Change." In *The Complete Book of Everyday Christianity: An A-to-Z Guide to Following Christ in Every Aspect of Life*, edited by Robert Banks and R. Paul Stevens, 713–18. Downers Grove, IL: InterVarsity, 1999.

———. "Organizational Values." In *The Complete Book of Everyday Christianity: An A-to-Z Guide to Following Christ in Every Aspect of Life*, edited by Robert Banks and R. Paul Stevens, 718–21. Downers Grove, IL: InterVarsity, 1999.

———. *The Other Six Days: Vocation, Work and Ministry in Biblical Perspective.* Grand Rapids: Eerdmans, 1999.

———. "Resistance: Grappling with the Powers." In *The Other Six Days: Vocation, Work and Ministry in Biblical Perspective*, 215–39. Grand Rapids: Eerdmans, 1999.

———. *Seven Days of Faith.* 2nd ed. Eugene, OR: Wipf & Stock, 2021.

———. "So What about the Church? The Kingdom People." In *The Kingdom of God in Working Clothes: The Marketplace and the Reign of God*, 152–61. Eugene, OR: Wipf & Stock, 2022.

———. "The Uselessness of Work: A Professor's Meditation on Ecclesiastes 2.22." *Regent World*, May 1990.

———. *Work Matters: Lessons from Scripture.* Grand Rapids: Eerdmans, 2001.

Stevens, R. Paul, and Alvin Ung. *Taking Your Soul to Work: Overcoming the Nine Deadly Sins of the Workplace.* Grand Rapids: Eerdmans, 2010.

Stockard, Jim. "Commissioning Ministries of the Laity: How It Works and Why It Isn't Being Done." In *The Laity in Ministry: The Whole People of God in the Whole World*, edited by George Peck and John F. Hoffman, 71–79. Valley Forge, PA: Judson, 1984.

Stone, Howard W., and James O. Duke. *How to Think Theologically.* 2nd ed. Minneapolis: Fortress, 2006.

Stott, John. *Issues Facing Christians Today.* Basingstoke, UK: Marshalls, 1984.

Straw, Carole. *Gregory the Great: Perfection in Imperfection.* Berkeley: University of California Press, 1988.

Taylor, John. "Labor of Love: The Theology of Work in First and Second Thessalonians." In *Work: Theological Foundations and Practical Implications*, edited by R. Keith Loftin and Trey Dimsdale, 49–68. London: SCM, 2018.

Teresa of Ávila. *Interior Castle.* Translated by E. Allison Peers. New York: Doubleday, 1989.

Terkel, Studs. *Working: People Talk about What They Do All Day and How They Feel about What They Do.* New York: Ballantine, 1972.

Torrance, Thomas F. *Trinitarian Perspectives: Toward Doctrinal Agreement.* Edinburgh: T. & T. Clark, 1994.

Twain, Mark. "A Humorist's Confession." *New York Times*, November 26, 1903.

Tyndale, William. *The Parable of the Wicked Mammon.* Cambridge: Cambridge University Press, 2016.

Bibliography

Underhill, Evelyn. *The Fruits of the Spirit.* Wilton, CT: Morehouse-Barlow, 1981.

Volf, Miroslav. "Work as Cooperation with God." In *Work: Theological Foundations and Practical Implications,* edited by R. Keith Loftin and Trey Dimsdale, 83–109. London: SCM, 2018.

Volf, Miroslav, and Dorothy C. Bass, eds. *Practicing Theology: Beliefs and Practices in Christian Life.* Grand Rapids: Eerdmans, 2002.

Waltke, Bruce K. "The Fear of the Lord: The Foundation for a Relationship with God." In *Alive to God: Studies in Spirituality,* edited by J. I. Packer and Loren Wilkinson, 17–33. Downers Grove, IL: InterVarsity, 1992.

———. *An Old Testament Theology: An Exegetical, Canonical and Thematic Approach.* Grand Rapids: Zondervan, 2007.

Ward, Benedicta, trans. *The Sayings of the Desert Fathers: The Alphabetical Collection.* London: Cistercian, 1974.

Williams, Charles. *The Descent of the Dove: A History of the Holy Spirit in the Church.* New York: Meridian, 1956.

Wingren, Gustaf. *Luther on Vocation.* Translated by Carl C. Rasmussen. 1957. Reprint, Eugene, OR: Wipf & Stock, 2004.

Witherington, Ben, III. *Work: A Kingdom Perspective on Labor.* Grand Rapids: Eerdmans, 2011.

Wolterstorff, Nicholas. "More on Vocation." *Reformed Journal* 29 (1979) 20–23.

Wong, Siew Li. "The Intrinsic Value of Work: In Light of the Doctrines of Creation, Redemption and Eschatology." *Marketplace Theology* (blog), n.d. https://imtglobal.org/marketplace-theology/intrinsic-value-of-work.

Wright, N.T. *The Challenge of Jesus: Rediscovering Who Jesus Was and Is.* Downers Grove, IL: InterVarsity, 1999.

Wyszynski, Stefan Cardinal. *All You Who Labor: Work and the Sanctification of Daily Life.* Manchester, NH: Sophia Institute Press, 1995.

Author Index

Alexander, Irene, 26, 26n22, 27n83
Ames, William, 12, 12n26
Anderson, Ray S., 24, 24n19
Armstrong, Chris R., 158nn12–14
Auden, W. H., 181
Auer, Alfons, 157, 157n9

Bakke, Dennis W., 174n10
Banks, Robert, xviii3, 56n15, 83,
    83n2, 111, 111n1, 116n11,
    147, 147nn15–16, 150,
    150n21, 151, 151nn22–23
Barkman, Dale, 52n9
Barth, Karl, 24, 62, 68, 155
Bass, Dorothy C., 26n22
Baxter, Richard, 21
Benson, Iain, 130n8
Bergsma, John, 144n7, 145, 145nn8–
    11, 146, 146nn12–14
Bernstein, Peter L., 45–46, 45nn32–
    33, 46nn34–38
Best, Ernest, 189n8, 190n9
Boersma, Hans, 162–63, 162n27,
    162nn29–30, 163nn31–32
Bonhoeffer, Dietrich, 19, 20n7, 54,
    70, 70n5, 82
Boreham, Frank W., 88n17
Breuninger, Christian Beck, 19,
    19nn4–6, 37nn8–9
Bright, John, 175n11
Brooks, David, 186, 186n4, 188, 193,
    193n14
Bruce, A. B., 77n13
Bruce, F. F., 156n7, 176, 176n13
Brueggemann, Walter, 152, 152n28

Buber, Martin, 48

Calvin, John, 5n6, 30, 30n27, 70n6,
    100
Capon, Robert Farrar, 37, 38n11, 179,
    179n21
Carey, William, 116
Carlyle, Thomas, 159, 159n15
Chan, Simon, 12, 12n24, 12nn26–28,
    13, 13n30, 26n22
Charles, J. Daryl, 27n24, 28n24,
    37n10, 38, 38n12, 38nn14–
    15, 40n17, 42, 42n19, 42n21,
    43n22, 43n24, 44, 44n27,
    46n39, 47n40, 48, 48n48,
    49n49
Charry, Ellen T., 5, 5n6, 6, 6n6, 6n7
Collier, Winn, 63n24
Collins, Phil, 84n6
Congar, Yves, 179, 179n20
Cosden, Darrell, 52n7, 53, 53n11,
    154–55, 155n3
Costa, John Dalla, 185, 185n2
Covey, Stephen, 129
Crawford, Matthew B., 72, 72nn8–9,
    193, 193nn15–18
Cullman, Oscar, 58n18

Dahl, K. G. William, 142
Dale, Eric Steven, 185, 185n1
Davis, John Jefferson, 115–16,
    116n10, 116n12
De Beer, John, 26n22
De Sales, Francis, 101, 101n14

Author Index

Deissmann, Gustav Adolf, 164, 164nn33–34
Descartes, René, 21
Diddams, Margaret, 51n4
Diehl, William, 116n11
Dodd, C. H., 150, 150n20
Dreyer, Elizabeth A., 135n13
Droel, Bill, 166, 167n38
Duke, James O., 26n22
Dumbrell, William J., 14, 14n34
Dykstra, Craig, 21n11, 22, 22n13

Eastwood, Cyril, 50n2
Elliott, Brian, 84n5, 124n1, 125n3, 126n4, 189n8
Ellul, Jacques, 35, 35n2, 36–37, 37nn4–7, 44, 45, 45n28, 45nn30–31, 49, 49n50, 156, 156n8
Evans, Stanley, 100

Farley, Edward, 20, 20nn8–9, 21n10
Fee, Gordon D., 97n6
Flow, Don, 132
Follette, John Wright, 63
Forster, Greg, 116, 117n13
Forsyth, Peter T., xv, xvn1, 102–3, 102nn15–21, 103nn22–23, 159, 159nn16–19, 160n21, 161–62, 161nn23–25, 162n26, 165, 165nn35–37
Francis of Assisi, 19
Franklin, Benjamin, 53
Friedman, Edwin H., 76n12, 136, 137, 137n18, 189
Frost, Robert, 190n9, 191n12

Gandhi, Mohandas, 70
Garber, Steve, xvin4, 10n17
Goethe, Johann Wolfgang von, 21
Graham, Elaine, 26n22
Greear, J. D., 154n1
Gregg, Samuel, 114, 114nn6–8
Grenz, Stanley J., 21n12
Griffin, Emilie, 132, 132n11, 134, 134n12, 138nn30–31
Griffiths, Brian, 81, 81n1

Gundling, N. H., 20
Gutiérrez, Gustavo, 29n26

Hammond, Pete, 115
Haughey, John, 178, 178n18
Heidegger, Martin, 72
Heschal, Abraham J., 10n16
Hidy, Kathy, 166, 167n38
Houston, Drew, 124
Houston, James, 19, 48, 48n47, 98n9
Hume, David, 6n6

James, William, 193
John Paul II, Pope, 22, 61, 95
Jung, Carl, 63

Kaemingk, Matthew, 119, 119n15, 141, 141n3, 142nn4–5, 151, 152nn24–29, 153, 153nn32–33, 153nn35–36
Kant, Immanuel, 6n6, 21
Kidner, Derek, 41, 41n18, 44, 44n26, 45, 45n29, 47, 47nn41–43
Kierkegaard, Søren, 19, 19nn3–6, 35, 35n1, 37, 37n8, 71
Kolden, Marc, 67n1, 87n15
Kotiuga, Willy, xvin4

Ladd, George Eldon, 173, 173n8
Lawrence, Brother, 60, 61, 61n22, 101, 190
Leclercq, Jean, 167nn39–40
Lee, Jean, xvin4
Leech, Kenneth, 100n12, 120n16
Lewis, C. S., 28, 164
Lim, Clive, xvin3
Lin, Frank, 148n17
Locke, John, 6n6, 21
Luther, Martin, 3, 3n1, 7, 7n9, 12n29, 17, 17n1, 22n15, 23, 23n16, 42n21, 50, 53, 53n10, 67, 70n6, 105, 141, 141n1, 154, 154n1, 190, 191
Lyman, Stanford M., 105n28

MacDonald, George, 28, 28n25, 69, 69n3, 180

Author Index

MacLeod, George, 171, 172n2
Maddox, R. L., 12n29
Markus, R. A., 157n11
Marshall, I. Howard, 30n28
Matthew the Poor, 3, 3n2, 11, 11n22, 94, 94n2
McGrath, Alister E., 3n1, 7n9, 17, 17nn1–2
Melanie, Morrison, 20n7
Miller, David, 15n35
Moltmann, Jürgen, 9n14, 84
Moorhead, John, 158n11, 167n39
Morris, Leon, 149, 150nn19–20
Mouw, Richard, 10n16

Neill, Stephen Charles, 116n11
Newbigin, Lesslie, 171, 171n1, 182, 182n24
Newton, Isaac, 21
Nie, Bruce, 6
Nietzsche, Friedrich, 105, 105n29
Norris, Kathleen, xv, xvn2, 157, 157n10

O'Connell Killen, Patricia, 26n22
Oliver, Edumund H., 91, 91n21
Osthathios, Mar, 120, 120n16
Otto, Rudolf, 48

Packer, J. I., 7
Palmer, G. E. M., 185n1
Pattison, M. E., 137n17
Peabody, Larry, xvin4
Perkins, William, xvi, xviii, xvin5, 7, 7n10, 12, 12n25, 18, 31, 52, 94, 100, 100n13, 111, 142, 167, 192
Peterson, Eugene H., 63, 95, 95n3
Pink, Daniel, 50, 50n1, 54
Pinnock, Clark, 181
Potok, Chaim, 10
Preece, Gordon, 24n18, 51, 51nn5–6, 124n2

Reed, Gerard, 105n27
Ringma, Charles, 26, 26n22, 27n83
Rousseau, Jean-Jacques, 21

Satir, Virginia, 137, 137n19
Sayers, Dorothy L., 42, 42n20, 54, 54n13
Schaff, Philip, 160n22
Schein, Edgar H., 127, 127n6, 128n7, 135, 135nn14–15, 136n16
Schmemann, Alexander, 143, 143n6, 152, 152n30, 153n31
Schumacher, Christian, 85, 85n8, 87, 87n13, 87n16
Sherman, Amy L., 171n1, 173n9, 175n12, 192n13
Simmel, Georg, 193
Singh, Sadhu Sundar, 60, 60n20
Smith, Adam, 21, 113–14, 114n5
Soloveitchik, Joseph, 186
Spangberg, Mr., 88
Spidlik, Tomas, 3n3, 11, 11n19, 11n21
Stevens, R. Paul, xvin3, xviiin6, 8n11, 9n13, 10n15, 13nn31–32, 24n17, 25n20, 31n31, 43n23, 44n25, 54n12, 57n16, 58n19, 70n6, 71n7, 84n6, 86n10, 86n12, 96n5, 98, 99n10, 104n26, 119, 120n17, 122n18, 126n5, 172nn3–6, 173n7, 177n17, 181n22
Stockard, Jim, 153n33
Stone, Howard W., 26n22, 31n29
Stott, John, 52, 52n8
Straw, Carole, 158n12

Taylor, John, 113, 113nn2–3
Terkel, Studs, 113, 113n4, 114, 115n9
Thoreau, Henry David, 82–83
Torrance, Thomas F., 83, 83n3
Twain, Mark, 73, 73n10
Tyndale, William, 50, 50n3

Underhill, Evelyn, 98, 98n8
Ung, Alvin, xviiin6, 96n5, 98

Van Duzer, Jeff, 4
Voetius, Gisbertus, 20
Volf, Miroslav, 26n22, 176, 176nn13–16

Author Index

Voltaire (François-Marie Arouet), 21

Wace, Henry, 160n22
Waltke, Bruce K., 14, 14n33, 48, 48nn44–47, 85, 85n9
Weber, Hans-Ruedi, 116n11
Weil, Simone, 193
Wesley, John, 88
Williams, Charles, 181, 182n23
Willson, Cory B., 119, 119n15, 141, 141n3, 142nn4–5, 151, 152nn24–29, 153, 153nn32–33, 153nn35–36

Wilson, Jonathan, 4n4, xvin4, 85n7, 106n30, 131n9
Wingren, Gustaf, 67n1
Wolterstorff, Nicholas, 124, 124n2, 138
Wong, Siew Li, 55, 55n14
Wright, N. T., 178, 179n19
Wyszynski, Stefan Cardinal, 22, 22n15, 61, 61n21, 61n23, 63, 64n25, 67, 67n2, 92, 92nn22–24, 95, 96n4, 99, 99n11, 187, 187n5

Subject Index

ability to make things, common to
    God and man, 54
Abraham, God making his promise
    to, 145–46
accountability group, asking for, 107
Adam and Eve
    broke their covenant relationship
        with God, 145
    called to extend the sanctuary
        garden, 126
    forced to leave the garden, 144
    as priests of creation, 143
    testing of, 57
    as vice-regents over everything
        on earth, 13
administrator, 67, 68, 74
almsdeeds, corporal (bodily) and
    spiritual, 117
Anglican Prayer Book, on the three
    dimensions of resistance, 122
anti-kingdom, 8, 86
applied theology, 20–22, 27
arenas of conflict, as agents of
    spiritual growth, 96–98
"arrow prayer," of Nehemiah, 103
artifacts, 128, 135
ascetic theology, 13
Augustine
    on acting on lust, 105
    on the contemplative life, 158
    on God as lover, beloved, and love
        itself, 84
    on God without us, 175, 192
    on the Triune God, 6n6, 189
autonomy tree, 56–57

avodah, meaning both "to work" and
    " to worship," 144

Babel tower, people of unwilling to fill
    the earth, 144
bad work, doing, 52
badminton club, 126
Baptist "area minister," as author
    assignment #2, 67–68
beatific vision, 154–67, 156n7
behavior, guiding by rules, 129
being in communion, God as, 84
being-redeemed-community,
    expressing God's kindness,
    134
beliefs, 128, 132
believers, in the marketplace, 138
Benedictines, balanced life of, 62, 161
Bezalel son of Uri, 91, 148
Bible
    virtues in, 131–32
    wholistic living in, 24
    wisdom literature in, 38n14
biblical theology, 8, 25, 54, 55
bibliography, for doing theology from
    below, 26n22
blessing, 48, 56, 82, 83, 112
blessing God
    doing God's work with God,
        147–50
    by gathering for worship and
        mutual edification, 150–53
    as priests of creation, 143–44
    by ruling as royal sons and
        daughters, 145–47

Subject Index

blessing God (*continued*)
    through worship, 141
    ways to realize, 106–7
blessing to God, 142
bodily almsdeeds, 117–18
bodily life, presenting as an offering to God, 144
"body" metaphor, used by Paul, 84
body of Christ, as the community of God's people, 190
"bottom up" ("from below") theology, 15–16
bread, offered in remembrance of Christ, 152–53
business, exchange as, 4, 114
"Business as Mission," forms of, 8
businesses, seizing on values as rallying cries, 129

callings, 42, 181, 190n11, 191. *See also* vocation
capitalism, 46
Carey Theological College, 73
carpentry and business, author assignment #5, 71–72
case study, doing theology "from below," 25
Catholic sensibility, as really the beatific vision, 166
change
    cultural approach to, 135–36
    in an organization, 126–27
    situations when a church or an organization is likely to accept fairly radical, 66
    systemic approach to, 136–38
character, 70, 98, 130–32, 187
charisma, without character as dangerous, 70
chastity, as the ordering of our desires, 106
chores, God doing, 149
Christ. *See* Jesus Christ
Christianity
    deeds of following them into the new heaven and new earth, 178
    as an existence for Kierkegaard, 19
    practice inside, 25–27
    as responsive and always God-centered, 131
    service careers in, 42
    social achievements of, 91
    spiritual theology, 13
    theology based on the Bible, 11–12
    virtue influenced and deepened by faith, 130
Christlikeness, developing, 98
church(es)
    being frozen out in, 126
    gathering for worship and mutual edification, 190
    ministry of planting, 73
    with a simple group ministry, 66
    situations when change is relatively easy, 135
civility, as an indirect result of trade, 114
coaching and counseling, as author assignment #3, 68–69
co-creativity (sub-creativity), of Adam and Eve, 143
co-Creators, sharing work with God as, 27
coherent self, gaining from God by prayer, 193
communion, with God, 143
"communion" mysticism, in Christ, 164
community-building, of Adam and Eve, 143
compensatory theology, marketplace theology and, 8
computer science, as close to what God does, 82
Confucian culture, 11n20, 31n30, 76
Confucian tradition, in the Chinese culture, 7
"conscience," Greek concept of, 131
"consolation," in contrast with "desolation," 89

Subject Index

consummated kingdom, activity of the people of, 181
Consummator, God as, 82, 150
contemplation, 158, 193
contentment, 188–89
contextualization, within biblical history, 54
continuity, between this life and the next, 177
conversion, as continuous, 188–89
corporate worship, scattering workers, 153
corporations, values of, 130
covenant love (*hesed*), 134
coworkers, 82, 164
creation
    anointing of capacity for, 91
    of everything, 55–56
    God working in, 149
    Spirit anointing talents for, 90
    stewarded by humankind, 8
    waiting for the day it will be set free, 58
creational work, described, 175
creative action, faith inspiring, 133
creative idea, from a worker, 85
creator, God as, 150
crisis, as an opportunity, 137
criticism, not liking, 65
cross, taking up, 87
cultural approach, to change, 135–36
culture
    cannot be manipulated, 135–36
    enticing us to see our work only extrinsically, 98
    understanding organizational, 126–28
    unique expectations of leadership and service, 76
    work of, 175
    in the workplace, 126
culture-change mechanisms, 135
The Curate's Awakening (MacDonald), 69

daily life, theological meaning of, 24
daily work, 72, 157, 191

Daniel, answering for occupational riddles, 148
the dead who die in the Lord, as blessed, 183
death, separating us from those gone before, 190
delight, finding mainly in God, 100
democratic expectations, for the pastor in North America, 76
de-Westernization of theology, marketplace theology requiring, 8
dialectical theology, pub theology as, 27
direct change, promoting in a culture, 136
discernment, God the Spirit giving, 91
discipleship, identified with the consumption of religious goods, 116–17
disintegration, of faith and work, 52
disobedience, of Adam and Eve, 145
divine work, themes of, 84–85
"doctor of desire," Gregory the Great as, 167
doing theology from below, 26n22, 27–31
"drivenness," self-control as the opposite of, 99
dualism, 147, 158, 191–92

earth, groaning and waiting for liberation, 178
economic flourishing, 119, 121
economic system, dealing with, 113
Eden, as the home of humankind, 144
Eliphaz, not speaking well of God, 28
emotional flourishing, 119
emotions, expressing to God, 30
empowering leader, Jesus as, 77
"eternity," joy mirroring the inbreaking of, 47
eucharist, as the end of cult, 152
eulogy virtues, 186
evangelist, work as, 43–33

Subject Index

Eve. *See* Adam and Eve
everyday work, seeing God in, 166–67
exchanges, in the ancient world, 4
experience, theology wrung out of by Job, 28
extreme work, 62
extrinsic value, of work, 54
the eye and the body, parable of, 186
"eye of the soul," seeing traces of God, 163

face of God, seeking in Jesus Christ, 162
faith
    engaging the whole person, 23
    expressing itself through love, 10
    of Job, 29
    reconnecting with work, 120
    vision and as a sign of Kingdom culture, 138
    in a workplace context, 133
faith, hope, and love, working with, 163–64
faith and work, 115, 151–52
faith-action, unselfconsciousness of, 23
"faithfulness," meaning of, 98
fall of humankind, kingdom of God and, 56–58
families, context of counseling, 137
Father, God as, 85–86, 93
Father, Son, and Spirit, in a reciprocal unit, 83
fear, derived from grace bringing blessings, 48
fear of God, 41, 47–49
feedback, learning to be less dependent on positive, 78
fire of judgment, meaning transformation, 178
"flesh," Paul using the word, 5n5
the flesh, 96, 100–101
"flexible work," 125
flourishing, xvii, 119
Flow Automotive Companies, 132–33
followers, Jesus laid down his life for his, 77
"forbearance," meaning of, 99
foreverness, of work, xix
forgiveness, for sin in our work, 60
free markets, 114
free-flowing theology, theology in the pub as, 26
friends, of Job, 29, 160
"from above" theology, 3, 27
"from below" theology, 16, 17–31
fruit of the Spirit, provision of, 98–100
futility of life, the Professor starting with, 36
future, gaining the meaning of work from, 175–76

garden of Eden, 176. *See also* sanctuary garden
gathered life community, 151
genitive theology, marketplace theology as not, 8
"gentleness," meaning of, 98–99
gift, work as, 42–43, 60
gifts of God, virtues as, 131
gladness of heart, God giving, 40
God. *See also* Triune God
    blessing of working with, 85–86
    blessing through our work, 138
    giving us joy in work, 72
    giving wisdom, knowledge, and happiness, 40
    images of as a worker, 56
    involved in our lives, 43
    joy of in creation, 92
    keeping the world running, 82
    as operative in human affairs, 46
    in ordinary work, 156–57
    preparing a replacement pastor, 66–67
    seeing in prayer at work, 159–60
    seeing in work, 160–67
    speaking to the powers, 86
    in the way we work, 163
    work of, 44–45, 84–85, 147–50
    as a worker, xix, 10, 27, 145

Subject Index

God the Worker (Banks), 147
goel (redeemer-relative), of Job in heaven, 29
good people, appreciating beauty, 100
Good Samaritan, as an example of kindness, 99–100
good work
    definition of, 52
    extending the kingdom of God, 58
    as God's work, 63
    towards a theology of, 22–24
goodness, xvii, 100
gospel, as good news, 13n31
gospel confidence, persons having, 23
government, attempting to control us, 98
grassroots theology, reflecting lived theology, 26n22
gratitude, loving organization evoking, 134
gratuitousness, as a sign of Kingdom culture, 138
Great Commandment, xviii
Great Commission, 115–18
Greater Commission, 118–21
Greatest Commission, 121–23
Greek cultural world, early Christians and, 52
ground, cursed in Genesis, 42
a group, drawing out leadership, 70

Hagar, seeing God, 157
head, in theologies of work, 51, 54
heaven, contributing to a down-to-earth, 171–83
hebel (meaninglessness)
    appearing thirty-eight times, 42
    joy as the antidote to, 48
    Paul on creation subjected to, 49
    "a puff of smoke," 28
    usually translated "meaningless," 36
Holy Spirit. *See also* Spirit
    empowering believers, 9
    led Jesus into the wilderness, 103
    as the Spirit of worldly engagement, 176
    working with, 88–93
holy work, definition of, 52
homemaking, as author assignment #9, 77–78
homeostasis, concept of, 136
homo adorans, humankind as, 144
hope, in a workplace context, 133–34
the horizontal, blessing our neighbor, 187
horizontal extension, of the Kingdom, 116
human beings
    doing God's work, 82, 147
    filling the earth with God's glory, 85, 143
    "in the image of God," 56, 145
    loving the praise of, 99
    responsibility to rule, 14
    as sub-Creators, 8
human existence, as self-contradictory, 37
human flourishing, dimensions of, 119
human work, 59, 83–84
humanistic psychologists, examples of, 130
humility, marketplace theology inspiring, 187

I and Thou (Buber), 48
icons of God, coworkers as, 164
image of God, being made in, 180
imaginary locutions, 89
imago Dei, principle of, 6n6
indirect communication, by the Professor, 37
indirect ways, of loving and blessing neighbors, 114
Institute for Marketplace Transformation (IMT), 8, 17, 21, 61, 75, 192–93
institutions, unaware of actual values, 130
integrating theme, for marketplace theology, 13–15

Subject Index

integration, arenas of, 186–87
integrity, as a sign of Kingdom culture, 138
intellectual locutions, 89
InterVarsity staff worker, author assignment #3, 68–69
interviews, of ordinary people in the workplace, 26
intrinsic value, of work, 55
investment, Professor wisely counseling, 46
invisible hand, being led by, 113–14

Jacob, 149
Jesus Christ
    asking what meaning we are discovering in work, 44
    coming to in the fear of God, 48
    crucified by government, culture, and religion, 97–98
    on his Father as always at work, 63
    Jesus Christ, 157
    on the pure in heart as fully consecrated to God, 155
    receiving our service in the final judgment, 178
    resurrected body of bore scars from this life, 177
    reunited the royal and the priestly roles, 146
    tested vocationally in the areas of provision, pleasure, and power, 104
    as the ultimate servant leader, 77
    using indirect communication, 37
    as worker, xix
    works of, 58
Job, 28–29, 160
job-concept of work, those hardest hit by, 51
Pope John Paul II, on working in the world, 95
Joseph (son of Jacob), 106, 149
joy, 47, 48, 92, 100, 189
Judge, God described in Ecclesiastes as, 47

judgment criteria, 59

"kindness," 99–100
Kingdom culture, life signs of, 138
kingdom of God
    consummated, 14, 172–77
    as the integrating theme in the Bible, 8
    Jesus announced as come in him, 119
    Jesus commissioning his followers to participate in, 121
    marketplace theology based on the coming of, 191–92
    as personal, social, political, economic, and cosmic, 58
    rich diversity of people in, 120
    starting in Genesis, 13
    themes around the coming of, 55–59
The Kingdom of God (Bright), 175
kingdom of the world, 14
kingdom work, 52, 174
knowing, 6, 19

labor in the Lord, as not in vain, 59, 173, 178–79
laity, less-than-adequate equipping of, 116n11
"lay" theology, theology in the pub as, 26
leaders, 70, 137, 138
leadership, 70, 127, 136
Levites, 145, 146
life
    commending the enjoyment of, 41
    experiences in the New Testament, 30–31
    Job praying about, 28–29
    making sense of, 5
    theological reflection on, 26
    thinking about in Ecclesiastes, 27–28
"a life of prayer," living, 63
life on life, Jesus as, 77

Subject Index

life or work situation, starting with in a case study, 25
life sings, of Kingdom culture, 138
life's work, survival and transfiguration of, 177–79
liturgy, as work for the common good, 152
"living by the Spirit," 101
"locutions," 89–90
Lord's Table, 152
Lord's work, the blessing of doing, 81–83
love, 92, 100, 112, 134
"love children," born in the love of God, 189
love of God, world created through, 84
"Love your neighbor as yourself," as the Second Great Commandment, 112
loving and compassionate actions, 23
"lust of the eyes," 104
Luther, Martin
   on arousal, 105
   on the call to church leadership, 70n6
   on the medieval monastery, 53
   on one's daily work, 67
   on secular works as a worship of God, 141
   on taking up a cross in the marketplace, 22
   on theology wrung from life, 7
   "Treatise on Good Works," 23
   on true theology as practical, 12
   on work as masks of God, 154

"maker of all things," God as, 44, 156
management, as a practical way to love, 74
manna, God provided or spoke, 161
manual work, requiring brains, 72
marginalized and the outsider, engaging with, 69
marketplace
   beatific vision and, 154–67
   common grace in, 4
   cross to be taken up in, 87
   described, xx
   inclined to embrace short-term goals, 156
   meaning of, xv–xvi
   purifying result of, 67
"marketplace hermeneutic," 116
marketplace theology
   from above, 3–16
   as always in process, 192–93
   awakening passion, 10
   from below, 17–31
   concerning the integration of faith and work in the world, 185–86
   defined, xvi–xvii, 7, 8–9, 111–12, 171
   dimensions of, xviii
   doing, 15–16
   as an example of faith active in love, 187
   goodness of, xvii
   integral (wholistic) shape of, 9–12
   integrating theme for, 13–15
   as not a mere segmented sphere of application, 7–8
   prayer needed to develop, 159–60
   requiring thought, prayer, and practice, 160n20
   as the study of God in our work, 11
   taking time, 187–88
   as wholistic, 22
Mary and Martha, false distinction, 158
material flourishing, 162
meaning, 15, 43, 186, 187
meaningful activity, meaninglessness and, 41
meaninglessness, 39–40, 43
meditation, 193
mental and physical flourishing, 119
mental flourishing, 121
messiah, 120
messy middle, living and working in, 97
Methodist quadrilateral, 31

Subject Index

mind without a soul, as not wanted, 10
ministerial flourishing, 119, 121
ministry, exercising to each other's benefit, 151
Mishnah, on Sabbath-breaking, 129
misinterpretation, of work as worship, 152
mission
   of marketplace theology, 15
   without mysticism as inert, 187
   of work, 186
mission trips, going on short-term, 153
missionary, on the top of the holiness hierarchy, 52
"the mixed life," Mary and Martha symbolizing, 158
Monday work, as an extension of Sunday worship, 153
money, as a test in the workplace, 104
monks, embracing poverty, 106
moral theology, expanded, 20
morality (ethics), 15, 186, 187
morphogenesis, 136
motivation, related to culture, 127
motivational switch, as both inside and outside, 165
motive, of doing the Lord's work, 173–74
mouth, person coming out of, 160
mouth of God, every word coming from, 161
Moveable Mover, God as, 141
mutual edification, described, 151
mysterium tremendum and "numinous dread," in the presence of God, 48
mystery, in God, 44
mystical theology, 13
mysticism, 15, 186, 187
mystics, managing to find God in a life of noise, 157

need to be me, 76
need to be we, 76
needs, Jesus attended to his own, 77

negotiation, stages of, 137
neighbor, blessing your, 111–23
new heaven and new earth, 59, 165
new starts, marketplace theology as a series of, 188
New Testament
   early Christians aware of good qualities outside the family of God, 131
   final destination as a glorified material destination, 59
   starting with life experiences in, 30–31
New Testament Church, 175
next life, restful work in, 179–83
Noah, 145

observation, of work, 54
"old self," bearing vocation's cross, 67
Old Testament, the righteous doing justice and living by wisdom, 131
opportunity of every crisis, systemic leader welcoming, 137
opposites, values having no, 129
opus dei, as the work of God, 163
ordinary work, Luther exalted dignity of, 53
organizational change, making, 135–38
organizational culture, 126–28, 134
organizational faith, expressing, 133
organizational hope, 133–34
organizational love, inspiring caring loyalty, 134
organizations, nonverbal messages in, 126
ortho, for "right" or "true," 9
orthodoxy, 9, 13
orthodoxy-orthopraxy tension, in the West, 24
orthopathy, 9–10, 10n16, 14
orthopraxy, 10, 15, 22–24
overcomer, being, 100–103

Parable of the Ten Minas, in Luke 19, 15

Subject Index

parental approval, longing for, 99
pastor
    author assignment #1, 65–67
    author assignment #4, 69–71
    author assignment #6, 73
    the top of the holiness hierarchy, 52
pastoral or missionary service, as the Lord's work, 81
pastoral service, hazard of, 69
"Pastor's Toolbox," 153
"patience," 99
Paul. *See also* Saul
    constrained and restrained by the Spirit, 88
    on the creation subjected to frustration (*hebel*), 49
    crisis faced by on his way to Rome, 149
    on fruits of the Spirit, 98
    on God in his tent-making work, 157
    on "God's beloved," 132
    on Holy Spirit changing a person's status before God, 6n6
    interpreting Scripture differently from his peers, 31
    listing commendable virtues, 131
    not losing his personality on the Damascus Road, 164
    not mentioning Christians gathering to worship, 150–51
    praxis of Pentecost for, 24
    as a self-employed tradesman, 51
    on Spirit gifts, 90–91
    suggesting that work built on Christ will be saved, 178
    telling slaves that they are "working for the Lord," 173
    using the word "flesh," 5n5
peace, 31n30, 100
people, judging themselves, 182
people of God, 9
Perkins, William
    defined theology, xvi, 7
    definition of marketplace theology, 192
    on not needing to work, 94
    on vocational contentment, 100
PERSIST acronym, 192
persistence, as a sign of Kingdom culture, 138
personal experience, stories wrung out of, 26
personal faith, described, 133
personal flourishing, 119, 121
personal hope, meaning never giving up on people and helping people, 133
personal love, reflecting the love of God, 134
Peter, 31, 131–32
physical layout, of a workplace, 128–29
pleasure, as the second test which Jesus faced, 104
pleasure type, of testing, 57
Potiphar's house in Egypt, toxic culture of, 127
power, 105
powers, 57–58, 86, 97, 175
practice (*praxis*), 18, 31
prayer
    becoming a Christian through, 101
    as bent and drift of the soul, 161
    biblical marketplace theology an, 18
    chief object of all, 102
    emotional in Psalms, 30
    gaining answers to questions about work, 60
    habit of attention as the substance of, 193
    seeing God in, 159–60
    as work, 61–62, 63–64
prayerful theology of work, toward a, 60–64
prayerlessness, as the worst sin, 102
pride, as the primary vice, 187
priests of creation, 63, 143–44
principalities and powers. *See also* powers
    affecting work, workers, and workplace, 8

Subject Index

principalities and powers (*continued*)
  engagement and grappling with, 86
  experiencing, 97
  as fallen, 58
  inciting prayer, 63
  working without resistance from, 181
Principle-Centered Leadership (Covey), 129
"prisoners of hope," 133
process leadership, 137–38
procreators, humans as, 45
professor, as author assignment #7, 73–75
the Professor
  author of Ecclesiastes as, 35–36, 156
  believing that God has made everything beautiful in its time, 45
  doing theology from below, 36
  going to work with, 35–49
protective work, as God's work, 85–86
Protestant Reformation, 46, 53
provision, trusting God for, 106
provision type, of testing, 57
pub theology, as an exercise of testimony, 26
Pub Theology (Alexander and Ringma), 26–27
public marketplace, in Kenya, 4

Qoheleth, based on the Hebrew word *qahal*, 35
quadrant, marketplace theology as, 15
"quotidian," meaning "occurring every day," 157

redeemer, God as, 82, 150
redemption, scope of, 58
redemptive work, described, 119
"reflection in the mirror," as beautiful to behold, 167
The Reformed Pastor (Baxter), 21
refuge, God as our, 86

Regent College, academic dean of, 73–74
relational work culture, building, 84
resistances, trilogy of, 122
resume virtues, 186
resurrected persons, in a renewed creation, 180
revelation, through action, 31
right action, as a most basic level orthopraxy, 24
risk, work involving, 45–46
Roman Catholic Church, on work and the workplace, 95
royal sons and daughters, blessing God by ruling as, 145–47
rules, 129, 193

Sabbath, keeping, 107
Sabbath rest and contemplation, as a sign of Kingdom culture, 138
sacrament, work as, 146
sacramental moments, toil and turmoil as, 166
sacramental work, doing, 82
sacred-secular dualism, 158
salty kingdom values, listing of, 174n10
samah (to enjoy), appearances in Ecclesiastes, 42
sanctification, of the personality, 164n33
sanctuary garden, 126, 143–44
sapiential theology, 5
satisfaction, finding primarily in God, 43
Saul. *See also* Paul
  on the Damascus road, 30–31
schedule, workplaces flexible in, 125
school space, as a place of joy and learning, 125
science, xviii, 18
Scripture
  on God as involved in our work, 149n18
  locutions agreeing with, 89
  models of doing theology from below, 27–31

Subject Index

verses of applying to a case study, 25
on working with God in daily work, 148
Second Great Commandment, 112–15
secular work, 146–47
"self-control," meaning of, 99
self-giving, of the son, 87
seminaries, offering courses for non-clergy people of God, 21
servant leadership, example of, 74
service work, described, 174
Seven Deadly sins, recognizing the presence of, 107
sexual pleasure, as morally disordered, 104–5
shape, of marketplace theology, xvi
Sheep and Goats, parable of, 23, 141
simha (enjoyment), appearances in Ecclesiastes, 42
sin, residing in our persons, 97
single eye, seeing with, 155–56
situational leadership, of Jesus, 77
skill, God the Spirit giving, 91
social work, described, 175
society, rebuilding through work, 119–20
the Son, providing a model of how we are to work, 93
Son of God, blessing of working with, 87–88
Son of Man, Jesus as, 30
soul, 62, 95–96
The Soul of Prayer (Forsyth), on prayer, 102
space, turning raw into a place, 125
speaking, as more than mouthing words, 161
Spirit. *See also* Holy Spirit
being led by, 89
confirming in our hearts that we belong to God, 88
in conflict with the flesh, 96
implementing the Father's work, 85
Spirit fruit, 98

"Spirit gifts," 90
Spirit work, glorifying God, 91
spiritual almsdeeds, 117
spiritual flourishing, 119, 121
spiritual growth, 78, 96–98
spiritual locutions, 89
spiritual or rational "worship" (*latreia*), 151
spiritual theology, 5, 12, 13
spiritual work, 59, 175
spirituality, 11, 106–7
status quo (homeostasis), 136
Stephen, seeing Jesus, 30
stewards, of God's created world, 56, 85
"street theology," 8
struggle to pay attention, 193
subjective experience, selecting values as, 129
Sunday worship, as not a "moment" of worship, 153
sustainer, God as, 150
systematic theology, exploring work, 53–54
systemic approach, to change, 136–38
systems thinking, as essential, 84

talents, as creational aptitudes build into us by God, 90
telos, to pursue for all human cultivation, 7
temple sanctuary, of gods as a garden, 144
temptation, test becoming, 57n16
"tent-making" ministry, as life giving, 72
tent-making pastor, working as a among street people, 71
testing, 57, 103–4, 106, 107
theologian, in the Western Church, 10
theological curriculum, divisions of the modern, 5n6
theological learning, handiness of, 65–78
theological reflection, 25
theological virtues, 132

Subject Index

theology
   from above, xviii
   from below, xviii, xix, 12, 36–39
   as compressed prayer, 160
   defined, xvi
   divisions of, 11
   doing today, 6–7
   Enlightenment definitions of, 21
   gained through practice, 65
   meant to be applied, 8
   modern fragmentation of, 5
   as off-putting, xv
   problems with the fragmentation of, 12
   ways of doing, 31
"theology of application," shifting to, 27
"theology of the laity," emergence of, 116n11
theology of work, 52, 53–54, 78, 116
theophanies, Boersma on, 162n29
thought (*theoria*), biblical marketplace theology involving, 18
thought experiment, of what life is like without God and with God, 38
thoughtful theology of work, executive brief on, 53–54
"top down" ("from above"), 15
top-down theologians, Job's friends as, 29
"trade," as risky, 46
trades-person, Jesus came to earth as, 9
transcendence, as a sign of Kingdom culture, 138
transcendent help, needing from outside, 193
transcendent orientation, needed outside of ourselves, 185–86
transfiguration, of our work, 174
trees of life, on each side of the river of life, 181
Trinity, working with, 81–93
Triune God, 8, 122, 189. *See also* God
trivial toil, seeing God in, 157–58

troublemakers, working without, 181
trust, required in free markets, 114
truth, search for as a cognitive enterprise, 6

"under heaven," 36, 40–41, 188
"under the sun," 27–28, 36, 39–40, 188
"union" mysticism, 164
universe, present material to be replaced, 176

"value-free" education, as really impossiblw, 130
values, 5, 128, 129
"veiled truth," 37
the vertical, discovering God's intention for our work, 187
vertical penetration, of the Kingdom, 116
vices, 130, 131
virtual first, emphasis on, 125–26
virtualism, wedding of futurism to, 72
virtues, 131–32, 186
virtuous workplaces, with hints of God's presence, 126
visible signs of the culture, 128
vocation, 53, 103–6, 190–91. *See also* callings
vocational discernment, Spirit leading in, 88
vocational pursuits, of the author, 78
vow of obedience, testing power, 106

Wedding Supper of the Lamb, 180, 183
whole-life discipleship, including in work life, 116
Why Business Matters to God (Van Duzer), 4
wisdom, 38, 91
word, as a form of worship glorifying God, 60
Word of God, as a single integrating principle for marketplace theology, 13
work

Subject Index

allowing perception of the work of God, 44–45
arenas of, xvi
assignments of the author, 65–78
by the author over the years, 50–51
becoming "painful toil," 57
blessing our neighbor through, 111–23
brief history of, 51–53
categories of, 147
in Christ as a way to bless God, 146
command given before the fall, 56
done in faith, hope and love as lasting, 178
earthly, leaving traces on resurrected personalities, 176
as energy expended, xvi
as an evangelist, 43–44
extrinsic and intrinsic value of, 54–55
functions of the world of, 87
gaining a worldview for, xvii
as a gift, 42–43
of God, not understanding, 44
God is in, 163
as God's work, 44–45
growing spiritually through, 94–107
"under heaven," 40–41
involving risk, 45–46
as joyful in God, 47
kinds of, 174–75
kingdom of God and, 59
in the Lord will not be in vain, 191
loving our neighbor through, 84
as meaningful when we fear God, 47–49
as ministry, 148
in the next life, 179–83
not leaving prematurely, 78
nothing better than enjoying, 40
practice of, 65–78
as prayer, 61–64, 160–63
prayer inhibiting, 60
rebuilding society through, 119–20
reserved for slaves in the Greek world, 52
secularization of, 53
seeing God in ordinary, 156–57
soul revealed through, 95–96
story of the author, 65–78
"under the sun," 39–40
thinking and praying about, 50–64
toward a thoughtful theology of, 53–54
ways to be blessed while, 106–7
worship and, 141–53
work, worker, and workplace, seeing God in, 163–65
work above, defined, xviii
work and workplace, kingdom of God and, 58–59
workaholism, idolatry of work in, 57
workers, 10, 81–93, 164
working
  exploring the meaning of, xviii
  fleshly ways of, 163
  in God, joy of, 92
  preventing our being a burden on others, 113
  for someone else, 51
"working blessedly," exploring, xviii
workplace
  blessing, 124–38
  effects of the fall and, 42
  engaging physically, 128–30
  finding one's calling to, 78
  flourishing, 91, 119
  forming character in, 130–32
  fundamental beliefs, 132–34
  hints of sanity and grace in a miserable, 165
  interviewing ordinary people in, 26
  as the primary location for spiritual growth, 172
  questions arising in, 96
  Spirit inspiring creativity in, 91
  spiritual dimensions of, 118

workplace (*continued*)
    taking up the cross in, 123
    of "thorns and thistles," 57
    truth about, 10
    as where work is done, 126
"works of the flesh," 96, 97

world, taking the sanctuary into, 144
worship, work and, 120, 141–53
worship service, as often a performance, 151
Wright, Walter, example of servant leadership, 74

Scripture Index

OLD TESTAMENT

Genesis

	42, 54, 55, 82, 144
1–3	145
1:1	55
1:21	100
1:26–28	56
1:26	145
1:27–28	180
1:27	27
1:28	13, 56, 88, 126, 145
1:31	55, 56, 72, 88
2	145
2:5	55
2:11	144
2:15	55, 56, 145
3	56, 57
3:16	57n17
4:1	148
4:7	57n17
8:20–22	145
11	57
16:13	157
18	162n29
28	162n29
31:10–13	149
32	162n29
41	149

Exodus

19:6	146
28:2	91
31	93
31:1–11	148
31:2–5	91
31:3	90
33–34	162n29

Leviticus

	146
19:18	112

Numbers

12:7–8	162n29

Deuteronomy

	161
6:13	105
8:3	161
17:20	87n14
28:12	149n18

1 Kings

22:19	162n29

Nehemiah

2:4–5	103
8:10	92

Job

	31, 38
1:9	29
9:32	29

Scripture Index

Job (*continued*)

13:15	29
16:19	29
19:25–26	29
19:26–27	162n28
26:14	44
38–41	29, 149, 156
42:6	160
42:7	28, 160

Psalms

	29, 30, 31, 38
1	38n13
2	104n24
16:6	100
16:11	92
23	56
37	38n13
37:7	86n11
41:11	23
46:2	86
46:3	86
46:4	86
46:6	86
46:9	86
46:10	86
49	38n13
69:2	158n11
73	38n13, 152
78	38n13
90:17	149n18
91	38n13
126	38n13
127	147
127:1	147, 171
143:10	56

Proverbs

	38
2	131n9
8:27	92
8:30	92
16:11	58
20:10	58

Ecclesiastes

	xviii, 27, 27n24, 28, 28n24, 31, 35, 38, 41, 42, 42n21, 82, 156
1:1	35
1:2	36
1:3	36, 36n3, 39
1:9	36n3
1:13	43
1:14	36n3
2:3	36
2:4–11	39
2:11	36n3
2:17–23	39
2:17	36n3
2:18	36n3
2:22	36n3
2:24–26	40, 47
2:24	41, 43
2:25	41
3:10	43
3:11	39, 47, 48
3:12–14	40
3:13	56
3:16	36n3
3:22	40
4:3	36n3
4:7	36n3
4:8	39
4:15	36n3
5:1–7	39n16
5:2	40
5:7	40
5:10	39
5:12	39, 72
5:18–20	40, 47
5:18	36n3, 56
5:19	47
6:1	36n3
6:12	36, 36n3
7:16–18	39n16
8:9	36n3
8:12–13	41
8:15	36n3, 41
8:16–17	41
8:17	36n3, 39

Scripture Index

9:3	36n3
9:6	36n3
9:9–10	40
9:9	36n3
9:11	36n3
9:13	36n3
10:5	36n3
11	44
11:1	45
11:2	46
11:4	46
11:5	41, 44, 149n18, 156
11:6	41
11:7—12:1	47
11:9	41
12:13–14	41
12:13	28, 48
12:14	47
26:29	52
27:2	52
38:34	150

Isaiah

	38
5:1–7	56
6:1–5	162n29
11:1–9	59
42:1	104n24
49:4	174
55:11	161
58:13–14	92
58:14	93
61:1–7	12, 14
61:1–2	118
61:1	119
61:2	119
61:3	120
61:4	119
61:6	119
64:8	149n18
65	59

Jeremiah

18:6	56

Ezekiel

1:4–28	162n29
8:1–4	162n29
27	2
27:15	2

Daniel

2	148
5	148
7	30
7:13–14	30

Hosea

2:18–23	59

Amos

5:10–12	58
9:13	59

Micah

4:3–5	59

Zechariah

	38
9:12	133

DEUTEROCANONICAL BOOKS

Ecclesiasticus	52, 150

NEW TESTAMENT

Matthew

	5n6
4:1–10	57
4:1–11	104
4:1	103

Scripture Index

Matthew (*continued*)

5:8	154, 155, 162n28
5:13–17	58
5:16–17	58
5:37	174n10
5:41	174n10
6:22	155
8:16	56, 58
10:19–20	149
12:1–8	146
14:15–21	58
14:23	77
16:13–20	19
17:1–8	162n29
18:10	167
18:21–35	174n10
19:21	18
19:28	120, 177
22:39	112, 174n10
25:14–30	174n10
25:23	92
25:31–46	23, 178
25:31–36	59
25:35–46	141
25:40	92
28:18–19	105
29:19–20	115

Luke

3:37	145
4	118
4:16–21	14, 87
4:18–19	12
4:21	119
5:1	18
5:27–31	174n10
5:27	18
9:1–2	18
9:59	18
10:9, 17	173
10:17	173
10:25–37	99
10:28	18
10:38–42	61
16:16	14, 101
16:31	18

17:7–10	174n10
17:10	91
18:1–8	28
19:13	11n20, 15
22:44	159

Mark

6:3	58
12:30–31	xviii

John

	9, 121
1:12	133
1:14	122
3:3	14
3:5	14
3:16	84n4
3:19	182
5:17	27, 56, 63, 146, 149
5:44	99
7:17	18
8:31	18
8:51	18
11:43–44	58
12:43	99
13:4–5	58
13:34	84n4, 112
13:35	112
14:23	9n12
15:10	18
17:18	121
17:23	84n4, 112
17:24	162n28
20:21	9, 93
20:22–23	105
20:27	177
21:17	70

Acts

	92
6:2	56
6:4	56
9:3–9	162n29
10	31
14:15	49n49
15:1–29	136

Scripture Index

15:1–35	137
16:6–8	89
27:23–25	149

Romans

	38
1:21	49n49
2:4	134
5:3–5	63, 99
5:5	100
8	49
8:15–18	88
8:19–23	58
8:19–22	178
8:19–21	49, 176
8:21	176
10:14–17	133
12:1–2	119, 144, 151, 162
12:6–9	90–91
12:8	68
14:17	172

1 Corinthians

	181
1:22–25	131
2:9–10	181
3:9	82, 85
3:12–15	178
3:20	49n49
7:10	164n33
7:17	101
7:20	101
9:12	55
10:13	106
12:1	90
12:11	149n18
12:28	68
13:12	162n28, 163, 164, 165, 167
13:13	59, 112, 132, 163, 178
14:12	151
14:19	151
14:26	151
15	59
15:10	164n33
15:17	49n49
15:58	59, 149n18, 173, 178, 179

2 Corinthians

5:6	162n28
5:20	102
5:21	122
12:1–4	162n29

Galatians

2:11–21	136
2:20	164n33
3:28	120
5	101
5:6	10, 22, 111
5:13	97n7
5:17	96
5:19–21	96, 163
5:22–23	92, 98
5:23	98
5:24–25	101
5:25	101

Ephesians

	16
2:14–18	120
3:18	16, 31
4:7	90
4:10	88
4:11–12	xix, xixn7, 68, 174n10
4:17	49n49
4:28	55
4:31	131
5:2	131
6:12	63

Philippians

2	93
2:6	87
2:7	87
2:8	87
2:12–13	23
2:12	68

Scripture Index

Philippians (*continued*)

3:21	59
4:4	174n10
4:6	74, 100
4:8	131
4:11	74

Colossians

1:5	132
1:15–20	58, 84
1:16	58, 86
1:24	87, 123
1:27	164
1:28	149n18
2:15	58, 97
3:12	132
3:22–24	55
3:22–23	92
3:22	146
3:23–24	149n18
3:23	14, 173
3:24	146, 173
4:1	174n10

1 Thessalonians

1:2–3	59, 132
1:3	112
2:9	55
5:11	151
5:17	63, 160

2 Thessalonians

3:6–10	55

Titus

3:9	49n49

Hebrews

3:13	151
4:15	106
10:6	63, 99
10:24–25	151
11:3	133
11:4–16	133
11:27	162n29
12:14	156n7
13:21	149n18

James

1	107

1 Peter

1:12	167
2:9	131

2 Peter

1:3	131, 132
1:5	131
3:7	178
3:10–13	177
3:13	177, 178

1 John

2:16	57, 104
2:17	104n25
3:2	162n28
4:7–12	84n4

Revelation

	54, 55
1:12–16	162n29
4–5	162n29
5:9	59
11:15	14
14:13	59, 176, 178, 183
19:7	183
21–22	59, 177
21	176
21:5	56, 176
21:8	181
21:24	59, 174, 180
21:24	59
21:26	59, 174, 181
22	176
22:2	181
22:3	180
22:5	180, 181

Scripture Index

EARLY CHRISTIAN WRITINGS

Anselm of Canterbury	5n6
Anthony (Abba)	94
Aquinas, Thomas	5n6, 114, 117
Summa Theologica	
Part II of second part,	
Q 32, art 2 (p.241)	117n14
Athanasius (Athanasius of Alexandria)	5n6
Augustine of Hippo	5n6, 6n6, 9n14, 84, 105, 141, 158, 175
Literal Meaning of Genesis	
46	141n2
Basil the Great (Basil of Caesarea)	5n6, 160
Duns Scotus	20
Evagrius Ponticus	1, 10
Gregory of Nyssa	162, 163
Gregory the Great (Pope Gregory I)	157, 158, 162, 167
Homilaie xl in Evangelia	
30.1	167n40
Irenaeus of Lyons	154, 155
Against Heresies	
4.20.7 (p. 490)	154n2, 155n4
5.9.3 (p. 535)	155n6
Preface (p. 526)	155n5
Julian of Norwich	5n6
Teresa of Ávila	89
Interior Castle	89nn18–19
142–143	90n20

GREEK AND ROMAN LITERATURE

Anaxagoras	72
Ptolemy of Lucca	
De Regimine Principum	
bks II–IV	114n8
Socrates	19

www.ingramcontent.com/pod-product-compliance
Lightning Source LLC
Chambersburg PA
CBHW031355230426
43670CB00006B/546